THE MANY FACES OF COINCIDENCE

Laurence Browne

imprint-academic.com

Copyright © Laurence Browne, 2017

The moral rights of the authors have been asserted.
No part of this publication may be reproduced in any form
without permission, except for the quotation of brief passages
in criticism and discussion.

Published in the UK by
Imprint Academic, PO Box 200, Exeter EX5 5YX, UK

Distributed in the USA by
Ingram Book Company,
One Ingram Blvd., La Vergne, TN 37086, USA

ISBN 9781845409159

A CIP catalogue record for this book is available from the
British Library and US Library of Congress

*For my daughters,
Sally and Eloise*

Contents

Preface	ix
Chapter One: The Composition of Synchronicity	1
Chapter Two: The Dance of Chance	30
Chapter Three: Cosmic Coincidences	58
Chapter Four: Enigma Variations	86
Chapter Five: Coincidence Explanations	113
Chapter Six: Exploring the *Tao*	142
Appendix	170
Afterword	176
Bibliography	181
Index	197

Figures and Illustrations

Fig. 1: English Speaking Alien	40
Fig. 2: Invention Pyramid	44
Fig. 3: Goldilocks and the Fine Structure Constant	65
Fig. 4: The Earth and Moon from the Galileo Spacecraft	77
Fig. 5: Interference Pattern	90
Fig. 6: Box-pair Experiment	95
Fig. 7: Delayed Choice with a Vengeance	97
Figs. 8–17: The Oxherder	136–8
Fig. 18: Fishermen's Evening Song	157
Fig. 19: The Flammarion Woodcut	170
Fig. 20: Double Mandalas	173

Acknowledgements

I would like particularly to thank Phil Dowe for his encouragement and guidance with my PhD thesis, from which this book has evolved; also my wife Tianyan for putting up with my long hours and late nights in the back room of our house. Many others have supported me along the way and provided important feedback on various chapters, including Lance Storm, Michelle Boulos Walker, Dominic Hyde, Victor Marsh, Carole Ramsey, Adam Williams, John Stanley, Dieter Graf, Garnet Brose, Colin Biggs, and Michael Muirhead. In addition, I would like to express my appreciation to the Australian Government Department of Education and Training for the grant of an APA research scholarship, without which it is unlikely this project would have come to fruition.

Permission for the following figures and illustrations was kindly given by Nick Harding (Fig. 1), Kevin Kelly (Fig. 2), Phil Disley (Fig. 3), Fred Kuttner (Fig. 6), The Nelson-Atkins Museum of Art (Fig. 18), Inner City Books (Fig. 20). Permission for the following quotes and poetry was kindly given by Taylor and Francis (C.G. Jung, *Synchronicity: An Acausal Connecting Principle*), Faber and Faber (T.S. Eliot, *Four Quartets*), Penguin (D.C. Lau, *Lao Tzu: Tao Te Ching*), Harper Collins (Stephen Mitchell, *Tao Te Ching: An Illustrated Journey*), Jessica Kingsley (Chung Chang-yuan, *Creativity and Taoism*), Alfred Music (Joni Mitchell, *Woodstock*). All reasonable effort was made to obtain permissions for illustrations and excerpts not referred to above, with the exception of those in the public domain.

Preface

A coincidence can be broadly defined as 'a notable co-occurrence of events' which may have causal or non-causal origins. Some coincidences have discernible causal connections, though these may be quite subtle and complex. Others are clearly attributable to the random play of chance or luck, while certain ostensibly random coincidences can be distinguished by the numinosity and meaning they hold for the individual involved. C.G. Jung coined the term *synchronicity* for such coincidences. However, there is currently no generally accepted overarching theoretical framework that deals comprehensively and inclusively with the several disparate categories under which different sorts of coincidences might be appropriately classified. A primary aim of this book is to remedy that omission.

Just as planets and stars appear as points of light in the night sky and are indistinguishable to the untrained eye, so coincidences may seem on the surface to be all of one kind. This, unfortunately, has led to a tendency towards either/or explanations to account for them, a situation exacerbated by the ideological and metaphysical presumptions that have historically been equated with particular explanations. And there is more than a grain of truth to the notion that how we personally interpret coincidences is a reflection of our underlying beliefs about the nature of the universe and whether or not there is more to our existence than meets the eye.

The first chapter begins with a conceptual investigation into synchronicity and also the circumstances through which Jung came to develop the theory. His collaboration with the physicist Wolfgang Pauli is now well known and the subject of a number of scholarly and popular studies. However, it may well be that this association was not as important for Jung's conceptualisation of synchronicity as his friendship with the sinologist Richard Wilhelm during the 1920s. Wilhelm bequeathed to Jung an intuitive understanding of the Chinese concept of *tao*, which was to become for Jung very much associated with the *meaning* in meaningful coincidences.

In the second chapter probability theory, with all its power and ammunition against unwarranted subjectivity in the analysis of coincidences, is introduced. This sets the scene for an attempt at an overall categorisation of the various types of coincidence, including those that potentially have causal explanations. An example of the latter is the simultaneous development of the radio during the late nineteenth century, which led to acrimonious disputes over who actually invented it: was it Nikola Tesla or Guglielmo Marconi, or was it perhaps the Kentucky farmer Nathan Stubblefield, who eventually died of starvation as a reclusive pauper?[1] Whoever it was, it would certainly not have been possible for any of them to come up with the idea of transmitting radio waves had not the scientific and technological groundwork already been in place though the prior inventions of the telegraph and telephone.

In the third chapter another set of coincidences is examined: those behind the apparent fine-tuning of the universe, without which there would be no stars, no planets and no possibility of sentient life. This is an extremely rich field for coincidences and some of the parameters are so mind-blowingly precise that it is difficult not to wonder whether perhaps the whole thing really *is* some kind of 'put-up job', as the astronomer Fred Hoyle conjectured in his amazement at certain of the processes that had to have occurred for life as we know it to come into being.[2] Alongside these remarkable measurements are the rather odd anomalies and coincidences associated with quantum physics. These are discussed in the fourth chapter, as are some of their fascinating and perhaps unnerving implications.

The fifth chapter provides a summary of the various coincidence categories, as well as some examples as to how particular coincidences might be analysed. And because the whole concept of synchronicity is a fairly tricky one, it is revisited here with certain caveats as well as indications as to how meaningful coincidences might profitably be incorporated into the fabric of our everyday lives. It was Jung's conjecture that synchronistic events point to an underlying psychophysical unity, which he called the *unus mundus*. This was a view also shared by Pauli, and is one that appears to sit comfortably with certain interpretations of quantum physics.

The main focus of the sixth and final chapter is on the Chinese notion or principle of *tao*, as already mentioned a key concept for Jung as regards the underpinnings of synchronicity. An important question that naturally arises, particularly given its ubiquity in Chinese thought, is whether or not the *tao* has any sort of genuine objective reality in addition to its being a philosophical principle. If it does, it may provide a significant boost for the proposition that synchronicity is an authentic phenomenon in its own right and not just a subjective projection onto naturally occurring chance circumstances or causal mechanisms of one sort or another.

Endnotes

1. Rhoades, 'Just Who Invented Radio and Which Was the First Station?'
2. Hoyle, 'The Universe: Past and Present Reflections'.

'You never enjoy the world aright,
till the sea itself floweth in your veins,
till you are clothed with the heavens
and crowned with the stars…
till you are intimately acquainted
with the shady nothing
out of which the world was made.'

Thomas Traherne (17th C)

Chapter One

The Composition of Synchronicity

While there are a number of possible approaches to the whole question of coincidences, this work begins with an attempt to understand the concept of 'synchronicity', the term coined by C.G. Jung to refer to the phenomenon of meaningful coincidences. One might reasonably ask why he thought it necessary to present to the public a new word for a familiar notion. For Jung, however, synchronicity was much more than simply a synonym for meaningful coincidences: it was certainly that, but he also conceived of it as an *acausal connecting principle* for all types of phenomena that could not be fully explained by standard notions of causality, including ESP and the anomalies of quantum physics. In addition, and no doubt partly because of this wider conception, Jung seems to have had considerable difficulty in articulating a consistent and readily accessible definition for the term.[1] Not that this was necessarily a bad thing, and in his defence his associate Marie-Louise von Franz makes the point that for Jung synchronicity was essentially a working hypothesis rather than a definitive conception.[2]

It is only rarely that new words introduced into the public arena by a particular author are readily accepted as part of general discourse, and it is highly doubtful that Jung himself could have predicted how popular his invented term would become. An internet search for 'synchronicity' brings up numerous offerings, from serious philosophical proposals in regard to the ground of being to New Age miracle solutions and dismissive remarks by sceptics. For the theistically inclined, meaningful coincidences are readily interpreted as messages or signs from the divine, while for those from the opposite end of the spectrum, coincidences of any stripe tend to be viewed as interesting anomalies explainable by the laws of probability. The gap between these two viewpoints has long appeared all but unbridgeable, which is one reason why Jung, with his theory of synchronicity, was interested in developing an explanatory model that would be able to contribute towards bridging that gap.

It is understandable that the possibility of a theoretical explanation for meaningful coincidences should catch popular imagination so readily. The usual physicalist explanation that all such occurrences are simply random events, however meaningful they might appear, does not satisfy those for whom such coincidences have been literally life-changing. There is also an uncanniness that often accompanies these experiences, as if an ancient memory of the mysteriousness and inter-connectedness of life is suddenly and unexpectedly evoked. To have that sudden sense of proximity with the numinous explained away as an example of regression to magical thinking in the face of blind chance is for many deeply unsatisfying, and it is no wonder that people should thirst for richer and more convincing explanations. Von Franz explains this impasse well:

> The difficulty for the Western mind in attaining a proper understanding of synchronistic phenomena lies not so much in their occurrence, since every introspective person can easily recognise them, as in their fundamental acceptance in the realm of scientific thought.[3]

Some examples will give a sense of the multi-layered complexity that can be involved in synchronistic experiences. In his major treatise on the subject, *Synchronicity: An Acausal Connecting Principle*, Jung gives an account of a young woman patient of his whose personal problem was linked with what he describes as her rigid Cartesian conception of reality. She had had a dream in which she was given a golden scarab and as she was describing her dream to Jung there was a gentle tapping at the window. He looked out and saw a flying insect, which he grabbed and brought inside. It was a scarabaeid beetle, or rose-chafer, the closest thing to a golden scarab to be found in that part of Europe. The coincidence of this triggered a shift in the patient's conceptual rigidity and from then her condition began to improve. An added dimension to this story is that in Ancient Egypt the scarab was a symbol of rebirth, which according to Jung was exactly what took place psychologically for the young woman at that moment.[4]

Another compelling synchronicity story is one recounted by the astronomer and popular science writer Camille Flammarion, after whom the widely reproduced *Flammarion Woodcut* is named (see Appendix). Flammarion liked to collect curious and intriguing anecdotes, including the famous story of M. de Fortgibu and the plum-pudding, which he gave as an example of a triple coincidence. Jung includes this story as a footnote in his treatise, and it has been quoted so often that it has become somewhat emblematic of the phenomenon of meaningful coincidence, perhaps justifiably so as it succeeds in conveying the often enigmatic flavour of such coincidences in a much more immediate and graphic way than can be provided by any sort of formal definition:

> A certain M. Deschamps, when a boy in Orléans, was once given a piece of plum-pudding by a M. de Fortgibu. Ten years later he discovered another plum-pudding in a Paris restaurant, and asked if he could have a piece. It turned out, however, that the plum-pudding was already ordered — by M. de Fortgibu. Many years afterwards M. Deschamps was invited to partake of a plum-pudding as a special rarity. While he was eating it he remarked that the only thing lacking was M. de Fortgibu. At that moment the door opened and an old, old man in the last stages of deterioration walked in: M. de Fortgibu, who had got hold of the wrong address and burst in on the party by mistake.[5]

Jung describes this nineteenth century anecdote as 'edifying', and there is a rather enjoyable aesthetic quality in some of the stories of this kind, as if created by a joker or trickster. Jung also relates the remarkable account of a woman who took a photograph of her young son in 1914 and left the film to be developed in Strasbourg. Because of the outbreak of the war she was unable to pick up the film and so let it go. In 1916, she bought another film in Frankfurt to take a picture of her recently born daughter. But when this film was developed it was found to be doubly exposed, with the picture of her daughter superimposed on the 'lost' one of her son. Apparently the original picture of her son had not been developed and for some reason had got mixed up with a batch of new films.[6] This story is also edifying but has a slightly different flavour, with less humour perhaps but equally arresting. One suspects that this highly improbable occurrence would have been profoundly moving as well as meaningful for the woman.

These stories and others are all to be found in *Synchronicity: An Acausal Connecting Principle*, which was first published jointly with an essay on Johannes Kepler by the physicist Wolfgang Pauli in 1952 as *Natureklärung und Psyche*. Their book was later translated into English and came out in 1955 under the title *The Interpretation of Nature and the Psyche*. Although the joint publication gave the impression of being two essentially unrelated monographs, in actual fact Pauli had a significant influence on Jung's theoretical formulation of synchronicity.[7]

Influences and Predecessors

Paul Kammerer

Jung's essay is an attempt to provide an explanation of how and why meaningful coincidences occur, and also why he felt it necessary to coin a new term for a well-established phenomenon. His predecessors in this field include the philosophers Leibniz and Schopenhauer, as well the Austrian biologist, Paul Kammerer, who for over twenty years kept a log book of coincidences. This was eventually published in 1919 as *Das Gesetz der Serie* (the law of seriality), which Einstein is reported to have described as 'original and by no means absurd'.[8] Kammerer noted that coincidences often came in series or clusters, and he records that on one day his brother-in-law went to a concert and had both seat No. 9 and cloakroom ticket No. 9. The next day he went to another concert where he had seat No. 21 and cloakroom ticket No. 21.[9] According to Jung, there is nothing particularly meaningful about such coincidences and therefore they cannot be described as synchronistic events.[10]

Nevertheless, their occurrence was clearly significant for Kammerer and he classified such seemingly mundane coincidences with what Arthur Koestler describes as 'the meticulousness of a zoologist devoted to taxonomy'.[11] He did this because he thought coincidences, whether single or recurrent, were manifestations of an acausal principle in nature that ran parallel to causation. In his view, this principle was behind *laws of seriality*, which he thought were as important as the laws of physics but were as yet unexplored. For Kammerer, each coincidence we perceive is a fleeting glimpse or tip of the iceberg of the underlying activity of seriality, which he held to be 'ubiquitous and continuous in life, nature and cosmos. It is the umbilical cord that connects thought, feeling, science and art with the womb of the universe which gave birth to them'.[12] In Koestler's reading, Jung's notion of an acausal connecting principle contains rather too many elements of Kammerer's position.[13] Jung, however, does not acknowledge this and in fact criticises Kammerer for making unsubstantiated claims:

> Kammerer's factual material contains nothing but runs of chance whose only 'law' is probability; in other words, there is no apparent reason why he should look behind them for anything else. But for some obscure reason he does look behind them for something more than mere probability warrants—for a *law of seriality* which he would like to introduce as a principle coexistent with causality and finality. This tendency, as I have said, is in no way justified by his material.[14]

Interestingly, it is quite possible that had Kammerer not introduced the term *seriality*, Jung would not have found it necessary to come up with *synchronicity*, and when he first explains the concept in his essay, he wants to assure the reader that it is not to be confused with *synchronism*, which 'simply means the simultaneous occurrence of two events' and does not contain the added and all-important dimension of *meaning*. According to Jung, 'Synchronicity… means the simultaneous occurrence of a certain psychic state with one or more external events which appear as meaningful parallels to the momentary subjective state — and, in certain cases, vice versa'.[15] A more accessible definition of the term is given by von Franz, much of whose writing on the subject serves to clarify Jung's often difficult and meandering conceptualisations:

> This phenomenon consists of a symbolic image constellated in the inner psychic world, a dream, for instance, or a waking vision, or a sudden hunch originating in the unconscious, which coincides in a 'miraculous' manner, not causally or rationally explainable, with an event of similar meaning in the outer world.[16]

Arthur Schopenhauer

Jung seems to have been keen to distance himself from Kammerer, and one reason for this might well have been a fear of how his theoretical position on this topic would be greeted. Was it strong enough to withstand the inevitable counter-arguments from the scientific community? Before exploring the finer details of his synchronicity hypothesis more fully, it is worth remarking on some of Jung's major influences in addition to Kammerer. One of these was Arthur Schopenhauer, whose essay 'On the Apparent Design in the Fate of the Individual', in Jung's words, 'originally stood godfather to the views I am developing'.[17] According to Schopenhauer, 'Coincidence is the simultaneous occurrence of causally unconnected events' that can only be explained by the action of a *transcendent will* which orchestrates the lives of individuals, both subjectively and objectively, in accordance with 'the most wonderful pre-established harmony'.[18]

Jung criticised this position as being too deterministic and also far too broad in comparison with his idea of synchronicity as 'it credits meaningful coincidences with occurring so regularly and systematically that their verification would either be unnecessary or the simplest thing in the world'.[19] Although Jung rejected Schopenhauer's explanation, he commended him for having the courage to attempt to find a transcendental solution to the conundrum of meaningful coincidence 'at a time when the tremendous advance of the natural sciences had convinced everybody that causality alone could be considered the final principle of explanation'.[20]

The 'causality' Jung refers to here is clearly material or physical causation, the subtleties and philosophical difficulties concerning which he seems either to have been unaware of or considered irrelevant to the point he was intent on making: that the whole idea and thrust of *causality* needs to be balanced by an equal and opposite *acausality*. And perhaps, like the vast majority of the populace both then and now, he was unaware of the questioning within mainstream philosophy of the very *notion* of causality. For example, in a paper addressed to the Aristotelian Society in 1912, Bertrand Russell declared that 'The law of causality, like much that passes muster among philosophers, is a relic of a bygone age...'[21] Because everything is in one way or another contingent on something else, it is technically impossible to pin down with certainty a definite 'entity' that can invariably be identified as a specific cause for a specific effect, or vice versa.

This point was well made as early as the eighteenth century by the Scottish philosopher David Hume who proposed that the term *constant conjunction* replace that of causality. This is not an unreasonable suggestion, as is apparent when one considers the use of statistically based research methods. For example, the idea that smoking causes cancer does not mean that every smoker invariably gets cancer but that there is a statistically significant 'constant conjunction' between smoking and lung cancer.[22] But it was clearly not from Hume that Jung inherited his philosophical leanings, it was rather from the earlier and more organically-minded Gottfried Wilhelm Leibniz.

Gottfried Leibniz

Unlike Schopenhauer, whose major works were written in the first half of the nineteenth century, Leibniz lived in the transition period between the medieval and the modern eras. Just before he died in 1716, he proposed in his posthumously published *Monadology* that, contrary to being a vast machine, the universe was 'a vast living organism, each part of which was also an organism'.[23] Each organism or 'monad' exists independently from all others but is perfectly synchronised within the *pre-established harmony* of the whole. Thus, every little piece of the total puzzle, from the smallest particles of matter to living creatures and everything else known or unknown, is a part of an integrated and harmonious totality. A simple comparison would be with a symphony orchestra, in which each instrument has its part to play in the 'pre-established harmony' of the musical score.

This notion of a pre-established harmony, which Schopenhauer also refers to, comes from Leibniz but the thinking behind it did not originate with him. Not only were there medieval conceptions of the transcendent unity of the microcosm and macrocosm with which he would have been familiar, there was also the likely influence of Chinese ideas, which would have come from his contact with the Jesuits in Peking. Joseph Needham, author of the multi-volumed *Science and Civilisation in China*, observes that it is not difficult to find this influence in Leibniz's writing, as in the following excerpt from the *Monadology*: 'Every portion of matter may be conceived of as a garden full of plants or a pond full of fish; but every stem of a plant, every limb of an animal, every drop or sap of blood is also such a garden or pond.'[24]

One of Leibniz's achievements was that he was able in his *Monadology* to break away from the grip of magical causality that so profoundly characterised the medieval mind, while retaining an organic conception of the universe. He conceived his monads as having 'no windows'; in other words, they were connected *only* to pre-established harmony and *not* to one another. Because they had no causal interconnections, monads could not directly influence each other. This effectively meant that magical action-at-a-distance was not possible for individual monads which, in the case of living organisms, Leibniz referred to as 'souls'.[25] Needham argues that he was able to do this as a result of his understanding and appreciation of the subtleties of Neo-Confucian thought, of which he was kept abreast by the Jesuits in Peking, in particular through his correspondence with Father Joachim Bouvet. Leibniz rejected the mechanical universe of Descartes and Newton but in doing so did not retreat to the magical, and therefore deeply superstitious, thinking of the medieval mind, which at the time was a very significant accomplishment.[26]

Jung was very much in accord with Leibniz's idea of pre-established harmony, apart from one very important point: the frequency of occurrence of synchronistic events.[27] In the *Monadology*, each soul has a constant connection with pre-established harmony, as does the body, and their relationship is like that of two synchronised clocks. In Leibniz's words, 'The soul follows its own laws, and the body its own likewise, and they accord by virtue of the harmony pre-established among all representations of one and the same universe.'[28] As Jung remarks:

> Leibniz postulates a complete pre-established parallelism of events both inside and outside the monad. The synchronicity principle thus becomes the absolute rule in all cases where an inner event occurs simultaneously with an outside one. As against this, however, it must be borne in mind that the synchronistic phenomena which can be verified empirically [Jung's use of 'empirical', it should be noted, does not refer to formal scientific testing but rather to the traditional meaning of observation and experience], far from constituting a rule, are so exceptional that most people doubt their existence. They certainly occur much more frequently in reality than one thinks or can prove, but we still do not know whether they occur so frequently and so regularly in any field of experience that we could speak of them as conforming to law. We only know that there must be an underlying principle which might possibly explain all such (related) phenomena.[29]

Contemporary Influences

Richard Wilhelm

Jung first introduced publicly the idea of a *synchronistic principle* during his memorial address at the funeral of the sinologist Richard Wilhelm in 1930.[30] However, it took him another two decades to develop the idea fully and present it to the public. During the 1920s, Jung had formed an important friendship with Wilhelm who had a profound impact on Jung's understanding of Chinese philosophy and its fundamentally synchronistic approach to the interpretation of events. Of particular importance for Jung was Wilhelm's seminal translation of and commentary on the *I Ching* or *Book of Changes*, about which he spoke during the memorial address: 'Wilhelm has succeeded in bringing to life again, in a new and vital from, this ancient work in which not only many Sinologues but even many modern Chinese as well can see nothing but a collection of absurd magical formulae... Despite its fabulous age, it has never grown old, but still lives and operates, at least for those who understand its meaning.'[31]

Indirectly, the long shadow of Leibniz can be felt here, for it was very much his interest in Chinese philosophy, including the *I Ching*, which helped spark the West's fascination with Oriental ideas, an infatuation that continues unabated to this day. There is no doubt too that Jung's close association with Wilhelm was a crucial ingredient in his development of the notion of synchronicity. He refers to both Wilhelm and the *I Ching* in his treatise, and in 1949 he wrote the foreword for Wilhelm's translation. In it he described synchronicity as 'a certain curious principle... [which] takes the coincidence of events in space and time as meaning something more than mere chance...'[32] He also explained clearly and with practical examples how synchronicity is involved when the *I Ching* is consulted.

J.B. Rhine

But it was not so much his great respect for Wilhelm, nor his interest in the *I Ching*, which gave Jung the impetus to go public with what he felt was a difficult and challenging theoretical construct; it was the decisive influence of two other investigative pioneers from very disparate fields. The first of these was the parapsychologist J.B. Rhine. In 1934, Rhine sent Jung a complimentary copy of his book *Extra-Sensory Perception*, on the assumption that he might be interested in his research. In the following year, Rhine established the Duke Parapsychology Laboratory, and in 1937 the *Journal of Parapsychology* was launched. In 1940, after receiving his third book, *Extra-Sensory Perception after Sixty Years*,

Jung wrote the following to Rhine: 'It is a most interesting and valuable piece of work you have produced with your collaborators. I'm glad that somebody has undertaken the enormously patient work to produce an unshakable basis for ESP.'[33]

It is not really surprising that Jung was interested in the ESP research conducted by Rhine. His childhood had been very much involved with spiritualism. His cousin was a medium, family séances were a common occurrence in the Jung household, and his doctoral dissertation, published in 1902 as *On the Psychology and Pathology of So-Called Occult Phenomena*, was based on observations of his cousin in trance.[34] Paranormal events occurred for Jung throughout his life, including one that took place during an important meeting with Freud in 1909, during which Freud formally 'anointed' Jung as his 'successor and crown prince'.[35] Later in the evening, Jung felt a red-hot sensation is his diaphragm and then there was suddenly a loud report that came from a nearby bookcase, startling them both. Shortly afterwards, Jung announced that there would be another report. There was, as he had predicted, and the shock of this apparently deeply unnerved Freud and may well have been a symbolic foreshadowing of their break, which came three years later.[36]

It is, of course, quite possible that there is a more mundane explanation for the occurrence, which was understood somewhat differently by Freud.[37] But whatever the actual circumstances surrounding this incident, it should be emphasised that, for Jung, verifiable evidence of parapsychology was not only of great importance to him personally, but also for his attempt to establish a scientific footing for his theory of synchronicity. Indeed, in 1951, not long before the publication of his treatise, he wrote the following to Rhine:

> I regretted very much not seeing you when you were in Europe. Soon after you left I recovered from my illness and I have been able to finish a paper that is largely based on your ESP experiment which, by the way, is intensely discussed over here by psychologists as well as physicists.[38]

Wolfgang Pauli

It may be that such private communication contains a certain amount of friendly hyperbole, as Jung almost certainly would not have expressed anything like this in public, nor did he. However, the notion that his essay on synchronicity was largely based on Rhine's work would most definitely not have met with the agreement of his most active collaborator, Wolfgang Pauli, whose influence on Jung as regards the conceptualisation of synchronicity has become increasingly apparent since the release of their mutual correspondence.[39] For example, in regard to the remark Jung makes in his treatise about

Schopenhauer's essay 'On the Apparent Design in the Fate of the Individual' originally standing 'godfather to the views I am developing', we gain a somewhat different impression from their correspondence. In June 1949, Pauli wrote to Jung specifically recommending that he reference the essay, which he said had 'had a lasting and fascinating effect on me and seemed to be pointing the way to a new trend in the natural sciences'.[40] Although there is no further mention of Schopenhauer's essay in their correspondence, the fact that Jung makes such enthusiastic mention of it in his treatise was almost certainly the result of Pauli's prompting.

Wolfgang Pauli was a brilliant physicist who had collaborated closely with Nils Bohr and Werner Heisenberg on the development of quantum theory during the 1920s, and after whom the 'Pauli Exclusion Principle' is named. When suffering a personal crisis as a result of his failed marriage in 1930, Pauli was advised by his father to make contact with Jung, which he did, to the lasting benefit of both. Pauli's dreams became the subject of extensive analysis by Jung who considered him to be 'chock-full of archaic material',[41] and at the same time, Pauli explained to Jung some of the principles of quantum mechanics, in particular the unpredictable behaviour of particles at the sub-atomic level. Their association and friendship lasted until Pauli's death in 1958.

In Pauli's view, the parallel discoveries by Planck in physics and Freud in psychology right at the turn of the twentieth century were a significant coincidence. He was also intrigued, as was Jung, with the speculative possibility that the deepest level of the human psyche shares a fundamental unity with the quantum level of matter.[42] This interest was almost certainly augmented by the tendency for various sorts of calamitous accidents to occur in his presence, which became known amongst his colleagues as the 'Pauli Effect'. He appears to have shared this talent for unconscious psychokinesis with Jung, and it may well have brought an added dynamism to their relationship. One of Pauli's nicknames was *'der Geissel Gottes'*, which translates as the 'scourge' or 'whip' of God. As with the Pauli Effect, this term was used with a certain amount of humour, and it referred to his often fierce and merciless insight into the theoretical weaknesses of his colleagues.[43] Although Jung was twenty-five years older than Pauli and much venerated within his circle, Pauli was not afraid to criticise Jung when he considered his thinking sloppy.[44] Much has been written on their relationship, about which the author Robert Moss makes the following observation:

> Pauli was probably the only person in Jung's life from whom the great psychologist tolerated challenging feedback and criticism on matters most precious to him for a period of time anywhere near this long. This,

in itself, is amazing, since many people found Pauli's rudeness and incinerating criticism unbearable.[45]

One reason why Jung was reluctant to publish anything on synchronicity for so long was because of its likely ridicule from the scientific establishment. He was not scientifically trained and his language tended to be imprecise and intuitive, suitable perhaps for interpreting dreams but not for proposing a conceptual framework for meaningful coincidences, which could be so easily dismissed as subjectively determined. So the active encouragement of a Nobel prize-winning physicist was very welcome to Jung. In 1949, he wrote a draft of his essay and sent it to Pauli for criticism. Unlike Jung, Pauli was terminologically very precise. For example, he objected to the obvious etymological difficulties in the word 'synchronicity', particularly as the inner and outer correspondences that make certain coincidences meaningful do not necessarily occur at the same time. Pauli made clear his objection to this: 'The word "synchron" thus seems to me somewhat illogical, unless you wish to relate it to a chronos that is essentially different from normal time.'[46]

Instead of 'synchronicity', Pauli preferred the term *meaning-correspondence*.[47] But Jung *did* want to relate synchronicity to a chronos that is essentially different from normal time, as Pauli put it. Jung held that the 'meaning' in meaningful coincidences is *not* subjectively determined but arises from a realm *outside* the temporal world, and it is the breaking through of this timeless realm into the temporal sphere that constitutes the 'syn-chron'.[48] In other words, it is time and the timeless that become synchronised in a synchronistic event, and this has very little to do with chronological determinations. It is indeed quite common, even likely, for the various elements that go to make up a meaningful coincidence to occur over a period of time. A case in point would be the story of M. de Fortgibu and the plum-pudding, which unfolds over several decades.

So in a synchronistic occurrence, more significant than any temporal element is the *equivalence of meaning*, wherein the pattern of meaning in the psyche of the person experiencing the coincidence is reflected in the physical event. And according to von Franz, 'the factor of meaning is an inalienable part of the synchronicity phenomenon. What this meaning factor might consist of largely eludes our cognitive capacity.'[49] Significantly, Jung equated this elusive 'meaning factor' with the Chinese concept of *tao*, and was particularly pleased with Wilhelm's translation of it as 'meaning'.[50] To convey a flavour of the *tao*, and thereby what he considered to be at the very core of the equivalence of meaning that occurs during a synchronistic experience, Jung included a number of verses from Wilhelm's version of the *Tao Te Ching* in his treatise, beginning with Chapter 25:

> There is something formless yet complete
> That existed before heaven and earth,
> > How still! How empty!
> Dependent on nothing, unchanging,
> All pervading, unfailing.
> One may think of it as the mother of all things under heaven.
> I do not know its name,
> But I call it 'Meaning'.
> If I had to give it a name, I would call it 'The Great'.[51]

The Rupture of Time

In an interview with the acclaimed historian of religion Mircea Eliade in 1952, Jung explained synchronicity as a *rupture of time* which 'closely resembles numinous experiences in which space, time and causality are abolished'.[52] He was discussing Rudolf Otto's characterisation of religious experience as *numinous* and there are clear parallels here with profound experiences of synchronicity, which are often accompanied by a breath-taking sensation of mysteriousness and awe, and can, like religious experiences, be life changing. For in the moment of synchronistic awareness, there is, as Jung puts it, an 'absolute knowledge' which is not dependent on either the sense organs or on cerebral processes and which exists 'in a space-time continuum where space is no longer space, nor time time'.[53]

Victor Mansfield, author of *Synchronicity, Science, and Soul-Making*, argues that 'absolute knowledge' is too strong an expression and would prefer to tone it down by saying, 'we have sporadic access to knowledge that surpasses the ego's normal sense channels and modes of reasoning'.[54] But whatever the terminology, this flash of immediate insight, which Jung called absolute knowledge, is not to be confused with the *meaning* that occurs in the correspondence of inner and outer events inherent in a synchronistic experience, though they are both essential ingredients. Von Franz elaborates:

> The 'meaning' of a synchronistic phenomenon visibly participates in the nature of this 'absolute knowledge' of the unconscious, which is nevertheless only a 'cloud of cognition' for our conscious intelligence. The realisation of 'meaning' is therefore not a simple acquisition of information or of knowledge, but a living experience that touches the heart just as much as the mind. It seems to us to be an illumination characterised by great clarity as well as something ineffable.[55]

A modern example of a synchronistic event of this calibre concerns a rabbi from Israel on a visit to New York. Because the rabbi had a serious heart condition, he was under the care of a local doctor, whose telephone number he carried with him at all times (this was before the days of mobile phones). One day he started to feel severe heart pains and so immediately called the number and asked if the doctor was there. The person who answered the phone seemed a little puzzled but said that the doctor was, and would fetch him. The doctor came to the phone and assured the rabbi he would be over soon; but before hanging up he asked the rabbi how he knew his whereabouts as he was on an emergency call and had not told anyone where he was going. The rabbi, somewhat surprised, said that he had simply dialled his regular number. The doctor then looked down at the telephone number displayed on the dial of the phone he was using and saw that it was *exactly* the same as his, except for one number which was one digit off.

Later, after his arrival at the hospital, the rabbi was told that his life had been saved only by the timely intervention of the doctor.[56] Jung would have described this remarkable turn of events as an authentic *act of creation in time*. In a critical situation, an intricately simple but profoundly meaningful solution to the rabbi's predicament breaks through, or ruptures, the space-time continuum at that moment to produce a powerful synchronistic outcome that is causally 'unthinkable'.[57] Of course, it could be argued that the rabbi could just as easily have called an ambulance, or that probability theory renders the outcome highly unlikely but within the realms of possibility; but that is not what occurred. Instead, out of the blue, an exact mistake was made that was mathematically so unlikely in its precision, yet so appropriate.

As mentioned in the case of M. de Fortgibu and the plum-pudding, there is often a *trickster* element in synchronicities. In their investigation of synchronicity, Allan Combs and Mark Holland devote a chapter to the mythological figure of the trickster: Hermes for the Greeks, Loki for the Norse, Coyote for the Plains Indians, and Ananse for the Ashanti of West Africa.[58] These trickster gods are mythological embodiments of meaningful coincidence and it is through their manipulation of unpredictable and paradoxical circumstances that they teach important lessons to people, particularly when they are caught up in rigid ways of thinking, which might well have been the case for M. Deschamps. And in relation to the implicit confrontation between synchronicity and science, both philosophical and methodological, Combs and Holland write: 'The world of modern mechanistic science is a world bounded by the rigid constraints of causality. It is the Trickster's predilection to cross such boundaries, bringing the unexpected to the commonplace.'[59] There is every likelihood that both the rabbi and the doctor were profoundly moved by their experience, for as Jung suggests in the foreword to his treatise, the implications of the phenomenon of synchronicity are 'philosophically of the greatest importance'.[60]

Jung considered the creativity displayed in synchronistic events to be evidence of the ancient idea of a continuous creation, or *creatio continua*. In this view, creation is not a one-off event but rather an ongoing activity which underlies our existence at each moment. In Jung's articulation of this process, the *creatio continua* is born out of the original undifferentiated unity of all existence, the *unus mundus*, a conception derived from medieval philosophy. The *unus mundus* is a key concept in Jung's explanatory framework for synchronicity, specifically so because it represents the idea of psychophysical unity, 'where there is no incommensurability between so-called matter and so-called psyche'.[61] In other words, mind and matter are undivided in the *unus mundus*. And out of it comes the *creatio continua* which, as von Franz explains, 'should be seen not only as a successive series of creative acts but equally as the eternal presence of the *one* creative act'.[62] In addition, and importantly for the overall understanding of Jung's theoretical position: 'Synchronistic events are "singularities" in which the oneness of psyche and matter, the *unus mundus*, becomes sporadically manifest.'[63]

Two Types of Synchronicity

An essential element of Jung's theory of synchronicity is the distinction he made between the wider *principle* of synchronicity, the 'acausal connecting principle' of the subtitle of his treatise, and the narrower category of synchronistic *events*, which he described as 'a special instance of general acausal orderedness'.[64] It is synchronicity as an acausal connecting principle that he, with input from Pauli, postulated as a complement and alternative to the causal principle. According to the depth psychologist Ira Progoff, much of the inspiration for the necessity of a principle in contradistinction to causality came from Jung's reading of Leibniz, whose notion of a pre-established harmony was very much a forerunner of Jung's acausal connecting principle.[65] As already mentioned in the brief section on Leibniz, in his conception there is no causal interaction amongst monads, each of which is synchronised with pre-established harmony. Progoff elaborates:

> The significance of the 'pre-established harmony' is that it sets the pattern within which the diversities of life may have their 'interconnections'… The harmony of this pattern is not to be explained. It is simply how the cosmos has been 'pre-established' to provide the conditions for life.[66]

This is essentially how Jung conceived of his acausal connecting principle, though it was for him much more limited in its application than it had been for Leibniz. It really only came into play when causal explanations failed — but where they *do* fail is by no means insignificant. One area is quantum physics, which of course underpins the entire universe as we know it. Another is mathematics, specifically the inherent properties of natural numbers, which acausally display what the physicist Eugene Wigner described as 'the unreasonable effectiveness of mathematics in the natural sciences'.[67] In addition to what he identified as the *a priori* factors of the discontinuities of modern physics and the properties of natural numbers, Jung was also keen to include J.B. Rhine's experiments within this wider conception of synchronicity.[68] But Rhine himself, notwithstanding his sustained correspondence with Jung, was reluctant to abandon causality as an explanation for parapsychological events.[69] This did not stop Jung from categorising the results of ESP experiments as acausal phenomena and therefore part of his principle of synchronicity. At the same time, he also singled out synchronistic events as a 'special instance' of the acausal principle because of their uniqueness and unrepeatability.

In order to clarify this distinction *within* acausality, Victor Mansfield, Sally Rhine-Feather and James Hall in a 1998 journal article differentiate between 'scientific' and 'historical' causality, neither of which pertain to synchronistic occurrences in the narrowly defined sense.[70]

Briefly, *scientific* causality refers to experimental replication, while *historical* causality refers to the determination of a 'historical' chain of events leading from the effect back to the cause. For example, in quantum measurements there is precise repeatability when large numbers of particles are examined but not so at the level of individual particles, which are entirely random. So from this perspective quantum physics is 'scientifically' causal though *not* 'historically' causal and therefore a natural candidate for Jung to include under the umbrella of his acausal principle. Similarly, parapsychological experiments are scientifically replicable but not historically so.

There is absolutely no debate about this at the quantum level, though there is for parapsychology, despite consistent statistically significant results for ESP experiments.[71] This is not, however, the debate we are concerned with here but rather whether replicability is *theoretically* possible for parapsychological research, and clearly it is. But there is still no identifiable causal mechanism or energy exchange behind ESP, and this makes it 'historically acausal'. By the same token, it very much appears that synchronistic events are *neither* historically *nor* scientifically causal. For ESP experiments standardised testing procedures are the norm; for synchronistic occurrences, however, that is another proposition entirely. Their occurrence is both sporadic and unpredictable and, as von Franz puts it, they are 'almost all one-time experiences and therefore not confirmable'.[72] In other words, under the umbrella of acausality it is *only* synchronistic phenomena that are completely acausal in their manifestation.

Meanwhile Pauli, foreshadowing what would subsequently become a significant criticism of Jung's treatise, told Jung that he thought Rhine's experiments were involved with a totally different phenomenon to synchronicity.[73] This sentiment is reflected in the same journal article by Mansfield, Rhine-Feather and Hall who say they 'do not understand Jung' when he ascribes *meaning* to Rhine's experiments, which he unequivocally does in his treatise: 'Rhine's experiments confront us with the fact that there are events which are related to one another experimentally, and in this case *meaningfully*…'[74] Because the presence or otherwise of meaning is a crucial differentiating feature between synchronistic and purely parapsychological events, they take Jung to task for blurring the boundaries here and argue that, unless synchronicity is interpreted strictly, it will be all too easily confused with parapsychological phenomena.[75] It is perhaps not insignificant that Sally Rhine-Feather, one of the three authors of the paper, which is titled 'The Rhine Jung Letters: Distinguishing Parapsychological from Synchronistic Events', is J.B. Rhine's daughter.

In an attempt to explain this tendency in Jung's thinking, the cultural historian Richard Tarnas makes the important distinction between his *initial* development of the idea of synchronicity, when the focus was much more on straightforward experiences of meaningful coincidence, and his later broadening of the concept. Thus, by the time he had come to write his treatise, Jung's 'increasing focus on parapsychology and physics had in a sense partly colonised the original concept and thus obscured the reality of how he had integrated his experience of meaningful coincidences into his life and clinical practice'.[76] Indeed, there is a considerable amount of reference to what can only be described as parapsychological rather than purely synchronistic phenomena in Jung's essay. For example, he spends three pages describing the details of an out-of-body experience of a woman who nearly died following complications during the birth of her first child.[77]

Pauli also thought that Jung was trying to include too many different kinds of phenomena into his concept of synchronicity and, according to Suzanne Gieser in her analysis of their collaboration, this was his main criticism: instead of drawing such a broad and intuitive brush, Pauli wanted Jung to specify the components of synchronicity with greater care and precision. As Gieser notes: 'With his critical disposition he found himself constantly irritated by Jung's careless concept formation and drifting perspectives, while at the same time he found the discussions with him stimulating and fertile.'[78] For example, Pauli objected to Jung's inclusion of Rhine's experiments in his synchronicity thesis because they did not involve 'archetypal contents becoming conscious'.[79]

The Surfacing of Archetypes

In Jung's psychological model, with which Pauli was familiar, archetypes are 'archaic remnants' or 'primordial images' from the collective unconscious,[80] which Jung postulated as existing at the deepest levels of the human psyche, below the level of the personal unconscious. His use of the term *archetype* is different from the Platonic conception in that it involves feeling and emotion[81] and is therefore more complex and 'earthy' than the abstract and rarefied Platonic world of ideal Forms. If, for example, we speak about an ideal or 'archetypal' rose, we are automatically invoking the Platonic Idea or Form of 'roseness', which is quite different from the Jungian conception. But Jung was not shy to appropriate and change the meaning of established ideas when it suited him. So, following Jung's terminology, when an archetype breaks through to consciousness, there is an *affective charge*—in other words, an intense burst of emotion—which can be enormously powerful and, during the time that an individual is under the spell of the archetype, all-consuming, as Jung explained in a 1957 interview:

> The archetype is a force. It has an autonomy and it can suddenly seize you. It is like a seizure. Falling in love at first sight is something like that. You see, you have a certain image in yourself, without knowing it, of woman, of *the* woman. Then you see that girl, or at least a good imitation of your type, and instantly you get a seizure and you are gone. And afterwards you may discover it was a hell of mistake.[82]

In his treatise, Jung describes archetypes as *unobservable* structures or 'patterns of behaviour' in the unconscious which, when activated, 'develop numinous effects which express themselves as *affects*'.[83] When archetypal contents become conscious, according to Jung, as for example when a person is swept up in a frenzy of creative inspiration, is consumed by fury, or falls deeply and dramatically in love, the luminosity and heightened awareness that come with the intense focus on a particular situation or content takes energy away from other parts of the consciousness, which then slip into unconsciousness. Into the space vacated, therefore, deep-seated unconscious material can then surface and, with that surfacing, the individual's normal orientation towards the world is suspended.

With the excitation of the archetype, not only can the contents of the unconscious break through, but also the *unus mundus* itself, and it is the surfacing of this unified realm of matter and psyche from the deepest layers of the collective unconscious that gives rise to synchronistic events.[84] And while such experiences can be very inspiring for someone who is psychologically balanced and whose ego structure is strong, for the mentally unstable there can be serious consequences, as von Franz observed from her clinical experience with psychologically disturbed patients:

> At the time of dropping into a psychotic interval most patients are in a highly excited, emotional state, and an archetype in the unconscious, or indeed the whole collective unconscious is violently activated. Hence synchronistic events occur with conspicuous frequency at such times (although they also occur with normal people when an archetype is activated). And at such times the patient will make a false interpretation of synchronistic phenomena in a way designed to confirm his morbid fantasies rather than to correct them.[85]

Synchronistic experiences are also more likely to occur at critical junctures in people's lives, especially at key times such as the death of close friends and relatives or the first youthful explosion of love. At such times, the archetypes in the unconscious are activated by the extreme situation, setting the stage for an increased probability of a synchronistic occurrence. Both Jung and von Franz are very insistent that an increased probability or tendency for synchronistic experiences to occur when an archetype is activated does *not* mean that archetypes *cause* synchronistic events.[86]

As the research psychologist Lance Storm explains it: 'The idea of the archetype having causal properties which bring about synchronistic events would be as untenable to Jung's idea of synchronicity as claiming, for example, that an immediate drop of land *causes* the phenomenon of the waterfall.'[87] Of course, a waterfall needs an immediate drop of land for its existence but there are so many other factors involved and countless cliff-like landscapes that do not sport waterfalls. Likewise, archetypes may set the scene for synchronistic events, but they do *not* directly cause them. Moreover, synchronistic events *always* occur in unexpected patterns and configurations, and consistently display a freshness and creativity that renders straightforward cause and effect inconceivable, or as Jung puts it, 'unthinkable'.

Jung's explanation of the operation of synchronistic events is certainly coherent in itself; however, when he states, as he does in his treatise,[88] that meaningful coincidences occur more frequently than probability should allow, he opens both himself and his theory to the risk of ridicule. Why he felt the need to do this is unclear but may be linked to his blurring of the boundaries between synchronicity and parapsychology. From a theoretical perspective, there is no intrinsic reason why the workings of synchronicity should not be entirely compatible with the laws of chance. To suggest otherwise, as Jung does, though with no empirical data beyond his own personal and clinical observations, naturally encourages statements to the contrary.

For example, the mathematician Steven Strogatz makes the point that 'no evidence... has ever been found for Carl Jung's idea of "synchronicity", the claim that meaningful coincidences in our lives occur more often than by chance alone'.[89] But as Strogatz makes abundantly clear in a rather remarkable and engaging coincidence anecdote of his own,[90] it is not the occurrence of meaningful coincidences *per se* that he is questioning but rather the suggestion that they occur more often than chance would allow. And as we shall see, particularly in Chapters Two and Three, the breadth of possibility that chance is able to cater for is very great indeed.

Synchronicity and the *I Ching*

A conceptually problematic but potentially useful dimension for an understanding of the workings of synchronicity is through the age-old activity of divination. Used regularly by pre-scientific cultures all over the world and throughout history, divination is essentially the use of ritual procedures to *provoke* synchronistic phenomena in order to foretell the future. The most basic divination techniques use random patterns such the tossing of chicken bones, examining the entrails of a sacrificed animal or reading tea leaves to determine whether a particular course of action is favourable or not. Through the chaotic pattern, which acts like a ceremonially created Rorschach blot, knowledge from the unconscious is released and the determination is made.[91]

While oracular methods are diverse and widespread, from the calendrical divination of the Maya to the oracle at Delphi and the augurs of Rome, it was only in China that a divinatory method with the sophistication of the *I Ching* was developed. It became the predominant oracle in China after the overthrow of the Shang Dynasty in the eleventh century BCE. The main method of divination for the Shang imperial court was based on the observation of cracks in tortoise shells, and during the reign of the dynasty literally hundreds of thousands of tortoise shells were painstakingly prepared and then ritually cracked with red hot pokers to create patterns which could then be interpreted for decisions on all manner of subjects, from military campaigns and the weather to dreams and toothaches.[92]

With the change of dynasty came a change of dominant oracle from the comparatively primitive interpretations of random patterns in tortoise shells to the much more sophisticated number oracle of the *I Ching*, described by Wilhelm as 'unquestionably one of the most important books in the world's literature'.[93] According to Wilhelm, the *I Ching* was far more important as a book of wisdom than as an oracle, and provided the source of ideas for both Confucianism and Taoism. In addition, in its function as an oracle, it did not just make prophesies about the future but gave advice for correct conduct in any situation, so that ethical responsibility rested with the individual.[94] Mathematically, the *I Ching* is based on the binary interplay and of *yin* and *yang*, the symbols for negative and positive, which are portrayed as broken and unbroken lines. These lines are combined into eight trigrams (three-line configurations) and then into sixty-four hexagrams (six-line configurations). Into each of these hexagrams certain images and archetypal situations were intuited and developed over many centuries by generations of scholars and sages.

When the oracle is consulted with integrity, there is a psychic *mirroring* between the state of mind of the questioner and the image or images provided by the arrangement of hexagrams at that unique moment in time. In addition to the impact of the image, there is the theoretical explanation and commentary, and the combination of these provides the questioner with a reading.[95] The *I Ching* was developed and refined over the centuries to stimulate a reflective apprehension of meaningful coincidence, which is so much a characteristic of the Chinese way of thinking. In addition, and perhaps more importantly, it encouraged an ethical response to any given situation through the wisdom of past generations that is provided in the commentaries.

The 'affective charge' that characteristically accompanies a synchronistic experience is also a characteristic of consulting an oracle such as the *I Ching*, especially for those for whom it is a living being. They approach it with reverence and sincerity, and in doing so invoke the deepest levels of their psyche, and then the answer from the reading is filled with a sense of uniqueness and meaning. This was Jung's own experience, as he details in his foreword to the Wilhelm translation. He personified the book, which in itself is an act of animistic reverence, and asked the *I Ching* about his intention to present it to the West. The answer he received was favourable, with certain caveats, and afterwards he felt that his question had been satisfactorily answered:

> I agree with Western thinking that any number of answers to my question were possible, and I equally cannot assert that another answer would not have been equally significant. However, the answer received was the first and only one; we know nothing of other possible answers.

It pleased and satisfied me. To ask the same question more than once would have been tactless and heavy-handed and so I did not do it... Moreover, a repetition of the experiment is impossible, for the simple reason that the original situation cannot be reconstructed. Therefore in each instance there is only a first and single answer.[96]

Jung was well aware of the standard objections to the validity of the *I Ching* and indeed to any divination method, the main one being that all divinatory or oracular interpretations are subjective and therefore dependent on the psychological processes of the diviner or interpreter. But it was exactly the mindset that adheres itself axiomatically to such objections that Jung called into question: 'While the Western mind carefully sifts, weighs, selects, classifies, isolates, the Chinese picture of the moment encompasses everything down to the minutest nonsensical detail, because all the ingredients make up the observed moment.'[97]

In Chinese thought, where the *tao* is held to be a gentle and veiled presence that nourishes all existence, the external world is both alive and filled with latent meaning. In the thinking style of the Chinese, which von Franz calls *field thinking*, meaning is present in both the individual and the environment and it is therefore natural for the Chinese, and other East Asians, to look at what else is happening at the same time as a particular event in order to grasp the overall picture.[98] This approach is reflected in an anecdote von Franz relates which concerns a Japanese man who came up to her after a lecture she was giving on synchronicity and causality, and said, 'Now I understand what causality is! When I was reading about Western physics, I always thought that it was all synchronistic. And now that you have taken so much trouble to show the differences, I am able to understand for the first time what causality is!'[99]

For Pauli too, it was important to distinguish between a spontaneous occurrence of synchronicity and an induced one, as in the case of consulting an oracle such as the *I Ching*. He made a comparison between the ritual preparation for divination and scientific experimentation. Both are controlled conditions and any new discovery requires that intuitive connections are made by the observer.[100] While the scientist is looking for causal links, the diviner is looking for constellated meaning in a particular instant of time. The main difference between the two is that in a scientific experiment chance is eliminated to the greatest possible extent, while in divination chance becomes the central factor and, via the method employed, the source of information.[101]

When there is total involvement and focus, the act of divination is filled with portentous significance and this can stimulate a temporary collapse in the usual boundary between the external world and internal processes of thought and feeling. Obviously, causality is involved in the setting of the scene during divination, but the actual experience of meaningful coincidence, when there is a synchronistic correspondence between physical events and psychological states, cannot, in Jung's view, be explained in terms of cause and effect. This applies both to spontaneous experiences of synchronicity as well as those experienced under the controlled conditions of divination.

The Presence of Affect

Pauli was comfortable with references to Chinese philosophy, including the *I Ching* with which, like Jung, he was very familiar. However, the same cannot be said about his feelings towards astrology, about which he felt instinctively suspicious.[102] He was therefore concerned when Jung proposed the inclusion of a chapter in his essay titled 'The Astrological Experiment'. He thought that it would easily be misinterpreted by believers in astrology as definite support by Jung for astrology, and therefore strongly encouraged him to make clear its limitations when clarifying the workings of synchronicity.[103] Jung did so, though for anyone looking for scientific or philosophical precision, the inclusion of several pages of astrological symbols in the text might seem a little disconcerting.

Jung had already shown the effectiveness of an *I Ching* reading in his foreword to the Wilhelm translation and quite possibly he wanted to attempt something similar for astrology. Although the experiment did not yield any statistically useful data in terms of astrological correspondences, it *did* reveal a relationship between the emotional state of those compiling the data from the experiment (Jung himself and an assistant) and positive correlations from the material. Jung reports that when they were excited and expectant, they came up with a surprising number of accurate correlations. However, as the data collection wore on and they began to feel bored, they came up with correlations that were no better than chance.[104]

A parallel pattern had also been revealed in Rhine's ESP experiments: there were statistically significant results when the subjects were fresh and interested, but these fell away as the exercise became more routine.[105] The common denominator appears to have been the presence of *affect*, and if what Jung is implying is correct, not only in clearly defined synchronistic experiences is there a connection between psyche and matter but also whenever an affective charge is produced as a result of the activation of an unconscious archetype. An example provided by Combs and Holland concerns a retired businessman who became very involved in doing odd jobs around the house. When he and his wife spent a week with their daughter and her family, all sorts of things went wrong in the house, which had hitherto been fine, and he was there to fix them. When the week was up and the parents went home, things returned to normal in the daughter's house with no major breakages or failures that required his odd job skills.[106] Although Combs and Holland describe this as a type of synchronicity, it may be more accurate to label it as a kind of low intensity psychokinesis, rather like the Pauli Effect, especially as the father would have been completely unaware of anything abnormal or unusual.

If there was a synchronistic element involved, it would have been of a much subtler order than what might be expected in dramatic synchronistic events. But as Combs and Holland point out, many synchronicities are actually very subtle and may be part of an ongoing process of inner guidance and self-understanding.[107] Everyday events or chance perceptions, such as glancing at the title of a book or noticing a sudden burst of sunlight through the clouds, may accord with unconscious processes to provide hints for intuitive decision making. While this kind of psychological openness to the surrounding environment may sound suspiciously akin to the superstitious associations that are rife in magical thinking, there is a significant difference, one that is reflected in the difference between primitive forms of pattern divination and the ethical reflectiveness that is so central to the oracular function of the *I Ching*. This also accords with the goals and aims of Jung's depth psychology, in which synchronicities are viewed as markers in the process of *individuation*, which represents the inward journey towards the integration of the psyche.

Synchronicity and Deliberate Intention

Joseph Campbell, who became widely known after his series of interviews on mythology with Bill Moyers on PBS in 1986, often spoke about the importance of *following one's bliss*, in other words, of being in accord with one's deepest needs for fulfilment and happiness. When asked during the interviews by Moyers whether he had ever had the sense, when following his bliss, of 'being helped by hidden hands', he replied:

> All the time. It is miraculous. I even have a superstition that has grown on me as a result of invisible hands coming all the time—namely, that if you do follow your bliss you put yourself on a kind of track that has been there all the while, waiting for you, and the life that you ought to be living is the one you are living. When you can see that, you begin to meet people who are in the field of your bliss, and they open the doors to you. I say, follow your bliss and don't be afraid, and doors will open where you didn't know they were going to be.[108]

It may seem here that Campbell is providing advice on how to increase the flow of positive coincidences in one's life, and this could well be the case. But it is one thing to suggest that one follow's one's bliss and quite another to attempt to manipulate synchronicity, and Campbell specifically warns against using the power of deliberate intention to achieve one's personal aims. He asks, rhetorically: 'Are you going to be a person of heart and humanity—because that's where the life is, from the heart—or are you going to do whatever seems to be required of you by what might be called "intentional power"?'[109] In regard to this very pertinent issue, Jung quotes at length from the Dominican scholar Albertus Magnus (1206–1280), who held that extreme intensities of emotion could cause magical effects: 'When… the soul of a man falls into a great excess of any passion, it can be proved by experiment that it binds things and alters them in the way it wants… Whoever would learn the secret of doing and undoing these things must know that everyone can influence everything magically if he falls into a great excess… and he must do it at that hour when the excess befalls him…'[110]

Jung includes this type of deliberate magic or enchantment within his synchronicity hypothesis, an inclusion which in effect opens the door to what Mansfield describes as 'the willful employment of acausal orderedness'.[111] There is much written along these lines in so-called New Age literature, where the power of intention is regularly extolled as an Aladdin's lamp to fulfil one's deepest dreams and desires. One such example is *Synchrodestiny: Harnessing the Infinite Power of Coincidence to Create Miracles* by the prolific and best-selling author Deepak Chopra. Some quotes from the book include: 'Intent creates coincidences; it is the reason why, when you're thinking of something, it happens.'[112] 'What most people call luck is the application of synchronicity to the fulfilment of our intention.'[113] And: 'Perhaps a miracle lies in the wings. You'll never know unless you form an intention, become sensitive to the clues from the universe, follow the chain of coincidence, and help create the destiny you most desire.'[114] A brief analysis of *Synchrodestiny* immediately reveals how far removed the concept of synchronicity has come in popular imagination from Jung's much more sophisticated conceptualisation.

One reason for this was surely his determination to include ESP and parapsychology as part of his hypothesis, thus leading to certain expectations of the 'hidden possibilities' of meaningful coincidence. In contrast to the ethical constraints incorporated into the deeply synchronistic fabric of the *I Ching*, Jung's mature presentation of synchronicity allows for a Pandora's Box of uses and interpretations. Much of the responsibility for this potential slippery slope must, therefore, go to

Jung's theoretical incorporation of synchronicity into parapsychology, which in fact became increasingly apparent in his later years, when he was no longer subject to the editorial gaze of Pauli. For example, in his 1958 publication, *Flying Saucers: A Modern Myth of Things Seen in the Skies*, he writes about '…remarkable relativisations of space and time which simply cannot be explained causally. They are the parapsychological phenomena which I have summed up under the term "synchronicity" and which have been statistically investigated by Rhine'.[115]

The blurring of boundaries in that statement is evident, as they are in the obscurities and inconsistencies of *Synchronicity: An Acausal Connecting Principle*, Jung's main work on the subject, which stands in stark contrast with his elegantly conceived foreword to Wilhelm's translation of the *I Ching*. It is as if, in the foreword, his original inspiration for the development of the concept of synchronicity had once again come to life, and his original inspiration was very much bound up with the character and achievements of Richard Wilhelm. Had Wilhelm not died so early, together they may have presented and developed a framework for synchronicity much more in keeping with the Chinese way of thinking embodied in the *I Ching*. If Jung's address at Wilhelm's memorial service is anything to go by, this could well have been the case, as can be seen in this brief excerpt from the eulogy:

> It is no small service to have given us, as Wilhelm did, such an all-embracing, richly coloured picture of a foreign culture; but much more important is the fact that he has transmitted to us the living germ of the Chinese spirit, capable of working an essential change in our view of life. We are no longer reduced to being admiring or critical observers, but have become participants in the Eastern spirit, to the degree to which we have succeeded in experiencing the effective potency of the *I Ching*.[116]

The Rainmaker

Most of the literature on synchronicity since Jung published his treatise places only marginal significance on the importance of Wilhelm in Jung's development of the concept. The overlay of quantum physics and particularly parapsychology has all but drowned out the possibility of a quintessentially Chinese interpretation of synchronicity, one that needs no recourse to paranormal explanations. An important acknowledgement of Wilhelm comes from Ira Progoff, who has described how he was shown personally by Jung how to consult the *I Ching*.[117] Progoff writes: 'Jung's association with Wilhelm was of major importance in his conception of Synchronicity, for it gave him an opportunity to draw upon Wilhelm's knowledge of the noncausal sense of "patterning" that plays so important a role in ancient Chinese thinking.'[118]

Another area that is rarely mentioned in the literature, but which has long been associated in the popular mind with meaningful coincidence, is prayer. Combs and Holland quote the famous saying of Archbishop William Temple: 'When I pray, coincidences start to happen. When I don't pray, they don't happen.'[119] However, they do not follow up on it, and Jung was of the opinion, as with his explanation of the phenomena described by Albertus Magnus, that 'the traditional belief in the efficacy of prayer', like magic wish-fulfilment, is 'based on the experience of concomitant synchronistic phenomena'.[120] The implicit reference here is to petitionary prayer, traditionally regarded as much more ego-centred and desire-laden an activity than the surrendered stillness of contemplative prayer or meditation.[121] And on a felicitous note, it appears that in Jung's mind the epitome of the latter was to be found in a story told to him by Wilhelm from his personal experience in China. It is the story of the Rainmaker who in his humility and openness to the *tao* became a living embodiment of the principle of synchronicity in all its natural goodness. Marie-Louise von Franz gives a lively version of the story, which Jung asked her friend and fellow analyst, Barbara Hannah, to repeat at every lecture she gave:

> In Kiaochou came a great drought so that men and animals died in the hundreds. In despair, the citizens called for an old rainmaker who lived in the mountains nearby. Richard Wilhelm saw how the rainmaker was brought into town in a sedan chair, a tiny little grey-bearded man. He asked to be left alone outside the town in a little hut, and after three days in rained, and even snowed! Richard Wilhelm succeeded in being allowed to interview the old man and asked him how he made the rain. But he answered, 'I haven't made the rain, of course not.' And then, after a pause, he added, 'You see it was like this—throughout the whole of nature and all the men and women here were deeply disturbed. They were no longer in tao. When I arrived here I became also disturbed. It was so bad that it took me three days to bring myself again into order.' And then he added, with a smile, 'Then naturally it rained.'[122]

Endnotes

1. Jung, *Synchronicity*, 36–42; Main, *The Rupture of Time*, 39–47.
2. von Franz, *Psyche and Matter*, 310.
3. von Franz, *Number and Time*, 6–7.
4. Jung, *Synchronicity*, 31–33.
5. Ibid., 21, 21n.
6. Ibid., 21.
7. Meier, *Atom and Archetype*; Gieser, *The Innermost Kernel*.
8. Koestler, *The Roots of Coincidence*, 87.

9   Ibid., 84.
10 Jung, *Synchronicity*, 11–12.
11 Koestler, *The Roots of Coincidence*, 85.
12 Ibid., 87.
13 Ibid., 95.
14 Jung, *Synchronicity*, 13.
15 Ibid., 36.
16 von Franz, *Number and Time*, 6.
17 Jung, *Synchronicity*, 16.
18 Koestler, *The Roots of Coincidence*, 107–108.
19 Jung, *Synchronicity*, 18.
20 Ibid., 19.
21 Russell, *Mysticism and Logic*, 171.
22 Smoley, *The Dice Game of Shiva*, 67.
23 Needham and Ronan, *The Shorter Science and Civilisation in China*, Vol. 1, 248.
24 Ibid.
25 Jung, *Synchronicity*, 114–115.
26 Needham and Ronan, *The Shorter Science and Civilisation in China*, Vol. 1, 248–249.
27 von Franz, *Psyche and Matter*, 26–27.
28 Jung, *Synchronicity*, 115.
29 Ibid., 116–117.
30 Wilhelm and Jung, *The Secret of the Golden Flower*, 141.
31 Ibid., 140.
32 Jung, foreword to Wilhelm, R., *I Ching or Book of Changes*, xxiv.
33 Mansfield et al., 'The Rhine Jung Letters', 13.
34 Main, *The Rupture of Time*, 66–67.
35 Ibid., 68.
36 Koestler, *The Roots of Coincidence*, 91–92.
37 Fisher, L., 'Jung's Explosive Visit to Freud'.
38 Mansfield et al., 'The Rhine Jung Letters', 3.
39 Meier, *Atom and Archetype*.
40 Ibid., 38.
41 Zabriskie, 'Jung and Pauli: A Meeting of Rare Minds', xxxii.
42 Lindorff, *Pauli and Jung: The Meeting of Two Great Minds*, 2–3.
43 Ibid., 11–13.
44 e.g. Meier, *Atom and Archetype*, 53–67.
45 Moss, *The Three 'Only' Things*, 212.
46 Cambray, *Synchronicity: Nature and Psyche in an Interconnected Universe*, 14.
47 Gieser, *The Innermost Kernel*, 287.
48 von Franz, *C.G. Jung: His Myth in Our Time*, 245.
49 von Franz, *Psyche and Matter*, 209.
50 Jung, *Synchronicity*, 95–96.
51 Ibid., 97 (for the English rendering see footnote 3).
52 McGuire and Hull, *C.G. Jung Speaking*, 223.
53 von Franz, *Projection and Recollection in Jungian Psychology*, 193.
54 Mansfield, *Synchronicity, Science and Soul-Making*, 45.
55 von Franz, *Psyche and Matter*, 257.

56 Krohn, *The Maggid Speaks*, 224.
57 Jung, *Synchronicity*, 140–143.
58 Combs and Holland, *Synchronicity: Science, Myth and the Trickster*, 79–102.
59 Ibid., 97.
60 Jung, *Synchronicity*, 6.
61 von Franz, *Psyche and Matter*, 217.
62 Ibid., 48.
63 Ibid., 101.
64 Jung, *Synchronicity*, 139–140.
65 Progoff, *Jung, Synchronicity, and Human Destiny*, 68–73.
66 Ibid., 73–74.
67 von Franz, *Psyche and Matter*, 216.
68 Jung, *Synchronicity*, 139.
69 Mansfield et al., 'The Rhine Jung Letters', 14.
70 Ibid., 15–21.
71 e.g. Radin, *Entangled Minds*, 282–292.
72 von Franz, *Psyche and Matter*, 22.
73 Cambray, *Synchronicity: Nature and Psyche in an Interconnected Universe*, 13.
74 Jung, *Synchronicity*, 27.
75 Mansfield et al., 'The Rhine Jung Letters', 19.
76 Tarnas, *Cosmos and Psyche*, 499n.
77 Jung, *Synchronicity*, 126–128.
78 Gieser, *The Innermost Kernel*, 283.
79 Cambray, *Synchronicity: Nature and Psyche in an Interconnected Universe*, 13.
80 Jung, *Man and His Symbols*, 57.
81 von Franz, *Psyche and Matter*, 6.
82 McGuire and Hull, *C.G. Jung Speaking*, 279–280.
83 Jung, *Synchronicity*, 29.
84 von Franz, *Projection and Recollection in Jungian Psychology*, 91–92.
85 Ibid., 197.
86 von Franz, *Psyche and Matter*, 29; Jung, *Synchronicity*, 138.
87 Storm, 'Synchronicity, Causality, and Acausality', 164.
88 Jung, *Synchronicity*, 14–16, 142–143.
89 Strogatz, *Sync*, 275.
90 Ibid.
91 von Franz, *On Divination and Synchronicity*, 39.
92 Peat, *Synchronicity: The Bridge between Mind and Matter*, 129.
93 Wilhelm, R., *I Ching or Book of Changes*, xlvii.
94 Ibid., liv.
95 Wilhelm, H., *Heaven, Earth and Man in the Book of Changes*, 12–14.
96 Jung, foreword to Wilhelm, R., *I Ching or Book of Changes*, xxix.
97 Ibid., xxiii.
98 von Franz, *On Divination and Synchronicity*, 8.
99 von Franz, *Psyche and Matter*, 82.
100 Gieser, *The Innermost Kernel*, 289.
101 von Franz, *On Divination and Synchronicity*, 50.
102 Gieser, *The Innermost Kernel*, 289n.
103 Main, *The Rupture of Time*, 88.
104 Jung, *Synchronicity*, 77–85.

105 Ibid., 34.
106 Combs and Holland, *Synchronicity: Science, Myth and the Trickster*, 118.
107 Ibid., 123.
108 Campbell, *The Power of Myth*, 120.
109 Ibid., 144.
110 Jung, *Synchronicity*, 45–46.
111 Mansfield, 'Distinguishing Synchronicity from Parapsychological Phenomena', 15.
112 Deepak Chopra, *Synchrodestiny*, 114.
113 Ibid., 123.
114 Ibid., 145.
115 Jung, *The Essential Jung*, 332–333.
116 Wilhelm and Jung, *The Secret of the Golden Flower*, 140.
117 Progoff, *Jung, Synchronicity, and Human Destiny*, 24–32.
118 Ibid., 21.
119 Combs and Holland, *Synchronicity: Science, Myth and the Trickster*, 58.
120 Jung, *Synchronicity*, 141.
121 Huxley, *The Perennial Philosophy*, 277–278.
122 von Franz, *Psyche and Matter*, 119.

Chapter Two

The Dance of Chance

It should not come as much surprise to the reader that ever since Jung first put forward his synchronicity hypothesis, the very idea that meaningful coincidences should somehow merit a special coincidence category of their own has met with persistent and significant opposition. For example, in a review shortly after the release of *Synchronicity: An Acausal Connecting Principle*, the philosopher Antony Flew made the point that meaning and acausality are *already* implied in our everyday understanding of coincidences. As he puts it: '…it is hard to see that this concept is either new or even potentially explanatory… Synchronicity is not a (new) *species* of coincidence: it *is* coincidence.'[1] Indeed, it is views such as this that hopefully this study will successfully be able to counter. In addition, a consistently strong source of dismissal has come from proponents of the explanatory ability of probability theory to account for coincidences, however unlikely, uncanny or meaningful they might appear to be.[2]

This chapter will look at different explanations for coincidences and will attempt to develop an overall model that is able to incorporate both synchronicity and chance as viable explanatory categories for coincidences. Causality too needs to be taken into consideration, and whether direct or hidden, it represents an essential element in any overall model. But let us commence with an event that goes right to the heart of both probability and credibility:

On a January evening in 1998, at a whist club in Bucklesham, Suffolk, a 'perfect hand' was dealt to eighty-seven year old Hilda Golding. It was the first game of the evening, and when she picked up her cards, she was amazed to see that she had all thirteen clubs. There was no reason to doubt the authenticity of the deal as the cards, routinely, had been shuffled and reshuffled and there were fifty other players in the clubhouse that night.[3] The odds against getting thirteen cards of one suit in whist, bridge or any of their variants which use a standard pack of fifty-two cards has been calculated at a massive 635,013,559,600 to one. Nevertheless, according to the mathematician Warren Weaver, this should not be viewed as a surprising event because it is a simple fact that *any* whist or bridge hand has exactly the same probability of occurring.

Indeed, Weaver suggests that anyone who is present at the table when such a hand is dealt should say, 'This is an improbable and a rare event, but it is *not* a surprising event. It is, however, an interesting event.'[4] No doubt Weaver had his tongue at least partly in his cheek when he included this suggestion in his book, *Lady Luck*, as he would have been well aware that if globally there are — for argument's sake — fifty million bridge players and they each play an average of four games a day, then a hand containing thirteen cards of a particular suit should occur by the law of averages only once every eight or nine years. Obviously, his primary aim was to emphasise that every hand is *equally* unlikely and should technically be viewed as equally astonishing.

However, Weaver does say that it would be surprising if *two* such perfect hands, or indeed any two identical hands, occurred on the same evening, as the odds against this happening would be extremely small indeed.[5] Yet something a good many times *more* surprising occurred on that January evening in 1998: not only was Mrs Golding dealt a full suit but so were each of the other players. Alison Chilvers had thirteen hearts; her mother, Hazel Ruffles, who was also the dealer, had thirteen diamonds; while the dummy hand (they were playing three-handed whist) had thirteen spades. Said Mrs Golding, according to the *Daily Mail*, 'I was absolutely bowled over when Alison revealed that she had all the hearts but the surprise was even greater when her mother showed a full set of diamonds.'[6]

Perhaps even more astonishing is that the likelihood of this extraordinary alignment of cards actually occurring is almost completely inconceivable, with odds against of an utterly staggering 2,235,197,406,895,366,368,301,559,999 to one. Following the event, a mathematician at Essex University was quoted in the same *Daily Mail* article as saying: 'The figures are astronomical. If the entire population of the world played whist all day the odds against this happening would still be equivalent to several lifetimes.'[7] It would have been interesting to have obtained a comment from Weaver, especially as he was an avid collector of coincidences, but unfortunately he passed away in 1978.

Another calculation as to how long it would take for such a hand to occur by chance is provided by the statistician Brian Everitt in his engaging book on probability, *Chance Rules*: 'Somebody with time on their hands once calculated that if all the entire adult population of the world played bridge continuously for the next 10 million years, the odds would still be 10 million to one against such a set of hands.'[8]

Everitt then goes on to list several reported instances, names and dates included, of claims for games where four complete suits were dealt, all occurring within the space of a decade. For example, R.R. Thomas of London, England, is quoted as saying of the perfect deal he witnessed in 1952: 'The pack was not a new one, was properly shuffled, cut and dealt.' Everitt, quite reasonably, makes the point that so many reports of a perfect deal in such a short space of time, given the odds, suggests that fraud is the likely explanation, and that the claimants had been 'duped by pranksters'.[9]

Fraud is certainly the likely explanation for what occurred at Bucklesham, though it would not have been that easy for a prankster to have been able to slip in a pre-arranged pack at the last minute. That leaves the possibility of substitution by one or more of the players, or a wider conspiracy involving other members of the club. However, in terms of credibility, given that there was no suspicion of foul play raised at the time, and given the nature of the occasion and the evident sincerity of the ladies involved, it is not unreasonable at least to *entertain* the possibility that the deal was in fact genuine. Alison Chilvers told a BBC reporter, who would naturally have been concerned about this: 'It was an ordinary pack of cards. I put all the cards out because I get the hall ready. They were shuffled before they went on the table, and Hazel shuffled them again before they were dealt.'[10]

Deal or No Deal?

Unless there was some extremely fine acting and subterfuge, for which there appears to have been no inkling of suspicion, both at the time and afterwards, the deal must seriously be considered to have been authentic. Naturally, it is well-nigh impossible to eliminate all possibilities for fraud in such situations, and stage magicians are skilled at showing how it can be done. At the same time, it is important to consider the context and the likelihood that any of the ladies involved would have had the sheer effrontery to pull such a stunt. According to Mrs Ruffles, 'I gave the cards a really good shuffle and then dealt them out in the usual way, starting with Hilda. Once we realised what we were holding it was obvious who was going to win every trick. It really was most extraordinary.'[11]

Her sincerity was backed up by the *Daily Mail* reporter: 'The players are adamant that the cards were properly shuffled, cut and dealt and have put the feat down to coincidence.'[12] In addition, there has never been any dispute or even much public discussion about the occurrence beyond the odds against it happening and the very ordinary but reputable circumstances surrounding the event. The poet and literary critic, Al Alvarez, also the author of a book on poker, was quoted in *The*

Guardian as saying, 'The pity is it happened to three ladies at a whist drive. They won't make any money out of it.'[13] Hilda Golding, however, was not unduly disconcerted: 'The prizes are always very good at Bucklesham: a chicken, joint of beef or a big tub of butter.'[14] Clearly for Mrs Golding, the friendly environment and social conviviality of the whist club represented a far greater prize than any gain or fame she might have received from so emphatically trumping the odds.

An alternative explanation for what occurred at Bucklesham has been suggested by Ray Hill, a mathematician at Salford University concerned with the use of statistics in cot deaths.[15] He noted that *The Guardian* article reported that a new pack of cards was used. In a new pack, the suits are arranged in order and therefore need to be thoroughly shuffled before playing. As mentioned in the media reports, the cards were shuffled twice and then cut. Hill surmises that if by chance two flawless 'riffle shuffles' had been made, then a perfect deal would automatically have occurred, no matter how the cards were cut before the deal. He asserts that by all accounts this would have been very unlikely, but that the chances of it occurring were immensely more probable than by randomness alone. It is also worth recalling that R.R. Thomas, who claimed a perfect deal in 1952, made a point of saying that the pack used then was not a new one. Perhaps he was aware of the increased chances of a perfect deal after shuffling a new pack. Hill explains the process thus:

> A riffle shuffle is one in which the pack is split into two roughly equal parts and the two parts merged by allowing the corners of cards from one part to fall alternately with cards from the other part. If one is lucky enough to split the pack exactly into half and then lucky enough to execute a riffle shuffle in which the cards in one half alternate exactly, one for one, with the cards in the other half (we call this a perfect shuffle), then the result will be that the first 26 cards in the pack will have, say, hearts and spades alternating, and the second 26 cards will have diamonds and clubs alternating. If one is then fortunate enough to execute a second perfect shuffle, then one will have a pack arranged in the order: heart, diamond, spade, club, heart, diamond, spade, club, and so on. This now produces a perfect deal! How the final cut is made is not relevant as its effect is just to rotate the four hands around the table.[16]

This is certainly a possible explanation, and it would be interesting to enquire into the shuffling methods characteristically employed at the Bucklesham whist club. But whatever the actual cause, a perfect deal is without question explainable as a random and, sooner or later, *expected* event by simple appeal to the law of large numbers. As Weaver puts it, 'If the probability of a certain outcome is only one in a thousand, this does mean after all that it is likely to happen on the average about once in a thousand times. And you just might start out with the unlikely event.'[17]

Bridge, whist and their forerunners have been played for around five hundred years and have at various times been very popular, particularly bridge in the first half of the twentieth century, before television. Again for the sake of argument, let us say that fifty million whist and bridge players have played an average of four games a day for the past two hundred years. This means a total of 3,650,000,000,000 (3.65 trillion) games, assuming four players for each game. If we round this up to four trillion (4×10^{12}) games, it is still only a minute fraction of the more than two octillion (2×10^{27}) games required for a perfect deal to occur by chance.

The odds of this occurring in the next two hundred years at the same rate of play are something like 500 trillion to one against, within the next one thousand years 100 trillion to one against, and in a billion years a mere 100,000 to one against! Perhaps it is because the odds are so utterly outrageous that what happened that evening at Bucklesham was not taken very seriously at the time, with more of a feel-good and sensationalist focus in the media than a serious consideration of the thought-provoking implications of the occurrence, if genuine, of this extreme statistical outlier.

Notwithstanding the immensity of the figures mentioned above, there are additional probabilities that should also be taken into consideration. The most significant of these concerns the timing, for almost as improbable as the actual event itself was *when* it occurred. Despite Weaver's remark about starting off with the unlikely event, for it to have taken place within the first five hundred years of the history of this type of card game is decidedly fortuitous when one considers how many billions of years would be required (at our rate of fifty million games a day) to ensure that all four players at a table are once again simultaneously dealt complete suits. A further item of statistical significance, though trifling in comparison, is *where* it occurred. There have certainly been other reported instances of a perfect deal, as mentioned by Everitt. However, this appears to be the only one to come anywhere *near* meeting the criteria for authenticity required for it to be taken seriously, and not simply dismissed as hearsay.

For example, the reaction to a perfect deal claimed by a foursome playing bridge informally at home would inevitably revolve around the issue of evidence, for how could such a claim possibly be substantiated, even if all those present passed lie detector tests and took oaths of honesty? This makes what happened at Bucklesham markedly more significant, and raises the possibility of another set of odds, this time for the likelihood of such a hand being dealt in circumstances that could even be considered credible. But whatever the odds, the problem of hard evidence, or the lack it, is crucial for such cases, as the parapsychologist John Beloff makes clear, for the critical issue is *'never whether the person in question would cheat but, only, whether he or she could have cheated in the conditions specified. It is their ability, never their morals, that are on trial'*.[18]

Taking into account all of the above, and notwithstanding the absence of any direct accusation of fraud, it is inevitable that a verdict of 'not proven' would be accorded the unanimous claim of the ladies involved that the deal was completely random. There is also, in this particular case, the added possibility of the exact card configuration occurring as a result of two instances of inadvertent perfect shuffling. And even if another such deal could be genuinely substantiated, say, in the next ten or twenty years, the question of fraud would never really be removed, essentially because it could never really be disproved. But suppose it *could* be removed, then what? Then surely the possibility of *another* explanation, apart from the laws of chance, becomes that much more likely. The odds of a single occurrence are vast enough, but the odds against four complete suits being dealt twice in authentic circumstances and within the current time frame are presumably an almost totally unimaginable 2,235,197,406,895,366,368,301,559,999 x 2,235,197,406,895,366,368,301,559,999 to one.

And if a third perfect deal were genuinely authenticated in our time, then probability as a blanket explanation for any random distribution of cards would almost certainly come into question. Nevertheless, even if a third or a fourth perfect deal were to occur—and fraud could be *completely* discounted—chance would still be the preferred explanation for many. They would argue that, whatever the odds, any combination of hands is equally unlikely, and the only reason why a deal of four full suits is seen as special is because of the arbitrary significance imposed on it by the human mind. Weaver actually makes this very point in his discussion of the chances of a full suit (just one) being dealt significantly more often than it statistically should:

> It is very easy—indeed almost trivial—to compound unlikely events to produce a miracle. The probability that a given hand will contain thirteen specified cards (say thirteen spades) is of the order of 10^{-12}. I have heard of it happening in n cases. The compound probability that all these n persons hold all these thirteen spades is 10^{-12n}. So what?[19]

The Reign of Probability

Now, if we look carefully at what Weaver is saying here, we will be struck by his use of 'n', which implies that even if there are a hundred claims of a full suit in the course of a year, his response remains, so what? To give Weaver credit, he does not immediately jump to the conclusion of fraud, which takes the discussion in a completely different and very predictable direction. Instead, he maintains that whatever the frequency of a rare hand, the explanation is *still* that it is due to chance. He would therefore concur with at least part of the following observation, made more than a century ago by the science writer Camille Flammarion: 'The little god Chance sometimes produces extraordinary results.'[20] In Weaver's view, clearly, chance is the reason behind many extraordinary results, and in his chapter devoted to coincidences and rare events he quotes the poet John Gay to that effect: 'Lest men suspect your tale untrue, keep probability in view.'[21] He would not, however, have agreed with Flammarion's ironic elevation of chance to the status of a 'little god'.

Flammarion, though, had good reason for doing this as during his time, like today, there was a marked predisposition within certain elements of the scientific establishment to explain all manner of coincidences, however extraordinary, as manifestations of chance and the laws of probability.

Brian Inglis, continuing in Flammarion's caustic vein, provides a brief synopsis as to how and why chance came to be so revered. He describes how the foundations of probability were laid by Blaise Pascal and others in the seventeenth century, spurred by queries from gamblers, particularly in connection with the odds for dice. The eighteenth century saw, as he puts it, the gradual *sanctification* of chance as a result of the predictive successes of probability theory and also the strong endorsement of influential mathematicians such as Pierre-Simon Laplace (the 'French Newton'), who found it extraordinary that 'a science which began with a consideration of the games of chance should have become the most important object of human knowledge'.[22]

Laplace was also instrumental in equating 'coincidence' with 'chance', an important association that has to a notable extent withstood the test of time.

If the sanctification of chance came with Laplace, its *beatification* came with John Stuart Mill who argued in his *A System of Logic*, published in 1843, that a seemingly chance occurrence, far from being contrary to natural law as had hitherto been accepted, 'is an effect of causes, and could have been predicted from a knowledge of the existence of those causes, and from their laws'.[23] Thus, during the nineteenth century, the proponents of probability as the explanatory principle behind coincidences became triumphalist in their attitudes, as exemplified by Edgar Allan Poe's fictional detective, M. Auguste

Dupin, who after a coincidental occurrence in *The Murders in the Rue Morgue* (1852) makes the following remark:

> Coincidences ten times as remarkable as this happen to all of us every hour of our lives, without attracting even momentary notice. Coincidences, in general, are great stumbling-blocks in the way of that class of thinkers who have been educated to know nothing of the theory of probabilities, that theory to which the most glorious objects of human research are indebted for the most glorious of illustrations.[24]

The *canonisation* of chance came, writes Inglis, with the publication in 1866 of *The Logic of Chance* by John Venn, of Venn diagram fame. Venn argued that if an action is repeated often enough, any chance occurrence will sooner or later occur, whether it is being able to recreate one of Shakespeare's plays by drawing letters out of a bag (later to become the proverbial monkey on a typewriter) or throwing double sixes with a pair of dice a thousand times in a row.[25] It was assumed, particularly by those who wanted to avoid a parapsychological explanation for coincidences, that because chance could account for *some* coincidences it could account for *all* of them. Thus, chance became what Inglis has described with a certain succinct precision as 'positivism's safety net'.[26]

Weaver's reaction to the possible occurrence of n cases of a particular hand of thirteen cards would clearly come into that category and suggests a strongly materialistic conception of nature and the universe. For him, as for anyone with implicit positivist sympathies, any *non-materialistic* explanation for what occurred during the whist drive at Bucklesham would be almost too bizarre to contemplate. As Hill wrote concerning his thoughts about the case prior to considering the possibility of two perfect riffle shuffles: 'One's first reaction should be that all such claims are fraudulent; the odds are far too high.'[27]

Such sentiments are an implicit element of popular books on probability designed for public consumption, in which there is generally a chapter on coincidences. And in the requisite chapter, a standard feature is the 'birthday problem', which demonstrates that in any group of twenty-three people there is a slightly higher than 50% chance that at least two people will share the same birthday. The purpose of this interesting and easily accessible display of the laws of probability is to show those who have the misfortune of being mathematically illiterate that 'an exaggerated appreciation of meaningless coincidence' is unwarranted.[28] The words in quotation are from John Allan Paulos, author of the widely acclaimed book *Innumeracy*, first published in 1988, in which he expresses a justified concern over the widespread public ignorance of mathematical reasoning and the workings of probability. In his view, this has resulted in a far greater acceptance of superstition and pseudoscientific ideas than is desirable or healthy in an educated populace.

Clearly, for Paulos, any explanation for coincidence that does not have probability theory at its core is essentially irrational, as are the thought processes of those who perceive certain coincidences as intrinsically meaningful: 'Whether we are comfortable with the insignificance of most coincidences or insist on always finding a Meaning behind them is, in the end, a critical and revealing aspect of our personalities and world outlooks.'[29] Paulos makes no bones about his philosophical materialism and this naturally predisposes him towards a belief that chance is indeed the 'safety net' explanation for coincidences, meaningful or otherwise, and that there really is no need to posit a hypothesis such as synchronicity.

A similar position is held by the mathematicians Persi Diaconis and Frederick Mosteller, whose 1989 paper, 'Methods for Studying Coincidences', has been very influential as regards statistical approaches to coincidence. An essential feature of probability theory is the 'law of large numbers', first stated by Jacques Bernoulli in the early eighteenth century. As an extension to this law, and specifically to deal with coincidences, Diaconis and Mosteller have posited the 'law of truly large numbers', which states that, 'With a large enough sample, any outrageous thing is likely to happen.'[30] And though more circumspect with their conclusions in the paper, an accompanying article in the *New York Times* states that in the opinion of the authors: 'No strange forces outside the realm of science are needed to explain coincidences.'[31]

Their paper does, however, pay tribute to both Kammerer and Jung, though with certain inaccuracies about Jung's position, which may suggest that they had not read his work in any great depth. In addition to the assertion that 'synchronicity has become a standard synonym for coincidence',[32] they 'argue (perhaps along with Jung) that coincidences occur in the minds of observers'.[33] Both statements are problematic: the first suggests that there is no longer any real distinction between meaningful and non-meaningful coincidences in common parlance, while the second ignores Jung's view of the *objective* nature of synchronicity, about which he is unequivocal: 'Synchronicity postulates a meaning which is *a priori* in relation to human consciousness and apparently exists outside man.'[34]

This is a clear example of very different disciplines talking at cross purposes about a common area they happen to share, like the shaded intersection of a Venn diagram. And given the mathematical and scientific status of probability theory, it is perhaps not a coincidence that the title of a very comprehensive and informative historical account of probability and its impact on our lives is nothing less than *The Empire of Chance*.[35]

The Naïve and the Sophisticates

While probability theorists have little disciplinary need to heed speculation on the nature of coincidences from depth psychology, they cannot be so cavalier when the very move of using chance as an explanatory safety net is questioned by a seasoned analytical philosopher. A paper by Elliott Sober, titled 'Coincidences and How to Reason About Them', goes to the heart of the 'safety net' issue, and in particular singles out Diaconis and Mosteller and their law of truly large numbers, which by definition is capable of accounting for the occurrence of 'any outrageous thing'.[36] Sober accuses them of *weakening the data* when it comes to reporting highly unlikely events. They do this, he argues, in order to boost the plausibility of chance as the best explanation for coincidences. One of Sober's professional concerns as a philosopher of science is the ongoing and often heated debate between creationists, who argue for existence of an Intelligent Designer, and the so-called 'new atheists', who assert that the theory of evolution provides sufficient evidence for the non-existence of any such Designer.

There appear to be echoes of this standoff in his paper on coincidences, in which Sober distinguishes between two groups that he calls, with a certain irony, the *naïve* and the *sophisticates*. The sophisticates represent the dominant mathematical and probabilistic way of thinking about coincidences, as epitomised by Diaconis and Mosteller, while the naïve he divides into two subgroups, both of which 'see causal connections everywhere'.[37] The first include those who see conspiracies behind highly unlikely events such as someone winning the lottery twice, which they therefore assume has been rigged; while the second will see the same event as the operation of some kind of paranormal agency, perhaps the hand of God. However, it is Sober's criticism of the sophisticates that is of particular interest. He cites the factual event of Evelyn Adams winning the New Jersey lottery twice, at astronomical odds against, in 1985 and 1986, and gives two descriptive statements that account for the occurrence, the first logically stronger than the second:

(1) Evelyn Adams, having bought four tickets for each of two New Jersey lotteries, wins both.

(2) Someone at sometime, having bought some number of tickets for two or more lotteries in one or more states, wins at least two lotteries in a single state.[38]

Sober uses the example of Evelyn Adams and the New Jersey lottery precisely because it is employed for the purpose of weakening the data by Diaconis and Mosteller, who ask: 'What is the chance that some person, out of all the millions and millions of people who buy lottery tickets in the United States, hits a lottery twice in a lifetime?' After reminding the reader that many people buy multiple tickets, they answer by citing statisticians from Purdue University who have calculated that it is 'practically a sure thing'.[39] This description of the situation is in marked contrast to the extremely high odds against a *particular* person, in this case Evelyn Adams, winning twice. Sober's response is clear: 'It is a theorem in probability theory that logically weakening a statement can't lower its probability — the probability will either go up or stay the same. In the case at hand, the probability goes up, *way up*.'[40] For further clarification concerning the weakening of observations to support a particular hypothesis, he includes the following cartoon:

Fig. 1: English Speaking Alien[41]

The possibility that both the being from outer space and the Earthling speak English is so unlikely that common sense says that there has to be a causal connection, the most obvious being that these aliens have been observing the human race for some time before landing, and with their superior technology and intelligence they have been able to master the major Earth languages before actually making contact. Nevertheless, it is *conceivable* that it is a genuine coincidence that both species developed English independently. A sophisticate might argue that when one considers the possibility of there being billions of inhabited worlds that surely must exist in an infinite universe, is it not *likely* that similar language patterns will emerge? After all, we need nouns and verbs to communicate clearly and it just so happens that the first aliens that land on Earth have coincidentally developed English. Sober, however, is not impressed with this move, and makes the following acerbic but pertinent comment:

> Sophisticates who constantly weaken their description of the data to avoid rejecting hypotheses of Mere Coincidence seem to think that *everything* is a Coincidence. These sophisticates are not just sophisticated —they are *jaded*. No correlation, no matter how elaborate and detailed, impresses them. In fact, none *can* impress them; their trick of weakening the data works against all comers. What we need is guidance on when the data may be weakened, not the imperative to always do so or the permission to do so whenever we please.[42]

For this guidance, he turns to the eminent biologist R.A. Fisher's theory of *sufficient statistics* which suggests that data may be weakened or simplified when sufficient information is included in the statistical analysis to come to the same conclusion as when *all* the available information is included.[43] Sober gives the example of fairly tossing a fair coin a thousand times in order to find the probability of its landing heads. Is it necessary to give the exact sequence of the tosses or would the totals be sufficient? As it turns out, just giving the totals would be sufficient in this case as the cumulative results for both procedures are equal, unlike for the two very different statements about the lottery win. The important point is that *both* sides of the equation must have the same value.

He therefore argues that the sophisticates would be far better served by *strengthening* rather than weakening their data, and he is by no means unsympathetic with their aim of showing how significant probability theory may be as an explanatory vehicle for certain coincidences. For the Evelyn Adams case, he makes the following suggestion:

> There is something right about the sophisticate's demand that the data about Evelyn Adams be placed in a wider perspective. We need to consider not just her double win, but the track records that others have had and whether she bought tickets in other lotteries that did not turn out to be winners. However, moving to this wider data set does not involve *weakening* the initial description of the data, but *adding* to it; the key is to make the data *stronger*.[44]

The Principle of the Common Cause

In other words, the sophisticates need to combat the naïve on the field of *evidence*, using probability theory for appropriate calculations and not as an ideological cudgel against potentially upsetting explanatory proposals. To some extent, this should not prove too onerous since the average sophisticate is unlikely to have much argument with the following query Sober makes concerning the conduct of state lotteries: 'Does any of us have frequency data on how often state lotteries, and the lottery in New Jersey specifically, are fixed? Surely if fixes occur, the parties will have every reason to prevent them from becoming public.'[45] This is an interesting question, and not one we would normally have cause to consider, on the assumption that major lotteries in democracies governed by the rule of law are clean and unbiased. But if we really wanted to find out, it might not be so easy, as Sober remarks: 'My hunch is that the slogan "the truth will out" is an exaggeration. In addition, how often the truth outs is more or less unknown. For this reason, we should be somewhat reluctant to interpret absence of evidence as evidence of absence.'[46]

It is therefore presumably in the interests of sophisticates to side with at least the more level-headed element of the 'conspiracy theorist' naïve. Indeed, their collective strength might be quite formidable, combining an investigative tenacity with statistical know-how. They will be aided too by what is perhaps the most definitive philosophical proposition in favour of a causal explanation for coincidences, Hans Reichenbach's *principle of the common cause*, which states: 'If an improbable coincidence has occurred, there must exist a common cause.'[47] If the 'must' seems a little strong here, Reichenbach does mitigate his position somewhat by saying that chance coincidences are not impossible. Nevertheless, he considers a common cause explanation for coincidences to be more probable:

> Suppose both lamps in a room go out suddenly. We regard it as improbable that by chance both bulbs burnt out at the same time, and look for a burned-out fuse or some other interruption of the common power supply. The improbable coincidence is thus explained as product of a common cause. The common effect, the fact that the room becomes completely dark, cannot account for the coincidence. Or suppose several actors in a stage play fall ill, showing symptoms of food poisoning. We assume the poisoned food stems from the same source—for instance, that it was contained in a common meal—and thus look for an explanation of the coincidence in terms of a common cause. There is also a common effect of the simultaneous illness of the actors: the show must be called off, since replacements for so many actors are not available. But this common effect does not explain the coincidence.[48]

Straightforward physical common causes, like a power outage or food poisoning, are comparatively easy to trace, especially in comparison with, for example, the cognitive processes that result in two people making the same suggestion at the same time, or one voicing what the other is thinking. Though the causal chains are subtler and more cerebral, it is both feasible and likely that both persons have made similar logical leaps from some prior suggestion, conversation or shared experience, as is well argued by the statistician Jeffrey Rosenthal in his book *Struck by Lightning*.[49]

Parallel developments in theoretical ideas, as with Charles Darwin and Alfred Wallace, or parallel inventions like the telephone or the electric light bulb, could be viewed as apparent coincidences explainable by the pre-existence of the appropriate theoretical and technological conditions for these developments. Indeed, in the case of evolutionary theory, both Darwin and Wallace had read Thomas Malthus's book on population growth just prior to coming up with the idea of natural selection, and there is the interesting coincidence of Alexander Graham Bell and Elisha Gray both applying on the same day, though three hours apart, for a patent for the telephone, resulting in a major public dispute and mutual accusations of intellectual theft.[50]

The history of mathematical, scientific and technological discovery is replete with instances of simultaneous or near simultaneous inventions with, according to technology writer Kevin Kelly, six inventors of the thermometer, five for vaccinations, four for the isolation of adrenalin, three for the hypodermic needle, three for decimal fractions, three for logarithms, four for photography, five for the telegraph.[51] Kelly provides a pyramidal model for a causal chain from idea to application, using the incandescent electric light bulb, for which there were a great many separate inventors, as an example (see Fig. 2). The common cause for the process was the harnessing of electricity combined with human ingenuity and a generally perceived need for an efficient form of lighting:

INVENTION PYRAMID

Inventors	Stage	Task
10,000–1,000	Think of Possibility	Recognise an opportunity for solutions
1,000	Idea of How	Imagining the crucial elements of the solutions
100	Details Specified	Selecting specific solutions
10	Working Device	Proving your solutions work reliably
1	Enabling Adoption	Convincing the world to adopt your solution

INVENTION PYRAMID cont.

Inventors	Example (electric light)
10,000–1,000	We should use electricity for lighting
1,000	An incandescent wire in a sealed bulb
100	Welded tungsten, vacuum pump, solder exhaust port
10	Prototypes by Swann, Latimer, Edison, Davy, etc.
1	Edison's bulb (electric system)

Fig. 2: Invention Pyramid[52]

The Blowgun Controversy

Determining the actual operation of causal chains can, however, be quite difficult and also contentious, especially when academic taboos are involved. Although at first glance an innocuous area of research, there is serious controversy over the origins of the blowgun (or blowpipe) which appears to have developed independently in both Southeast Asia and the Americas. The anthropologist Stephen Jett considers the shared complexities of the highly sophisticated blowguns of both regions to be far too great to accept the hypothesis of parallel invention and development. He argues that, as in the case of Madagascar, where the blowgun was introduced from Southeast Asia, ancient transoceanic journeys 'from Indonesia to tropical America seem the best explanation for the presence and detailed similarities of the blowgun complexes in the two hemispheres as well as for many other cultural and racial commonalities'.[53]

In other words, Jett believes that there are too many developmental correspondences between the two regions to accept that the blowgun complex was a spontaneous parallel invention. A significant problem for this viewpoint is that, despite the marshalling of considerable evidence, there is, as Jett puts it, an academic 'untouchability' when it comes to the subject area of 'Old World cultural influences on pre-Columbian America'.[54] And while Jett may be right in his findings, there is a marked contrast between his conclusion that 'similar environments and common human capabilities are not enough to account for striking and multifarious similarities between the peoples of distant areas'[55] and the exuberant certainty of Kevin Kelly's exposition of the dual origins of the blowgun:

> The gun as devised by these two separate cultures is expectedly similar —a hollow tube, often carved in two halves, then bound together. In essence it is a bamboo or cane pipe, so it can't be much simpler. What's remarkable is a nearly identical set of inventions supporting the air pipe.

> Tribes in both the Americas and Asia use a similar kind of dart padded by a fibrous piston, they both coat the ends with a poison deadly to animals yet which does not taint the meat, both carry the darts in a quill to protect the poisoned tip from being accidentally pricked, and both employ a similarly peculiar stance when shooting. The longer the pipe the more accurate the trajectory, but the longer the pipe the more it wavers during the aim. So both in America and in Asia the hunters hold the pipe in a non-intuitive stance with both hands near the mouth, elbows out, and gyrate the shooting end of the pipe in small circles. On each small revolution the tip will briefly cover the target. Accuracy, then, is a matter of the exquisite timing of when to blow. All this invention arose twice, like the same crystals found on two worlds. In prehistory, these parallel paths are played out again and again…
>
> Even if a few isolated ships from China or Africa might have reached, say, the shores of the new world pre-Columbian, these occasional landings would not be sufficient to kindle the many parallels we find. It is highly improbable that the sewed-and-pitched bark canoe of the northern Australia aborigines came from the same source as the sewed-and-pitched bark canoe of the American Algonquin. So we have to accept they are examples of convergent invention, and arose independently as part of parallel tracks.[56]

Like the parallel invention of the relatively simple bow-and-arrow, that of the bark canoe is hard to argue with, particularly as there is very little chance of contact between Australian aborigines and the Algonquin. The real difficulty occurs, of course, when propositions of independent parallel development are stretched to the point of incredulity, as in the cartoon depicting the alien speaking English, and as it would if an Amazon Indian tribe was discovered speaking Malay. The blowgun represents a special case because it stands on the cusp between the possibility of a direct causal connection with Southeast Asia and parallel evolutionary conditions providing the causal framework for parallel inventions.

Separated Identical Twins

A similarly fertile field for apparent coincidences with causal origins is in the area of twin studies. As with pre-historical parallel developments, separated identical twins are often found to have developed in uncannily identical ways. One pair, Mark and Jerry, who did not meet until they were thirty-one, had both become volunteer firemen. In addition, they had a number of identical mannerisms, including a particularly idiosyncratic way of holding their beer cans with their little fingers underneath. According to twins researcher Nancy Segal, 'Some people call it a coincidence, but they are ignoring the scientific side of the equation… The twins said that they use their pinky finger to support their can or glass as they drink. It is also likely that this position is comfortable for them because they have got the "same" hands and fingers.'[57]

This kind of trait might seem surprising to outsiders but it can be readily explained by genetics, as can the similarity in IQ scores for identical twins, which has been estimated at around 85%, as against 60% for fraternal twins.[58] Such findings, however, have regularly been the cause of heated and often bitter conflict connected with deep-rooted political and racial sensitivities that have surrounded the nature-nurture debate.[59]

In addition to the fallout from the extremely sensitive issue of the correlation between genes and intelligence, there is another awkwardness concerning twin studies, though a far more felicitous one, that comes from the frequency of astonishing coincidences that seem to occur around twins, especially identical twins. It is almost as if they are a 'fault-line' for coincidence: not only is there the biological 'coincidence' of their physical and gestural similarities that can often cause an observer to do a double-take, there is also in some pairs a level of unconscious behavioural mirroring that, arguably, stretches even the gene hypothesis a little too far. One set of identical twins, Dorothy and Bridget, who had been separated in Britain in 1945, met for the first time in 1979 as part of the Minnesota Study of Twins Reared Apart (MSTRA). When they met, they were both wearing seven rings on their hands, two bracelets on one wrist and a watch and a bracelet on the other. Both had a cat named Tiger, and when each married, both had worn exactly the same dresses and carried the same flowers. Dorothy had a son named Richard Andrew while Bridget's was called Andrew Richard. Dorothy's daughter was called Catherine Louise and Bridget's Karen Louise, though she had wanted to name her Catherine.[60]

Another pair, separated shortly after birth and who only met when they were thirty-nine, were both called Jim, had sons called James Allen and James Alan, were both married to women called Linda, whom each divorced, and then both remarried women called Betty. When they were children, they each had a dog called Toy. As adults, both used the same terms to describe their identical late-afternoon headaches and both inexplicably gained 10lbs at the same time in their lives.[61] They had both been firemen and sheriffs, both smoked Salem and drank Miller Lite, and just prior to meeting each, independently, had the idea of building a circular white bench around a tree in their yard. They lived in different parts of Ohio and coincidentally took their holidays at the same stretch of beach in Florida, regularly driving there in a light blue Chevrolet but never meeting. In addition, they died on the same day of the same illness.[62]

Such detailed and uncanny correspondences are not uncommon for separated identical twins, though the consistently remarkable intricacy of the coincidences surrounding the 'Jim Twins' (both of whose adoptive parents had christened them James) was regarded by the Minnesota study as a statistical outlier.[63] However, the observation that the case was an outlier does not in any way compromise its authenticity nor that of the many other reunited pairs with similar profiles. Though the more dramatic cases may represent statistical anomalies, essentially they are simply extreme instances of standard features displayed by reunited identical twins, which are generally understood to be the result of a combination of genetic predisposition and the play of chance within certain environmental constraints.

For example, one pair discovered upon meeting that they had each made a highly idiosyncratic but independent choice of a rare Swedish toothpaste, *Vademecum*. The choice of toothpaste might be random, but not the genetic predisposition behind the subtle causal chains that led each twin to purchase that particular brand, concerning the implications of which Segal writes, 'The matched presence of highly unusual or exceptional traits in identical twins… suggests that characteristic quirks and signature behaviours may partly reflect each person's unique genetic mix.'[64] In other words, we are far more influenced by genetic factors in our personal decisions and individual character makeup than we may think, as Segal, who was involved with the Minnesota study, makes abundantly clear:

> Contrary to what logic suggests, we learned that similarity in intelligence was unrelated to years of separation, contact time and age at reunion… We also learned that identical twins reared apart were as similar in personality traits as identical twins reared together, demonstrating that shared genes, not shared environments, primarily underlie family members' personality similarity. These findings are important because they uniquely demonstrate genetic influence on identical twins' coordinated development.[65]

Nevertheless, genetic similarity alone cannot adequately explain the fine detail and range of the coincidences experienced, almost certainly as profoundly meaningful, by the reunited pairs. Shared genes may provide a fertile ground for coincidences to occur, and may indeed act as a kind of fault-line for their frequency and level of correspondence, but they do not explain the coincidences themselves, nor why one set of identical twins should have so many more intriguing coincidences than another. The cases of Dorothy and Bridget, the Jim Twins and others may be outliers, but in any discipline or field of study it is often the outliers that in reality, if not in theory, determine general parameters, as has been forcefully argued by Nassim Nicholas Taleb, with particular reference to economics and the vicissitudes of the stock market, in *The Black Swan*.[66]

Unravelling the Roots of Coincidence

But what are outliers for twin studies are grist for the mill for the collectors of coincidence stories, epitomised in our time by Arthur Koestler, whose 1972 book *The Roots of Coincidence* arguably did more to raise public awareness of coincidences than even Jung's various publications on the subject. Following its publication, Koestler wrote to the *New Scientist* asking readers for reports of unusual coincidences, a selection of which he included, along with other accounts, in *The Challenge of Chance*, co-authored with Alistair Hardy and Robert Harvie and published in 1973. In it appear two contributions from a correspondent, Ivone Kirkpatrick: the first is a straightforward, if highly poignant, coincidence account, while the second would be more accurately categorised as an instance of ESP:

> One of the most remarkable coincidences I have experienced was one day before the last war. I happened to be reading a passage from Goethe's *Gespräche mit Eckermann* and I switched on my radio which happened to be tuned into a German station. To my astonishment the man was reading from the same page as I was.[67]

> My son was at The Pilgrims' School in Winchester. As you may know this is a prep school which provides the choristers for the cathedral. The headmaster's two sons are identical twins and were members of the school. One was a chorister. One afternoon, in the middle of choir practice, he let out a yell and cried: 'Somebody kicked me on the shin.' At the moment when he experienced the pain his brother was in fact kicked on the shin badly and was brought back from the playing field and put in the sick-bay.[68]

Notwithstanding the considerable body of anecdotal as well as some hard evidence concerning telepathy amongst twins,[69] the point about the juxtaposition of these two reports is that only the second has a conceivable cause for the coinciding events. Apart from fabrication, which is not generally difficult to ascertain, the most plausible explanation in this case is one that involves ESP. And even if the operation of this faculty remains elusive, it still implies a causal explanation, though not one that has been adequately identified, which is why Jung included ESP under the umbrella of his *wider* concept of synchronicity as an acausal connecting principle. It is not the purpose here to argue the case for ESP, for which there are already detailed expositions,[70] but to distinguish between two significantly different but essentially *anomalous* categories of coincidence explanation, neither of which can be adequately accounted for by the scientifically acceptable and invariably materialistic notions of cause and chance that are generally used to account for coincidences.

One difficulty, however, in making this differentiation is that both Jung and Koestler tended to conflate the two categories, very possibly because they were both enamoured with the parapsychological research of J.B. Rhine.[71] But in the first of Kirkpatrick's anecdotes there appears to be no possible explanation in terms of ESP: he is reading a passage from *Conversations with Eckermann*, an outstanding accomplishment of German culture and scholarship; the distinct possibility of war is in the air, the unconscionable belligerence of the Nazis a stark contrast to Goethe's humanity and brilliance. Kirkpatrick, clearly a German speaker, turns on the radio and hears, from the Nazi propaganda machine, exactly the same passage he is in the process of reading.

Kirkpatrick does not specifically mention whether the coincidence, in addition to its being astonishing, was personally meaningful to him. If so, and that would not be hard to imagine, it would come under Jung's definition of synchronicity as 'a meaningful coincidence in time'.[72] To someone who did not speak German it would probably have meant very little until Kirkpatrick had explained the circumstances, and even then it would have been he and only he who would have had the direct impact of the synchronicity. How statistically likely or unlikely the event might have been has no real bearing on the *equivalence of meaning* Kirkpatrick would almost certainly have experienced. The coincidence of Kirkpatrick turning on the radio and immediately hearing the same passage he was reading was *acausal* in the sense that any direct causal connection would be, to use Jung's language, 'unthinkable'.

It should also be emphasised that the acausality implied here is not to be confused with the 'acausality' that is often associated with highly unlikely chance events, such as the perfect deal at Bucklesham, assuming for the moment that fraud was not involved. If that was a genuine chance occurrence it has behind it, in all its remarkableness, a profound acceptance of causality as expressed through the laws of probability, and is therefore only *metaphorically* acausal. The acausality of synchronicity is in another category altogether because the connection between the objective and subjective elements is made through an immediately apprehended *meaning-correspondence* and it is *that* which, ultimately, distinguishes synchronistic events from 'mere coincidence'. In his thoughtful book on the subject Victor Mansfield emphasises this point (his italics): 'An important implication of acausal connection through meaning is that *in synchronicity the meaning is primary while the objective and subjective events that correlate are secondary and contingent.*'[73]

Readily identifiable accounts of synchronistic experiences are therefore unlikely to be strongly represented in the many compilations of coincidence stories, which tend to focus on the surprise factor, not on how personally meaningful a particular coincidence might be. In most cases one has to guess from the context, which is not always easy, though this very touching account is an exception: 'Stuart Spencer had been a widower for three years in January 2000 when his daughter gave him a present of a 1,000-piece jigsaw. She had found one of a paddle steamer on the Norfolk Broads, where Stuart and his late wife Anne had enjoyed many holidays. As he placed a piece to complete a figure in a wheelchair at the boat's stern, he saw it was his wife.'[74] This has the 'feel' of a synchronicity, in distinction to the many ESP stories that tend also to be included. A typical example is the following one, in which a woman who had been invited to dinner with a friend recalls, 'I was just about to begin eating when I had the strongest feeling I should return home immediately. This I did and my husband had just had a massive heart attack. I was able to get medical help and he survived.'[75]

This appears to be a straight case of telepathy or a strong intuitive sense with no immediate coincidence involved, until of course the woman returned home. Any synchronistic element in what occurred would have been to do with the fortuitous timing of her return home, but that would have been quite separate from the sudden sense that she should return, which certainly appears to have been somehow causally activated by her husband's heart attack. The timing of her return home is significant as she may quite easily have arrived too late to help. That, of course, can be interpreted as either luck or synchronicity. Indeed, many coincidence stories are structurally complex and do require careful analysis, as with this highly charged incident experienced by the novelist Frederick Forsyth:

> As a war correspondent in the Nigerian civil war in 1969, Forsyth felt uncomfortably that he was being stared at. He could see nothing to account for it, but suddenly there was a movement—a timber post twenty yards away toppled over. As he turned his head sharply to see what had happened: 'I felt the "whump" of a passing bullet slamming into the doorpost, then the "whack" of the sound. Jerking my head to the left had stopped it going through my forehead; instead, it went past my ear and buried itself in the door-jamb. I had indeed been stared at— by a Nigerian sniper in the forest fifty yards away.'
>
> The timber post, he later discovered, had been eaten away by termites; 'one termite must have given the last nibble that separated the last strand of wood.'[76]

Categorising Coincidences

Before examining the elements of Forsyth's remarkable escape, it is worth teasing out the main ways of accounting for coincidences that have been discussed or alluded to in this chapter. From this it is possible to discern essentially four broad categories, two of them distinctly causal and two not. Of the latter, the first is *chance coincidence* and the second, *synchronicity*: in other words, meaningless and meaningful coincidences, and in the case of both no direct causal connection can be discerned. The laws of probability are very successful in explaining the mathematical distributions of random events, and are therefore profoundly causal, though not so on the surface, which is why the ancient notion of luck has always had such currency. But while probability can explain the occurrence of random events, it cannot explain the equivalence of meaning that occurs in synchronistic experiences, which is why synchronicity, unlike chance or luck, is unequivocally acausal.

Of course, a chance coincidence may also be synchronistic, just as a synchronistic event can be seen as purely a matter of chance. The important point to understand here is that the operation of synchronicity does *not* depend on probability distributions. As the psychotherapist David Richo puts it, 'Chance and synchronicity will look the same in their display of an event but they are worlds apart… Chance happens to us, synchronicity happens in us.'[77] Nevertheless, perhaps there is a word in the English language that has arisen to cover the no-man's land or shared space between chance and synchronicity, and that is *serendipity*, generally defined as making chance discoveries when looking for something else. A pertinent example would be the accidental discovery of the mathematics of probability while looking to solve gaming problems.

Of the two causal categories, one involves a supernatural or paranormal element, while the other does not, and can be accounted for by standard theories of physical and mental causation.

It is worth mentioning as an aside that there is considerable debate within philosophical and scientific circles as to the nature of causation, especially when it comes to the subtleties of mind–brain interaction, as well as the connection between what appear to be the profoundly acausal micro-processes of the quantum level and the macro-processes of everyday causal interaction, a topic to be explored in Chapter Four. For the purposes of coincidence categorisation, however, the distinction between causal explanations that include the paranormal and those that do not is a reasonably clear-cut one. We might therefore refer to the categories as *conventional* and *paranormal causality*, with the caveat that 'conventional' here is used *solely* to distinguish it from 'paranormal' and not for any other reason apart from its conceptual clarity.

Thus, we have four broad categories for classifying coincidence explanations, each with blurred boundaries and the potential for further subdivision. For example, it would be sensible to make a distinction between paranormal explanations such as telepathy or remote viewing, which in practice as well as theory can be tested,[78] and those that invoke 'divine intervention' of one sort or another, which cannot. A similar distinction would need to be made within conventional causality when it comes to disputes over causal origins, as with the apparently independent development of the blowgun in both Southeast Asia and the Americas. Is there a direct causal connection between the two, or are they instances of common cause parallel invention?

Coincidence Categories
— Random chance explanations
— Conventional causal explanations
— Paranormal causal explanations
— Synchronicity explanations

Most coincidence compilations for popular consumption are a potpourri of all four categories, though the compilers often include them under different headings as, somewhat light-heartedly, Koestler does with such titles as 'the library angel', '*deus ex machina*', 'poltergeists', and 'the practical joker'.[79] Inglis, who was a close associate of Koestler and whose book *Coincidence* is a continuation and expansion of Koestler's investigations, includes the Forsyth anecdote as an example of the 'ghost in the machine', a reference to Koestler's book of the same title and also his category, *deus ex machina*, of cases involving machines.[80] Obviously, the machine in question is the sniper's gun, so not a very satisfactory approach to coincidence categorisation and quite a far cry from what might emerge based on the four categories delineated above.

A Sample Analysis

There are indeed a number of ways to make sense of this incident, and one that needs to be dealt with straight away is the hard-nosed conspiracy theorist approach, in other words, that the story is fabricated and that Forsyth has concocted it as he might one of his thrillers. For most people, such an attitude would be considered both unreasonable and ungenerous and that Forsyth, even without witnesses, should be given the benefit of the doubt, unless there is sufficient evidence to suggest otherwise. Still, there does need to be some checking that Forsyth's account is by and large accurate and not unduly distorted through exaggeration, embellishment, or faulty memory. Once that is satisfactorily established, or at least assumed for the sake of argument, possible explanatory scenarios for the coincidence can then be seriously entertained.

The most obvious interpretation, and technically the second on our list, is that Forsyth was simply *very* lucky that in an instance of pure chance the post fell, for whatever physical reason, at *exactly* the right moment for him to evade the bullet. Also, as a war correspondent in Africa, he was in an extremely precarious environment, and this would have made him hyper-sensitive to subtle signals such as a faint reduction in the surrounding noise level. We are not told if other people were about but, if so, they may have been aware of the sniper and had frozen their movements; the unnatural silence could easily have caused Forsyth to feel he was being stared at.

This allows for a conventional causal explanation for Forsyth's uncanny feeling that someone was staring at him. In his hyper-vigilant state, he would have naturally turned his head when the post fell, and could only be considered extremely fortunate that this happened to coincide with the sniper's otherwise very accurate shot. In addition, it is quite feasible that the sniper, also in a hyper-vigilant state, saw the post starting to fall and had to make a split-second decision about the right moment to shoot, especially as the sound of the post falling might disturb his target's walking rhythm and therefore the chances of an accurate hit. But perhaps he deliberated too long and was unable to get his shot off before the post hit the ground. So here we have a combination of chance coincidence and conventional causality, natural bedfellows for the materialistically inclined, and no need to entertain either the hypothesis of synchronicity or that of the paranormal.

A third interpretation makes the same initial inference regarding Forsyth's state of mind, that because of the dangerous situation Forsyth was both very aware of his surroundings and in an emotionally highly charged state. It also takes at face value his sense of being stared at, implying that his latent ESP had been activated: he could *feel* that someone was staring at him and at the same time had a strong premonition that he was in extreme danger. His excited state and emotional tension might then, in a similar manner to the 'Pauli Effect', have psychokinetically influenced the precariously fragile post to topple over at that precise moment, fortunately for him just at the right instant to prevent his certain death. The reaction of the sniper, presumably, would have been as in the second scenario, though he too would have been in a state of heightened emotional tension, and his concentrated focus on Forsyth may well have added to the latter's already stimulated psychic ability.

This is an interpretation from the point of view of paranormal causality; however, it is not likely to be one that parapsychologists would wish seriously to entertain, particularly as there is insufficient indication from Forsyth's account, apart from his sense that he was being stared at, that anything of a parapsychological nature took place. Still, it remains a possibility, as does a fifth interpretation in line with the subdivision suggested earlier for this category, which is that Forsyth was saved by divine intervention, perhaps in part so that he would be able to realise his potential as a talented thriller writer and through his novels bring pleasure and enjoyment to millions of readers. As for the sniper, perhaps he would simply have seen it as a bit of bad luck, though it is a little more romantic to conjecture that he might have interpreted the whole episode as part of the machinations of *Ananse*, or one of the other trickster gods of West Africa.[81]

In a final interpretation, Forsyth's sense of being stared at could have been caused by any of the reasons already suggested, or a combination of them (apart from fabrication). However, the important difference for this conceptualisation is the fascinating possibility that what in fact occurred was a genuine example of totally unrelated causal sequences coming together with utterly precise timing to create, for Forsyth, a most profoundly meaningful as well as life-saving coincidence. With an impeccable synchronistic flourish, the last termite ate through the post so that it fell at exactly the right moment for Forsyth to turn his head and therefore ensure that the sniper's bullet would miss him. No verification is required apart from ascertaining whether the relief Forsyth would undoubtedly have felt was accompanied by an 'absolute knowledge' of the *meaning* of the coincidence both at the time and possibly more significantly, afterwards, when he was told *why* the post had fallen. To clarify what he means by absolute knowledge, Jung refers to the following quote by Chuang Tzu: 'You use your inner eye, your inner ear, to pierce to the heart of things, and have no need of intellectual knowledge.'[82]

There is no clear evidence from Inglis's very brief report that Forsyth's experience could be classified as a synchronistic event, but if perchance it was, then obviously synchronicity as an explanatory category would come into play. If not, then one or more of the other categories would cover the contingencies. As already mentioned, most coincidence compilations include accounts, like Forsyth's, with a strong surprise factor, no doubt to attract the reader. Anecdotes with an evident synchronistic element are not normally specifically catered for, though Mansfield to some considerable extent makes up for this with the synchronicity stories he interweaves into the text of his book *Synchronicity, Science, and Soul-Making*.[83]

In the final analysis, however, most disputes over the nature of coincidences involve deeply held ideological or metaphysical beliefs, as has occurred in the explosive conflict over the influence of genes on intelligence, generated in particular by the consistency of results coming from twin studies. Similarly, the serious possibility that the evidence for the existence of psychic phenomena is irrefutable is so confronting for much of the scientific establishment that *any* explanation for coincidences apart from causal connectedness and chance probability is systematically refuted.

Hence the move by Diaconis and Mosteller and others to use mathematics to discount coincidence explanations that posit a 'supernatural' dimension, whether Jung's suggestion of the actuality of an underlying *unus mundus*, where psyche and matter are undivided, or the more straightforward question concerning the existence of *psi* phenomena. This issue, even more so than that of inherited intelligence, remains unresolved and virtually undiscussed, still largely a taboo area within mainstream academia. It is interesting, then, to read what Warren Weaver, writing in the early 1960s as a specialist in probability theory, which measures the metre of the dance of chance, had to say about Rhine's parapsychological experiments at Duke University:

> The Rhine E.S.P. results could be explained on the grounds of selection criteria or the falsification of data. Having complete confidence in the scientific competence and personal integrity of Professor Rhine, I find this explanation unacceptable to me. In any very long probability experiment there will occur highly remarkable runs of luck—as in the twenty-eight recorded repetitions of one colour at Monte Carlo... But I know of no analysis of Rhine data, based on such considerations, that makes it reasonable to believe that their success can be explained in this way.[84]

> As I have said elsewhere, I find that this is a subject that is so intellectually uncomfortable as to be almost painful. I end by concluding that I cannot explain away Professor Rhine's evidence, and that I also cannot accept his interpretation.[85]

Endnotes

1. Flew, 'Coincidence and Synchronicity', 199.
2. e.g. Paulos, *Innumeracy*; Diaconis and Mosteller, 'Methods for Studying Coincidences'.
3. Alleyne, 'The Perfect Hand'.
4. Weaver, *Lady Luck*, 221.
5. Ibid., 224.

6nbsp;nbsp;nbsp;Alleyne, 'The Perfect Hand'.
7nbsp;nbsp;nbsp;Ibid.
8nbsp;nbsp;nbsp;Everitt, *Chance Rules*, 68–69.
9nbsp;nbsp;nbsp;Ibid., 69.
10nbsp;nbsp;BBC News, 'Card Trick Defies the Odds'.
11nbsp;nbsp;Alleyne, 'The Perfect Hand'.
12nbsp;nbsp;Ibid.
13nbsp;nbsp;Elliott, 'Perfect Deal at Whist Drive Trumps the Odds'.
14nbsp;nbsp;Ibid.
15nbsp;nbsp;Hill, 'Cot Death or Murder – Weighing the Probabilities'.
16nbsp;nbsp;Ibid., 13.
17nbsp;nbsp;Weaver, *Lady Luck*, 172.
18nbsp;nbsp;Beloff, *The Relentless Question*, 183.
19nbsp;nbsp;Weaver, *Lady Luck*, 273.
20nbsp;nbsp;Inglis, *Coincidence*, 1–2.
21nbsp;nbsp;Weaver, *Lady Luck*, 211.
22nbsp;nbsp;Inglis, *Coincidence*, 100.
23nbsp;nbsp;Ibid., 101.
24nbsp;nbsp;Ibid.
25nbsp;nbsp;Ibid., 101–102.
26nbsp;nbsp;Ibid., 12.
27nbsp;nbsp;Hill, 'Cot Death or Murder – Weighing the Probabilities', 8.
28nbsp;nbsp;Paulos, *Innumeracy*, xi, 22–23.
29nbsp;nbsp;Paulos, *Once Upon a Number*, 64.
30nbsp;nbsp;Diaconis and Mosteller, 'Methods for Studying Coincidences', 859.
31nbsp;nbsp;Kolata, '1-in-a-Trillion Coincidence, You Say?'
32nbsp;nbsp;Diaconis and Mosteller, 'Methods for Studying Coincidences', 853.
33nbsp;nbsp;Ibid., 860.
34nbsp;nbsp;Jung, *Synchronicity*, 118.
35nbsp;nbsp;Gigerenzer et al., *The Empire of Chance*.
36nbsp;nbsp;Sober, 'Coincidences and How to Reason About Them', 2.
37nbsp;nbsp;Ibid., 1.
38nbsp;nbsp;Ibid., 2.
39nbsp;nbsp;Diaconis and Mosteller, 'Methods for Studying Coincidences', 859.
40nbsp;nbsp;Sober, 'Coincidences and How to Reason About Them', 2.
41nbsp;nbsp;Source for Fig. 1: by kind permission of the artist, Nick Harding.
42nbsp;nbsp;Sober, 'Coincidences and How to Reason About Them', 4.
43nbsp;nbsp;Fisher, *Statistical Methods and Scientific Inference*, 157.
44nbsp;nbsp;Sober, 'Coincidences and How to Reason About Them', 6–7.
45nbsp;nbsp;Ibid., 10.
46nbsp;nbsp;Ibid.
47nbsp;nbsp;Reichenbach, *The Direction of Time*, 157.
48nbsp;nbsp;Ibid.
49nbsp;nbsp;Rosenthal, *Struck by Lightning*, 21–22.
50nbsp;nbsp;Kelly, 'The Technium: Progression of the Inevitable'.
51nbsp;nbsp;Ibid.
52nbsp;nbsp;Source for Fig. 2: http://kk.org/thetechnium/progression-of/
53nbsp;nbsp;Jett, 'Further Information on the Geography of the Blowgun', 99.
54nbsp;nbsp;Jett, 'Confessions of a Cultural Diffusionist', 174–175.

55 Jett, 'Further Information on the Geography of the Blowgun', 99.
56 Kelly, 'The Technium: Progression of the Inevitable'.
57 Segal, *Indivisible by Two*, 22.
58 Allen, 'The Mystery of Twins', 2.
59 Segal, *Indivisible by Two*, 9–12.
60 Inglis, *Coincidence*, 185–186.
61 Holden, 'Identical Twins Reared Apart'.
62 Powell, *The ESP Enigma*, 50–51.
63 Allen, 'The Mystery of Twins', 2.
64 Segal, *Entwined Lives*, 119.
65 Ibid., 122.
66 Taleb, *The Black Swan*.
67 Hardy, Harvie and Koestler, *The Challenge of Chance*, 164.
68 Ibid., 185.
69 e.g. Playfair, *Twin Telepathy*, 101–109.
70 e.g. Dossey, *The Power of Premonitions*; Tart, *The End of Materialism*.
71 Jung, *Synchronicity*, 22–27; Koestler, *The Roots of Coincidence*, 12–15.
72 Jung, *Synchronicity*, 144.
73 Mansfield, *Synchronicity, Science and Soul-Making*, 26.
74 Plimmer and King, *Beyond Coincidence*, 210.
75 Inglis, *Coincidence*, 116.
76 Ibid., 94.
77 Richo, *The Power of Coincidence*, 102.
78 e.g. Radin, *The Conscious Universe*; Tart, *The End of Materialism*.
79 Hardy, Harvie and Koestler, *The Challenge of Chance*, 159–203.
80 Inglis, *Coincidence*, 89.
81 Pelton, *The Trickster in West Africa*.
82 Jung, *Synchronicity*, 100.
83 Mansfield, *Synchronicity, Science and Soul-Making*.
84 Weaver, *Lady Luck*, 272.
85 Ibid., 273.

Chapter Three
Cosmic Coincidences

The primary concern of the previous chapter was with the development of a possible, albeit simple, taxonomic system for the categorisation of various types of coincidences. So far all the coincidences discussed have been very much on a human scale, whatever their interpretation or categorisation might be. In this chapter, the focus shifts to cosmology, and in particular to what have been identified as the very precise parameters behind the structure and composition of our universe, also known as the 'cosmic coincidences'.[1] These coincidences are of a very different order to those considered so far and from any reasonable perspective decidedly more remarkable. They are also based on solid scientific evidence, a position shared by too few of the usual coincidence anecdotes. But before investigating this fertile field for the consideration of coincidences, it might be worth first examining one of the most remarkable, fortuitous and indisputably verified of what we might call 'everyday' coincidences, not only for its intrinsic interest but as a contrast to the array of cosmic coincidences that follow.

This particular event took place on March 1, 1950, in the town of Beatrice, Nebraska. It was a Wednesday evening, the regular time for choir practice at the West Side Baptist Church. With the weather still seasonally very cold, the Reverend Walter Klempel went into the church during the afternoon to light the furnace in preparation for the arrival of the choristers who habitually came at around 7.15 in time for the start of choir practice at 7.20. But that evening, at 7.25, there was a huge explosion which completely demolished the church and shattered windows in nearby homes. The blast was later thought to have been caused by the fire in the furnace igniting a gas leak from a broken pipe outside the church, though in the immediate aftermath of the devastation that was obviously not the main concern. However, concern soon turned into wonder when it became clear that at the time of the explosion the church had been empty.

Extraordinarily, and very much against character, *all* thirteen choir members for one reason or another were late. The minister and his wife were delayed because their small daughter's dress had been soiled and a fresh one needed to be ironed. The pianist had planned to come half an hour early but had fallen asleep; her mother, the choir director, had difficulty waking her so they did not leave the house until 7.15. A student, normally very punctual, was finishing a geometry problem and had she not been thus absorbed would have given a lift to a pair of sisters whose car refused to start. Another student was listening to a radio programme and wanted to wait until it finished; this resulted in her being late, and therefore also the friend who normally accompanied her to choir practice.[2]

The reasons go on and there were altogether nine distinct and unrelated explanations for the collective tardiness. Fifteen lives were thus 'saved': the thirteen choir members and two small children who would have come with their mothers. Weaver includes the story in his chapter on unusual coincidences in *Lady Luck* and estimates odds of a million to one against every member of the choir being late on the same evening.[3] Add that to the even more remote odds of this lateness occurring at the same time as an accidental explosion in a church or similar meeting-place and the extraordinary nature of the incident becomes evident. What occurred was not simply 'a coincidence'; it was far more than that, for it involved the synchronous alignment of *nine* discrete coinciding events of a certain type or order with a major event of an entirely different order.

Explanations have ranged from the play of chance, as assumed by Weaver, to divine intervention, the interpretation favoured by those involved who informed the correspondent for *Life* magazine when he came to investigate the story that it had been an 'act of God'.[4] At the same time, there are the more prosaic personal explanations of the participants: one choir member not yet mentioned said she felt a bit lazy and this made her late, while another wanted to finish a letter. Unlike a perfect hand at bridge or a run of twenty-eight reds in roulette, conscious decision was a central feature in the overall configuration. In his analysis of the event, the physician and author Larry Dossey argues in favour of the possibility of an unconscious *collective premonition* that subtly influenced the decisions of the choir members.[5] He also points out that such an explanation does not necessarily contradict the laws of physics, quoting the physicist Gerald Feinberg to that effect: 'If such phenomena do occur, no change in the fundamental equations of physics would be needed to describe them.'[6]

While there is already a large amount of data in support of the existence of presentiment or premonition,[7] the same cannot be said for 'acts of God'. The ability to sense premonitions, though their nature and even the validity of their existence might be disputed, is in principle as explicable as any other cognitive faculty. A full understanding of this capacity, therefore, is not intrinsically beyond standard scientific explanation, in contrast to the metaphysical and therefore non-scientific question of the actuality of a Creator, for obviously there cannot be an *act* of God (except in the metaphorical sense employed by the insurance industry) unless it is first established that there *is* a God. Perhaps a collective presentiment subconsciously urged the choir members to stay away from the church at the critical moment, perhaps it was simply luck. However, if a convincing case can be made for the existence of a greater intelligence or consciousness, then the very *possibility* of an act of God, a notion that has increasingly lost credibility with the progress and success of modern science, must once again be taken seriously.

The Precision of the Universe

Anyone who takes an interest in the sky at night, even the most amateur of astronomers, will know that after the Moon and Venus, and Mars when it is closest to the Earth, the brightest object in the night sky is Jupiter. With a backyard telescope the bands across Jupiter's surface are visible, as are four of its moons. And while Jupiter is famous for being the largest planet orbiting the Sun, it is less well known that without its great size and presence in the solar system, it is highly likely that we would not be around to appreciate its brilliance. This is because during the first billion years after the start of the solar system, the gravity of Jupiter, along with that of Saturn, helped clear asteroids and other forms of space debris left over from the creation of the planets. Had the force of Jupiter not pulled them away from the inner solar system, the Earth would most likely *still* be undergoing regular bombardment, making the equilibrium and stability needed for life to develop very difficult to sustain.[8]

The same goes for the Moon. According to the cosmologist John Barrow, without the pull of the Moon the length of our day would probably be a quarter of what it is now, resulting in extremely strong winds and very heavy erosion by both wind and waves, undesirable conditions for complex life to flourish.[9] In addition, the Moon, which Barrow aptly describes as 'Earth's dancing partner', stabilises the Earth's tilt and were it much smaller than it is it would be unable to do this. Only one or two degrees shift in the tilt is enough to cause an ice age, so shifts of much more than that would necessarily be catastrophic.[10] Peter Ward and Donald Brownlee, authors of *Rare Earth*, have this to say about the significance of the Moon for us:

> Without the Moon there would be no moonbeams, no month, no lunacy, no Apollo program, less poetry, and a world where every night was

dark and gloomy. Without the Moon it is also likely that no birds, redwoods, whales, trilobites, or any other advanced life would have ever graced Earth.[11]

Our blue and watery planet, so beautiful in photographs from space, is just the right distance from the Sun: a little too far away and the oceans would freeze; a little too close and they would boil and evaporate. The Sun is also stable, not fluctuating or part of a binary system, element-rich and, like the Earth, *just* the right size. Were the Earth a little smaller, its gravity would not hold down the oxygen; a little larger and it would have retained many of its original poisonous gases. As a result, according to the theoretical physicist Michio Kaku, 'Earth has "just the right" weight to keep an atmospheric condition beneficial to life.'[12] Indeed, the Earth is literally showered with so many finely balanced conditions that make it *just right* for life. These include the temperature range, the amount of oxygen in the air, the quantity of water in the oceans, the presence and distribution of tectonic plates, and the degree of tilt in the Earth's axis. We are therefore living, to use a popular expression, on a 'Goldilocks planet' in the 'Goldilocks zone' of our solar system.

In addition, as Kaku points out, our solar system is located in the Goldilocks region of our galaxy, about two thirds from the centre: too close and radiation levels would be too intense; too far away and there would not have been enough of the higher elements for life to form. There is also the remarkably good fortune, for us, that the Earth has an almost circular orbit, as an unstable or overly elliptical orbit would lead to such extreme temperature ranges that life would be untenable. Equally remarkably, the other planets of our solar system, apart from Mercury and Pluto (now categorised as a 'dwarf planet'), also have close to circular orbits, adding another vital element of stability to our solar system and therefore to the fragile Goldilocks zone we inhabit.[13]

If informed of the above, it is highly likely that many of the good citizens of Beatrice, Nebraska, especially those around at the time of the church explosion, would say, probably without much hesitation, that the hand of God which protected the choir members that night is the same as the one which made the conditions for life on Earth just right. But where, might ask the local sceptic, is the evidence of that? Could it not be, as with what occurred in Beatrice, simply *chance* that structured the solar system in the way that it has, particularly in view of the fact that there are countless billions of stars up there in the night sky, more than the grains of sand on every beach and desert in the world? Although by now she or he may well have created ideal conditions for a Mexican standoff, the sceptic does have a point and were the universe much smaller, say restricted to the Milky Way galaxy, it might be somewhat easier to defend the proposition that God had actively intervened in our particular corner of the cosmos to ensure that life on Earth could flourish with such exuberance.

But with estimates of up to and very possibly exceeding 10^{24} stars in the universe, and conceivably ten or twenty galaxies for every star in the Milky Way,[14] the chances of there being another planet with the requisite preconditions for life are *far* greater than if the Milky Way was surrounded only by a vast emptiness. Nevertheless, our sceptic would be well advised not to count his chickens prematurely, for supposing a planet *were* found with all the suitable conditions for life, there is *still* no guarantee whatsoever that even very primitive forms of life would evolve there. John Leslie, in his book *Universes*, cites a very pessimistic estimation by the astrophysicist Michael Hart, that 'even on an ideally inhabitable planet the chance that living things would develop would probably be lower than 1 in $10^{3,000}$... Indeed, even the 10^{11} galaxies inside our horizon would almost certainly all be uninhabited'.[15]

At the other end of the spectrum of astrophysical conjecture as regards extra-terrestrial life, a much more sanguine prediction was made following the announcement in September 2010 of the discovery of the first extrasolar Goldilocks planet, Gliese 581g, orbiting a red dwarf star within its Goldilocks zone, only twenty light years away. Astronomer Steven Vogt, part of the team that identified the planet, said at the press conference: 'Personally, given the ubiquity and propensity of life to flourish wherever it can, I would say, my own personal feeling is that the chances of life on this planet are 100 percent.'[16] Since then, however, the discovery of Gliese 581g has been disputed, though Vogt and his team have continued to marshal evidence for both its existence and its Goldilocks status.[17]

Perhaps an even more startling discovery was announced shortly afterwards, in December 2010, when astronomers working out of Keck Observatory in Hawaii found that the number of red dwarf stars in the known universe was *ten* times more numerous than had been previously thought, *tripling* the estimation of the total number of stars in the universe, and making the chances of finding habitable and life-supporting planets that much more likely, especially as many of the recently found 'exoplanets' orbit red dwarfs.[18] Thus, there was great excitement in early 2017 when the ultracool red dwarf star Trappist-1 was found to have seven roughly Earth-sized planets in orbit, three of which appear to be located in the system's Goldilocks zone.[19]

But whether life, intelligent or otherwise, exists elsewhere in the universe does not take away from the astonishing fact that not only life but advanced life capable of self-reflection, scientific inquiry, aesthetic appreciation, love and altruism has evolved on *this* planet. And if it can evolve here, it can presumably evolve wherever the conditions are right. So the deeper question that arises concerns the nature of the preconditions that allow for the development of life. As Paul Davies puts it: 'We are not concerned here with anything so parochial as life on Earth. The question is, under what conditions might life arise at least somewhere in the universe? If that life arises, it will inevitably find itself in a suitable location.'[20]

Essential to the conditions Davies refers to are the fundamental parameters of the universe, known as the *constants of nature*, invariant or close to invariant and apparently *arbitrary* numbers that underpin the laws of physics. The number of these constants is variously estimated at around twenty or thirty, the uncertainly being part of an ongoing debate amongst physicists as to how they might be best categorised.[21] There are, however, *three* that have been described as the 'pillars that seem to give physics its structure'.[22] They are: the speed of light (c), measured at close to 300,000 kilometres per second; Newton's gravitational constant (G), a fixed value in the equation for measuring the attractive force between objects; and Planck's constant (h), which is the relation between a photon (a quantum particle of light) and its wavelength. These are the most universal constants as they can potentially be used in the calculation of *any* physical phenomenon.[23] For example, from these three constants the smallest measurable length can be calculated, the Planck length (l_P) at 1.6×10^{-35} metres, as can the smallest possible measurement of time, Planck time (t_p) at 10^{-43} seconds. Any smaller, classical measurement ceases and quantum effects take over.

The Fine Structure Constant

Two of these 'pillars', the speed of light and Planck's constant, along with another fundamental physical constant, the charge of the electron (e), combine to make up what is regarded in physics as one of the most crucial and intriguing of the constants: the *fine structure constant* (a), which sets the scale for what are known as spectral lines. These are lines that appear on a spectrum of light when an atom is illuminated, and are considered the 'fingerprints' of that atom. When certain of these spectral lines are examined closely they reveal a 'fine structure', the spacing of which is determined by a number, and this number is the fine structure constant.[24] It was discovered in 1915 by the physicist Arthur Sommerfeld and was a major step in the early search for a connection between relativity and quantum theory. Einstein was delighted and wrote to Sommerfeld, saying, 'I do not believe ever to have read anything with more joy than your work.'[25] The fine structure constant was the first *dimensionless* constant to be discovered, as the science historian Arthur I. Miller explains:

> The three fundamental constants that make up the fine structure constant are the charge of the electron, the speed of light, and the Planck's constant, which determines the smallest possible measurement in the world. All these have dimensions… The fine structure constant is entirely different. Even though it is made up of these three fundamental constants, it is simply a number, because the dimensions of the charge of the electron, Planck's constant, and the speed of light cancel out. This means that in any number system it will always be the same, like pi which is always 3.141592…[26]

What was particularly intriguing about the fine structure constant was not only that it seemed to be 'exquisitely tuned to allow life as we know it to exist on our planet'[27] but that its value was almost exactly 1/137. According to Max Born, another of the major physicists of the era:

> If a [the fine structure constant] were bigger than it really is, we should not be able to distinguish matter from ether [the vacuum, nothingness], and our task to disentangle the natural laws would be hopelessly difficult. The fact however that a has just its value of 1/137 is certainly no chance but itself a law of nature. It is clear that the explanation of this number must be the central problem of natural philosophy.[28]

This is excerpted from an article Born wrote in the mid-thirties, entitled 'The Mysterious Number 137', and he was not the only scientist who betrayed a certain obsessiveness about 137, as the fine structure constant became popularly known. Wolfgang Pauli, Born's assistant at one stage, was deeply consumed by it, as was Arthur Eddington, who is reported to have insisted on hanging his hat on peg 137 at a conference in Stockholm.[29] The celebrated scientist Richard Feynman, who was familiar with Eddington's writings on 137, wrote about how annoyingly enigmatic the number was for physicists: 'Immediately you would like to know where this number comes from… Nobody knows. It's one of the *greatest* damn mysteries of physics: *a magic number* that comes to us with no understanding by man.'[30]

Perhaps the most profoundly affected by 137 was Pauli for whom it was, as Gieser puts it, '…a figure that had engrossed him for a large part of his life in the form of the fine structure constant and which to him concealed a large part of the mystery of existence.'[31] The fine structure constant and its enticingly mystical 137, a number that also has a particular association with the Kabbalah, was more than a fascinating conundrum for Pauli; it was *symbolically* important, not only for the progress of theoretical physics but as an archetypal and synchronistically resonant clue to the underlying unity of mind and matter, an abiding passion for Pauli, as his correspondence with C.G. Jung reveals.³² The synchronistic element is not just metaphorical: in December 1958, a few days after Pauli was rushed to hospital with crippling stomach pains, he asked his assistant Charles Enz, who had come to see him, whether he had noticed the number of the room he was in. When Enz said no, Pauli told him that it was 137, and the story goes that he then said he would never get out of there alive. And he never did, dying a week later from pancreatic cancer.³³

He was therefore not around for the accidental but highly significant discovery in the mid-sixties of cosmic background radiation, a discovery that resulted in the Big Bang theory becoming increasingly accepted by cosmologists as an established fact, which was certainly not the case in Pauli's time. Nowadays, there is a high degree of certainty not only that the Big Bang occurred but also when it occurred, and with his fascination for 137 there is little doubt that Pauli would have raised at least a quizzical eyebrow to learn that the birth of our universe had taken place some 13.7 billion years ago.³⁴

Unfortunately for the numerologically inclined, this figure was revised upwards in 2013 to 13.8 billion years.³⁵ But whatever the age of the universe turns out to be, the fine structure constant which, in Miller's words, 'very precisely describes the DNA of light',³⁶ remains of unimaginable importance. The physicist James Gilson gives a graphic description of just how significant it is:

> If a were to suddenly be switched off, here on earth, out there in those massive astronomical objects and indeed everywhere, atomic systems would shed all their orbiting electrons... [which] would slingshot tangentially out of orbit into a universal orgy of randomness. All atomic, molecular, biological systems would be destroyed in the process. All life including our own, all human aspirations, society and institutions would be consumed in the instant catastrophic fireball and there would be no record left that they had ever existed.³⁷

Fig. 3: Goldilocks and the Fine Structure Constant³⁸

The cartoon depicted in Fig. 3 accompanied a report in *The Economist* concerning astronomical observations that raise the possibility of the fine structure constant being very slightly different in different parts of the universe at different times. The figure given is 0.0006% for distant quasars existing 9 billion years ago, which provides food for thought but does little to disturb the current value of a at 1/137.036. The Goldilocks parameters for a appear to be around 4% greater or smaller, and outside this range stars would no longer be able to generate the preconditions for carbon-based life. So, as the report points out, '…you would have to go a very long way indeed to come to a bit of space where the fine-structure constant was more than 4% different from its value on Earth.'[39]

The Cosmological Constant

But a is only one of a number of equally crucial constants, some with Goldilocks parameters of far greater precision.[40] The most dramatic of these appears to be the *cosmological constant* (Λ), first proposed by Einstein as part of general relativity to explain why the universe was able to counteract the force of gravity. At that time a steady state universe was the accepted norm. But in 1929 the astronomer Edwin Hubble showed that the universe was expanding, prompting Einstein to abandon his anti-gravity proposition and to say that it had been his 'biggest blunder'.[41] Einstein's intuition, however, had been right and this was confirmed in 1998 when it was discovered that the expansion of the universe is accelerating, which could not occur unless there was indeed an anti-gravity or repulsive force in the universe.[42]

What is particularly extraordinary about the cosmological constant is that it was found to be, in the words of the theoretical physicist Steven Weinberg, 'vastly less than what would be produced by quantum fluctuations in any known realistic theory of elementary particles'.[43] Indeed, 'vastly' is a massive understatement here: the cosmological constant is in fact 10^{120} times *less* than what had been expected by quantum theory, and were it only 10^{119} times less, galaxies would not have formed.[44] Had it a negative value, the universe would have collapsed in on itself before life was even a possibility.[45] In addition, this 'nothing that weighs something' very much looks like the *dark energy* that makes up nearly three-quarters of the visible universe.[46] And the life-permitting precision of its value is described by Paul Davies in terms of the following analogy, one which makes the perfect deal of a full suit of cards for each player at bridge or whist at odds of 2×10^{27} to one against look like a walk in the park by comparison:

One measure of what is involved can be given in terms of coin flipping: odds of 10^{120} to one is like getting heads no fewer than *four hundred times in a row*. If the existence of life in the universe is independent of the big fix mechanism—if it is just a coincidence—then those are the odds against our being here. The level of flukiness seems too much to swallow.[47]

Explanatory Possibilities

The 'big fix' Davies refers to is taken from a reference to the 'dramatic suppression of dark energy',[48] in other words, the difference between its expected and its actual measurement. Davies himself calls it 'the biggest fix in the universe',[49] and the question begged—the more resoundingly so the more it is left hanging in the air—is that if there is a big fix, is there a *big fixer*? From a theistic perspective, the 'just so' parameters of the fundamental constants that underpin our bio-friendly universe are extraordinary coincidences, the precision and axiomatic necessity of which provide persuasive, if circumstantial, evidence that there is a designer behind the apparent design. Indeed, the precise dovetailing of certain constants with the nuclear resonances involved in the production of carbon and oxygen was so stunning for Fred Hoyle, the astronomer who first postulated in the early fifties how helium might be transformed into carbon, that his atheist convictions were severely shaken.[50]

With a certain measure of dry humour Hoyle later wrote: 'Some supercalculating intellect must have designed the properties of the carbon atom, otherwise the chance of my finding such an atom through the blind forces of nature would be utterly minuscule.'[51] In other words, had the properties of the carbon atom not been so finely tailored, intelligent life in the form of human beings would not be available to appreciate the arrangement. Further on in the same article he states unequivocally:

> If you wanted to produce carbon and oxygen in roughly equal quantities by stellar nucleosynthesis, these [the calculated levels for carbon and oxygen] are just the two levels you would have to fix, and your fixing would have to be just about where these levels are actually found to be. Is that another put-up, artificial job?... I am inclined to think so. A common sense interpretation of the facts suggests that a superintellect has monkeyed with physics, as well as with chemistry and biology, and that there are no blind forces worth speaking about in nature. The numbers one calculates from the facts seem to me so overwhelming as to put this conclusion almost beyond question.[52]

Although Hoyle's calculating superintellect has more in common with the 'Supreme Architect' of deism or freemasonry than the Christian God, his clear postulation of a designer behind the exquisite fine-tuning involved in the creation of chemical elements in collapsing stars accords with what the philosopher and theologian Keith Ward calls the 'New Design Argument'.[53] Ward concedes that the traditional argument from design, the 'Fifth Way' of St. Thomas Aquinas, which stems ultimately from Aristotle, has effectively been superseded by the Darwinian account of evolution through natural selection. But while the theory of evolution may be able to account for apparent design in nature, it is highly improbable it can explain the 'the precise structure of laws and constants that seem uniquely fitted to produce life'.[54] Therefore, according to Ward, a designer or creator God is a much more credible proposition.

This, however, is not a position shared by Stephen Hawking and his collaborator Leonard Mlodinow, who argue for the spontaneous self-generation from a multi-dimensional quantum field of up to 10^{500} possible universes.[55] We inhabit but one of these universes, one that is by chance superlatively 'designed' for life and for the existence of which there is no need to postulate a supernatural explanation. As Hawking and Mlodinow put it, 'Spontaneous creation is the reason there is something rather than nothing, why the universe exists, why we exist. It is not necessary to invoke God to light the blue touch paper and set the universe going.'[56]

There are clear echoes here of the response famously given by Laplace when asked by Napoleon why there was no mention of God in his description of the workings of the universe. Laplace reputedly answered: 'Sire, I had no need of that hypothesis.' This is a position shared by much of the scientific community, including the particle physicist Victor Stenger who argues that there is no evidence whatsoever that the apparent fine-tuning of the universe is in any way specifically designed for life. He is a strong proponent, like Hawking, of the idea of a multiverse and with so many possible universes with potentially different parameters, we naturally find ourselves in one that is suitable for our type of life. He believes that 'the pieces of our universe fell into the places where they are, not because of a guiding hand and a grand design, but through mere accident',[57] and that our particular universe 'is not fine-tuned to us; we are fine-tuned to our particular universe'.[58]

But whether the universe is deliberately fine-tuned for the possibility of sentient life or not, the fact that it exists *at all* and that we exist within it will not go away. *This* is the elephant in the room, and the main issue at stake is a simple one, if rather stark: *either the source from which everything evolved and continues to evolve is intelligent or it is not.* The multiverse explanation may well be a valid one but it should not be used as a smokescreen for questions concerning the nature of its ultimate origin.

It might be presumed that with the number of possible universes calculated at an inconceivable 10^{500}, the chances of at least *one* universe containing appropriate provisions for sentient life become overwhelming. But there is a danger in playing the probabilities game as it can lead to a type of one-upmanship that is more suited to a school playground than reasoned scientific and philosophical discourse. That said, there is one number that is so overwhelming and unimaginably vast in the remoteness of its probability that it beggars into insignificance *any* of the other enormous figures bandied about in the arguments over fine-tuning and the potential multiverse. This is the 'absurdly tiny' probability, as calculated by Roger Penrose, of our universe having at the Big Bang the state of low entropy needed to be compatible with the second law of thermodynamics and hence the structure of the universe as we know it.[59] The figure is one part in $10\exp(10^{123})$ which, if written out using the usual nomenclature for base-ten powers, would come out as $10^{1,000,000,000,000,000,000,000,000,000,000,000,000,000,000,000,000,000,000,000,000,000,000,000,000,000,000,000,000,000,000,000,000,000,000,000,000,000,000}$. Some idea of the cosmic scale of the sheer immensity of this number is provided by Penrose:

> This is an extraordinary figure. One could not possibly even *write the number down in full*, in the ordinary denary notation: it would be '1' followed by 10^{123} successive '0's! Even if we were to write a '0' on each separate proton and each separate neutron in the entire universe — and we could throw in all the other particles as well for good measure — we should fall far short of writing down the figure needed.[60]

In Penrose's view, the precision at the initial state of the Big Bang was so great that it simply dwarfs any other considerations, including the fine-tuning of the constants, which he considers to be 'chicken feed' in comparison. In the same way, the possibility that our universe is but one of an array of possible universes within a multiverse fails even to come close to accounting for these initial conditions. Our universe is *far* more special than it needs to be and we have no idea why that might be so, as he explains to the host of the PBS series *Closer to Truth*, Robert Lawrence Kuhn:

> You could imagine other big bangs that weren't so special, but that's not what we've got. We're here in this one — but we could have been here equally well in zillions of other ones... We don't need the universe to be that special for us. It's not any use to us at all why the distant universe is incredibly special and why it came from part of the big bang which is just as special as the part we came from... It needs a good physical theory to say why the Big Bang had the nature that it did and we have no theory which really explains that.[61]

Penrose argues that as regards possible universes, it would be much more economical, as well as more likely in terms of probabilities, for there to be *smaller* universes generated by the multiverse, each giving rise to life and consciousness, than it would be to create such a vast universe with the equivalent pockets of life that might be found in the smaller universes.[62] In other words, the calculation of one part in $10\exp(10^{123})$ is so extraordinary that it requires much more than anthropomorphic conjecture of any sort even to *begin* to explain it in any sense beyond the mathematical and physical. Penrose has his own speculative framework he calls *conformal cyclic cosmology*, or CCC, and which he lays out in his book *Cycles of Time,* first published in 2010.

He suggests a cyclic universe in which the final extinction of activity in one universe becomes the basis for a big bang in the next,[63] a proposal that he himself has described as 'outrageous'.[64] In addition, Penrose here *increases* the minuteness of the low entropy probability at the Big Bang to one in $10\exp(10^{124})$ in order to take into account the contribution of dark matter.[65] But outrageous proposals to explain the existence and nature of the universe are no strangers to cosmology, from the idea that at every moment the world forks into an almost infinite number of parallel universes to the possibility that we exist in an illusory virtual world, as depicted in the *Matrix* films.[66] Outlandish and intuitively unlikely as such proposals might appear, they are still logically possible, unlike empirically refutable propositions such as the Moon being made of cheese or the Earth being created less than ten thousand years ago: a belief apparently held by an astonishing 40% of the United States population.[67]

Robert Lawrence Kuhn, clearly inspired by the extensive number of highly stimulating interviews he has conducted with physicists, cosmologists, philosophers and theologians for the *Closer to Truth* series, has compiled a taxonomy of twenty-seven different explanations of the universe. He posits four overarching categories under which every logically permissible explanation for the question 'Why this universe?' must fall, irrespective of how accurate it may or may not turn out to be in reality, if ever that occurs. This list of twenty-seven 'reality generators' is neither exhaustive nor mutually exclusive, but each would have to come under one or more of the following four headings: One Universe Models, Multiple Universe Models, Nonphysical Causes, and Illusions.[68]

For example, under the dual categories of Nonphysical Causes and Multiple Universe Models comes a rich pantheistic model articulated by the visionary author Duane Elgin in his *The Living Universe*. Elgin speculates that the universe may not only be *alive* but that we, as an extremely rare evolutionary flowering of this aliveness, with our capacity for self-reflective awareness, are a crucial part of the universe's *own* evolution. He quotes, as Jung did to lend support to his articulation of the idea of synchronicity (see Ch. 1), from Chapter 25 of the *Tao Te Ching*,[69] with its ancient, subtle and by contemporary standards profoundly undogmatic cosmological conception of the source of the universe. Below is Stephen Mitchell's translation of the chapter; from it Elgin derives inspiration for his idea of a *mother universe*, a deliberately anthropomorphised version of the multiverse,[70] with which we are intimately and creatively entwined at every level of our being, as we are with the *tao*:

> There was something formless and perfect
> before the universe was born.
> It is serene. Empty.
> Solitary. Unchanging.
> Infinite. Eternally present.
> It is the mother of the universe.
> For lack of a better name,
> I call it the Tao.
>
> It flows through all things,
> inside and outside, and returns
> to the origin of all things.
>
> The Tao is great.
> The universe is great.
> Earth is great.
> Man is great.
> These are the four great powers.
>
> Man follows the earth.
> Earth follows the universe.
> The universe follows the Tao.
> The Tao follows only itself.[71]

Cosmology and Coincidence

One of the reasons for this brief investigation into cosmology and the 'cosmic coincidences' that underpin the narrow parameters for life in our universe has been to show how these figures dwarf into almost complete insignificance any of the low probability coincidences that are so often the cause of controversy here on Earth. The remote chances of being on the receiving end of two or three perfect deals at whist or winning the lottery four or five times are considerably *less* than chicken feed in comparison with the sheer statistical improbability of the existence of *any* Earth-bound observer.[72] And this is the case whatever the explanation for our universe turns out to be, whether theistic, atheistic, pantheistic or a holographic illusion. Another reason for this investigation is to see how the coincidence categories suggested in the previous chapter might stand up when cosmological realities are introduced. The categories are: a) random chance; b) conventional causality; c) paranormal causality; d) synchronicity.

There are clearly one or two adjustments that might be made. The most obvious is that for a discussion of the cosmic coincidences the term 'paranormal causality' is overly restrictive, a problem that could be solved by changing it to 'supernatural causality', which would adequately cover the key issue of whether there is a supernatural intelligence behind the apparent design of the universe. According to the *Oxford English Dictionary*, the term 'supernatural' has a wide range of meanings and can therefore readily accommodate not only the postulation of a creator God but also the possible existence of all sorts of anomalous phenomena, including ESP and telepathy.[73] In line with this change, it would also make sense to replace 'conventional causality' with 'natural causality' in order to distinguish it clearly from the idea of a supernatural cause. It is important to emphasise that the demarcation between the two is by no means black and white. For example, ESP and telepathy may in time be generally accepted as innate but scientifically explicable human capacities and therefore thoroughly 'natural'.

Another observation that emerges from a consideration of the cosmic coincidences is that at a certain level the very *notion of chance* becomes problematic and may even be redundant. This is because we are not dealing with everyday coincidences at our human level but with deeper questions about the origins of existence, and wherever possible we would want to trace any potentially random event to its causal source. As the physicist Freeman Dyson puts it, 'It is true that we emerged in this universe by chance, but the idea of chance is itself only a cover for our ignorance.'[74] In any case, what does it mean to say the universe exists by chance? Indeed, chance as we understand it may only be functionally possible in reference to a more encompassing reality that *allows* for random events. And if the universe, whether part of a greater multiverse or not, came into existence 13.7 or 13.8 billion years ago simply 'by chance', then what is the origin of that act of randomness?

There is an often quoted remark made by the physicist E.P. Tryon that the universe 'is simply one of those things which happen from time to time'.[75] Tryon's explanation for this chance event is that there is a quantum vacuum in which fluctuations occasionally occur. Hawking and Mlodinow, who essentially share this perspective, express it thus: 'Quantum fluctuations lead to the creation of tiny universes out of nothing. A few of these reach a critical size, then expand in an inflationary manner, forming galaxies, stars, and in at least one case, beings like us.'[76] It is interesting that they use the expression 'out of nothing' as it is reminiscent of the ancient philosophical notion of *ex nihilo* creation. If the universe was created *ex nihilo*, then the question turns to the nature of the creative agent, intelligent or otherwise. In this sense, then, the concept of chance becomes redundant or at the very least can be boiled down to whatever triggered the universe in the first place, and whatever that was, it was certainly not 'chance'.

Synchronicity appears to be less straightforward than the other three coincidence categories because it involves subjectivity, a synchronistic event being one in which there is an *equivalence of meaning* between an individual's psychic state and an external circumstance. Analogously, it could be fruitfully argued that everything we perceive is part of a universal 'meaningful coincidence' which knits our subjective perceptions to the apparently objective world. Indeed, one of Jung's motives for advancing the idea of synchronicity was to try to shed light on the conundrum of *psychophysical parallelism*, now commonly referred to as the mind–body problem, which Leibniz in particular had attempted to find a solution for through his *Monadology*.[77] But irrespective of the mechanism by which our subjective self-sense synchronises with our brain-mind-perceptual system, there is clearly an *a priori* meaning-correspondence between the awareness behind our eyes and the external world as it confronts us.

Without this meaning-correspondence we would simply be unable to operate in daily life. It might, therefore, not be too far-fetched to regard synchronistic experiences as specific instances of a *massive* synchronistic event that includes the collective self-sense of the entire human race and is taking place within a vast 'moment' of time that for each of us individually emerges at birth and ceases at death. In the unimaginable eons of time in which cosmology deals, the period in which self-aware human beings have existed on the face of the Earth is hardly equivalent to the blink of an eye. Perhaps one reason why synchronicities are so fascinating and genuinely numinous for those who experience them is that they somehow echo or resonate with the underlying parallelism of the vast and collective 'mega-synchronicity' in which we find ourselves.

When coincidences are discussed within cosmology, however, it is usually in terms of how finely tuned the constants are or how many Goldilocks zones we are fortunate enough to inhabit, for without the dovetailing precision of these 'anthropic' coincidences human beings would certainly not be able to ponder their significance. It is unsurprising then that these cosmic coincidences, while they are not themselves taken to be meaningful *per se*, are often used as compelling evidence for the argument from design, as for example in the following unequivocal assertion by the cosmologist Edward Harrison:

> Here is the cosmological proof of the existence of God—the design argument of Paley—updated and refurbished. The fine-tuning of the universe provides *prima facie* evidence of deistic design. Take your choice: blind chance that requires multitudes of universes, or design that requires only one… Many scientists, when they admit their views, incline towards the teleological or design argument.[78]

In *that* sense the anthropic coincidences are certainly meaningful. However, there are certain other meaningful coincidences within the purview of cosmology which are particularly pertinent to our time and perhaps to the future course of our planetary civilisation. In their book, *The New Universe and the Human Future*, Nancy Abrams and Joel Primack discuss what they perceive as the extraordinary confluence of *temporal* coincidences that humanity is currently in the midst of. They believe we are living at a 'cosmically pivotal moment', not only for the future of the human race but also, quite conceivably, for that of the *entire* universe.[79]

The Big Picture

To appreciate the sheer magnitude and immensity of our universe, or at least the section that is visible from Earth, it is worth envisioning how a much smaller universe might look, and not only much smaller but *billions* of times smaller. For this, we might consider how the night sky is likely to appear in the far distant future, perhaps a hundred billion years from now. By that time almost all the hundreds of billions of galaxies now within range of our telescopes would have sped over the cosmic horizon because of the ever-increasing expansion of space and the escalating enormity of that expansion.[80] The skies would still be full of bright stars, perhaps more than there are now, as a result of the predicted convergence in around five billion years or so of the Milky Way and Andromeda galaxies.

These two great spiral galaxies, the biggest in our Local Group, are moving towards each other due to their mutual gravitational attraction, along with a number of smaller and satellite galaxies, including the Triangulum galaxy, the only other spiral galaxy in the region and a possible satellite of Andromeda. But beyond the range of our Local Group of galaxies, the skies will be virtually empty. By that time the Earth will be long gone and the Sun will have become a white or even a black dwarf. Nevertheless, it is not inconceivable that our remote progeny will still be around in some form or another, especially if they will have found a way to emigrate to suitable exoplanets orbiting younger versions of our Sun. If that happens, as Abrams and Primack point out, they will almost certainly be dependent on records left by their ancestors to have a complete picture of the cosmos:

> The stupendously rich sky in the Hubble Ultra Deep Field, dense with galaxies, will be known to our distant descendants only historically through the records we leave. Those distant descendants' own deepest photos of space will show almost nothing. If we humans had not evolved to these abilities while the galaxies are still visible, it is possible that no intelligent beings in the distant future would ever be able to figure out how the universe operates. The astronomical observations and understandings that we pass on will be an irreplaceable part of our human heritage.[81]

Cosmologists Lawrence Krauss and Robert Scherrer describe this future scenario as an *apocalypse of knowledge*.[82] Not only will galaxies have disappeared but so will all but the faintest trace of background radiation from the Big Bang, which will be a *trillion* times more diffuse than it is now and might not even be detectable. With no other galaxies around apart from our Local Group, future astronomers without access to records from our era would very likely conclude that they were in a 'steady state' rather than an expanding universe, the general astronomical conception before the 1920s when Edwin Hubble discovered that distant galaxies are receding: the further they are from us, the faster they are moving away. In other words, our descendants would be extremely hard pressed to develop an accurate picture of the genesis and evolution of the universe. Therefore, as Abrams and Primack emphasise, it is indeed fortuitous that we have been able to develop the technology to map the furthest reaches of outer space when the most distant galaxies have *not yet* started to disappear over the cosmic horizon.[83]

From an evolutionary perspective it could quite easily have been many millions of years into the future before intelligent beings, whether *Homo sapiens* or some other species, made sufficient scientific progress to have an accurate idea of their place in the cosmos. Not inconceivably, this could have occurred far into the future of our planet, when the conditions for biological complexity will be *much* more tenuous than they are at present. We are currently in the middle of the billion-year period when the Earth is the most suitable for complex life.[84] At the end of that window of time, in five hundred million years, the heat of the Sun will be 6% greater than it is at present, and this will result in *sixty* times as much extra heat load as that created so far by all the greenhouse gases added to the atmosphere as a result of human activity.[85]

But perhaps the most remarkable of the temporal cosmic coincidences, and one that Abrams and Primack consider to be particularly felicitous, is that a profound conceptual upheaval within cosmology, potentially of the scale of the Copernican revolution, is taking place at so critical a time, when hugely important collective decisions must be made to determine the direction of our planetary future.[86] The revivifying fruit of this forthcoming conceptual revolution will be a *unifying cosmological vision* that provides 'a coherent, believable picture of the universe that applies to all of us and gives our lives and our species a meaningful place in that universe'.[87] Not only does it equip humanity with a clear idea of both the precise location and the unique evolutionary significance of the Earth in relation to the rest of the observable universe, it also reveals where human beings fit on a universal size scale.

Compared with galaxy clusters we are certainly next to nothing in size, but for elementary particles, atoms, molecules and cells, we are enormous. In fact, our size falls within the very narrow Goldilocks range for *any* kind of complex intelligent life, 'somewhere between a redwood tree and a puppy', as Abrams and Primack portray this narrow window. Much smaller and there would be insufficient atoms to cater for our complexity; much larger and the speed of light would limit the speed of our internal communications, including the speed of thought: 'Only near the centre of all possible sizes can consciousness as complex as ours arise, and this tells us something important about intelligent life anywhere in the universe: if it exists at all, it will have to be approximately our size.'[88]

Human beings are therefore by no means insignificant, especially as it is quite conceivable that *any* form of advanced life comparable with our own is simply non-existent in the Milky Way with its hundreds of billions of stars, and perhaps not even in our entire visible universe. On the other hand, it may be that in fact both our galaxy and the universe are teeming with life. But even if that is the case, there may be very few evolutionary pockets like ours that have been able to come anywhere near developing a species capable of self-reflective intelligence, let alone one that has been able to achieve, through the use of sophisticated astronomical instruments, a scientific account of both its own origins and that of the universe as a whole.

Furthermore, whatever the actual status of alien civilisations within and beyond our galactic borders, the human race has already evolved sufficiently to become, in a very real sense, *the universe's own awareness of itself*, its eyes and ears, as it were, and also its potential vehicle for profound self-understanding. And we simply do not know if this particular evolutionary leap has taken place elsewhere in the sheer

Cosmic Coincidences

vastness of space and time. If not, then our survival and our ability to care for our planetary home, is of *truly cosmic* significance. Abrams and Primack are very emphatic about this point:

> We humans might be the first. There may be microbial life on many other planets in this Galaxy, but it took a series of outrageously improbable events on Earth, plus multiple cosmic catastrophes to earlier species such as the dinosaurs, before humans could evolve. Earth is our only example of the evolution of life. If those improbable events were essential to make intelligent life, then our level of intelligence (and higher) may be extremely rare. Everyone is interested in discovering intelligent aliens out there, but suppose we are the only intelligence of our kind. Will there be consciousness and meaning in the future universe? Or will there just be sound and fury signifying nothing? This is what it means to be living at a cosmically pivotal moment.[89]

Hence the importance of an accurate cosmology: without it there would be no cosmic perspective, no real reason for human beings to think beyond survival and acquisition, and their own tribal and nationalistic concerns. A powerful piece of imagery in support of such a perspective entered into general awareness with the Apollo program and the first full photographs of Earth from space. In a moving response to these exquisitely beautiful images, the mythologist Joseph Campbell declared: 'All the old bindings are broken. Cosmological centres now are any- and everywhere. The earth is a heavenly body, most beautiful of all, and all poetry now is archaic that fails to match the wonder of this view.'[90]

Fig. 4: The Earth and Moon from the Galileo Spacecraft[91]

Certain popular songs have risen to Campbell's challenge, in particular John Lennon's *Imagine* and, before that, Joni Mitchell's *Woodstock*, which was composed around the time of the first Moon landing and has been recorded by over two hundred artists.[92] Its final verse is particularly potent:

> We are stardust
> Billion year old carbon
> We are golden
> Caught in the devil's bargain
> And we've got to get ourselves
> Back to the garden

From a cosmic perspective, the garden is the Earth and the devil's bargain our selfishness and greed. We may justify these euphemistically dubbed 'survival instincts' as inherited traits from our primitive ancestors, and we can say that on an evolutionary scale we are simply the descendants of early mammals and before them the earliest forms of life on Earth. But our origins are much more poetically and creatively charged: we are indeed composed of stardust and its array of rare heavy metals forged in stellar furnaces, with most of the iron in our blood coming from exploding white dwarfs and the oxygen we breathe largely a consequence of the supernova explosions of massive stars.[93]

The heavy metals and elements that make up the stardust from which we have evolved are in cosmic terms very scarce. Apart from hydrogen and helium, all the elements of the periodic table together make up only 0.01% of the atoms in the universe. Hydrogen and helium atoms, in turn, make up only 0.5% of the total and what is particularly striking about these relatively small proportions is that in total they constitute our entire *visible* universe. Invisible atoms floating through space and unlit by stars make up another 4%, while the other 95% of the density of cosmos is thought to be composed of dark matter and dark energy, making up 25% and a staggering 70% respectively.[94]

The amount of dark matter has not changed since the early universe, when the total quantity of dark energy was considerably less than it is now. The two were about equal around five billion years ago, at around the time our solar system was forming, but since then the proportion of dark energy has been steadily increasing. And it will continue to do at an accelerating rate until and beyond the time when all the galaxies have disappeared over the cosmic horizon, apart from our Local Group, which will continue to be held together by the gravitational attraction of dark matter.[95] As regards the nature and composition of dark matter and dark energy, by far the major players in the composition of the universe, it is not within the scope of this brief exploration of coincidences within the field of cosmology to discuss their nature in much detail.

Suffice to say that dark matter is comprised of extremely minute invisible particles that have yet to be fully identified, while dark energy is linked with the expansion of empty space, as measured by the cosmological constant. Its presence also means that empty space is not exactly empty and, as Krauss and Scherrer explain, in fact 'contains almost three times as much energy as all the cosmic structures we observe today: galaxies, clusters and superclusters of galaxies'.[96] The universe is clearly an incredible totality which functions with *unimaginable* precision. It has even catered for the evolution of intelligent beings capable of understanding the dimensions of that totality. Although there has been barely a ripple of appreciation or celebration beyond the disciplines involved, it is certainly coincidental that the creation of a scientifically accurate cosmology should have occurred at the same time as exponential growth, both in our population and our exploitation of resources, has resulted in a precarious future for the Earth's living systems.

The Nature of the Cosmic Coincidences

From the discussion so far, it appears that there are at least *three* distinct forms of coincidence that are integral to our understanding of how the universe is structured. First, and foremost, is the finely-tuned precision of the constants of nature and the initial conditions at the Big Bang, without which the makeup of the universe as we know it, and hence our existence, would simply not be possible. Second, there is the highly improbable confluence of Goldilocks conditions that have occurred in our galaxy and solar system, as well as on Earth, to set the stage for the conditions for our planet's rich and complex bio-diversity. As James Lovelock puts it: 'It almost seems as if our Galaxy were a giant warehouse containing the spare parts needed for life.'[97] Third, there are the temporal coincidences within cosmology, for example, that we are living at a time when the outer galaxies have not yet sped over the cosmic horizon. There is less than a 1% chance at any time of this being the case and the coincidence is that we are around to witness it.[98]

The reason for this equilibrium is due to the fact that in our current time period, the density of dark energy is roughly equivalent to the density of all the matter in the universe, both dark and visible.[99] As the density of dark energy increases so will its rate of expansion, and then the far galaxies will begin to disappear in earnest. In comparison with the precision of some of the fundamental parameters, 1% represents a huge probability margin. However, the fact that we are living at just this time, the best possible time for astronomy, as Abrams and Primack point out,[100] does suggest a certain synchronistic uncanniness and possibly a faint whiff of purpose or design.

To help further differentiate these three main forms of cosmic coincidence, the four categories of coincidence explanation introduced in the previous chapter are redisplayed below, with some appropriate changes in nomenclature to cater for the ultimate cosmological questions that arise naturally from this kind of discussion:

Coincidence Categories
— Random chance explanations
— Natural causal explanations
— Supernatural causal explanations
— Synchronicity explanations

The apparent fine-tuning for life of the universal parameters or constants of nature is *so* precise that it has led many scientists and philosophers to accept that this must be evidence of a creative intelligence. Many of those who refuse to accept this possibility hypothesise that our universe is one of the few life-permitting ones in a multiverse of potentially 10^{500} universes. But even if that were the case, and at present the multiverse remains but a hypothesis, what is the nature of its origin? The same question applies to other penultimate hypotheses, whether involving Platonic forms, angelic realms, or mathematically charged parallel worlds.[101] The design problem is merely pushed back another level and the question must eventually arise as to the nature of the origin, if indeed there is one, of the universe, multiverse, or whatever else is proposed.

Chance explanations also become problematic at this stage as all play of randomness requires a context within which to operate, likewise any explanation involving synchronicity. But the context for synchronicity is rather different, for any such consideration requires there to be a *conscious observer*. And this gives rise to the pertinent question of whether the presence of a conscious observer can *ever* be bracketed out from *any* explanatory model for the universe. Indeed, certain experimental anomalies at the quantum level bring this very question into particularly sharp focus, a matter that will be explored in some detail in the next chapter.

In his taxonomy of twenty-seven logically permissible explanations for the universe, Kuhn includes, as one of nine non-physical explanations, the pantheistic 'substance' of the philosopher Baruch Spinoza.[102] Interestingly, pantheism, the ancient idea that the universe *itself* is divine, has been described by Richard Dawkins as 'sexed-up atheism'.[103] And it is here perhaps that the boundary between the natural and the supernatural begins genuinely to blur. Straddling the two realms is the iconic figure of Albert Einstein, who famously wrote: 'I believe in Spinoza's God who reveals himself in the orderly harmony of what exists, not in a God who concerns himself with the fates and actions of human beings.'[104] Also straddling the two realms, though more like background noise than a symbolic figure, is the presence (or non-presence) of *nothingness*, though the quality of its non-existence is next to impossible for the intellect to grasp. Chuang Tzu, for whom the resolution of the conundrum of the interface of existence and non-existence is to be found in the *tao*, conveys the paradox of emptiness in this delightful allegory:

> Starlight asked Non-Being: 'Master, are you? Or are you not?'
> Since he received no answer whatever, Starlight set himself to watch for Non-Being. He waited to see if Non-Being would put in an appearance. He kept his gaze fixed on the deep Void, hoping to catch a glimpse of Non-Being. All day long he looked, and he saw nothing. He listened and he heard nothing. He reached out to grasp and grasped nothing.
> Then Starlight exclaimed at last: 'This is it! This is the furthest yet!
> Who can reach it? I can comprehend the absence of Being.
> But who can comprehend the absence of Nothing?
> If now, on top of all this, Non-Being is, who can comprehend it?'[105]

For all ultimate explanations for the universe, whether natural, supernatural or at the interface of the two, there will always be the enigma of nothingness, which the philosopher Robert Carter has described as 'the universal of universals'.[106] In other words, amongst such abstract qualities as goodness and beauty, the *most* abstract is nothingness. Yet it permeates everything; and whether or not creation emerged *ex nihilo*, whatever the quality of that *nihilo* may be, it is only when the manifest world appears that randomness and chance can genuinely begin to dance.

Chance is therefore very much in play as an explanation for the presence of biological complexity on Earth, the stability and metallic richness of the Sun, the size and position of the Moon, the near circular orbits of the planets of the solar system, and its location in the habitable zone of the Milky Way. For the science writer John Gribbin, the odds of all these and many more dovetailing Goldilocks conditions collectively occurring are incredibly remote: 'In an infinite universe anything is possible, but anything interesting may only be happening infinitely far away from us. The Milky Way contains a few hundred billion stars, but almost certainly contains only one intelligent civilisation. In that sense, our civilisation is alone, and special.'[107] But given the immensity of the universe, it is very hard to assert without direct evidence of divine, or at least alien, intervention that the extraordinary fecundity of the Earth is not simply the result of chance: a fortuitous combination of natural occurrences arising out of the structure and substance of the universe.

It is, however, possible to argue that the fact that we find ourselves on a beautiful, life-sustaining planet is a collective meaningful coincidence just as much as it is a chance event, especially given the distinction between the two made by David Richo and quoted in the previous chapter: 'Chance happens to us; synchronicity happens in us.'[108] And for certain individuals, for instance the visionary American priest Thomas Berry, there is a sense that our place in the universe is not just a chance occurrence but a profound synchronistic communion: 'We bear the universe in our being as the universe bears us in its being. The two have a total presence to each other and to that deeper mystery out of which both the universe and ourselves have emerged.'[109] But it is a rare individual for whom these words represent more than an occasional moment of wonder inspired perhaps by the beauty of nature or the magnificence of the sky at night.

In the same way, it is a rare individual who will find him or herself tangibly resonating with the temporal cosmic coincidences, all of which have considerable meaning for the future of the human race. To recap, they are: a) we are living at a time when the density of dark energy is still roughly equal to that of matter, which means that the distant galaxies are still visible; b) we are in the middle of the billion year optimum period for life on Earth, which means that there are potentially *millions* of years ahead for the human race, assuming we avoid irrevocably fouling our nest; c) we have developed a scientifically accurate picture of the universe at the *very* time that our planet is most at threat from the parallel dangers of exponential population expansion and the destruction of the natural environment. This is the most immediately meaningful of the temporal coincidences and one that could assist in shaping a vision for a genuinely harmonious and sustainable future. It is appropriate to give the last word in this chapter on the cosmic coincidences to Abrams and Primack:

> We few billion humans alive today represent through no democratic choice whatsoever the millions of our ancestors and the millions more generations of our potential descendants, with all their hopes and dreams and creations. We randomly-alive-today people actually have the power to end this evolutionary miracle, or not. Is suicide really the character we want to brand on the universe? Without human beings, as far as anyone knows, the universe will be silenced forever... It may seem strange that there should be a practical connection between the vastly different timescales of cosmology and our present environmental challenges, but there is a connection — it is crucial that people realise this very soon. By understanding how humanity fits into the timescales of the universe, we begin to grasp what is truly at stake for our planet and

for our descendants in the political and economic decisions being made today.[110]

Endnotes

[1] e.g. Bailey, 'What are the Cosmic Coincidences, and What Do They Mean?'
[2] Eadel, 'Why the Choir Was Late'.
[3] Weaver, *Lady Luck*, 218–219.
[4] Eadel, 'Why the Choir Was Late', 23.
[5] Dossey, *The Power of Premonitions*, 44.
[6] Ibid., 181–182.
[7] Radin, *Entangled Minds*; Dossey, *The Power of Premonitions*.
[8] Kaku, *Parallel Worlds*, 243.
[9] Barrow, *The Artful Universe*, 116.
[10] Ibid., 145–149.
[11] Ward and Brownlee, *Rare Earth*, 222–223.
[12] Kaku, *Parallel Worlds*, 243.
[13] Ibid., 223–224.
[14] Cain, 'How Many Stars Are There in the Universe?'; 'How Many Galaxies Are There in the Universe?'; 'How Many Stars Are in the Milky Way?'
[15] Leslie, *Universes*, 131–132.
[16] Blake, 'Alien Life Certain to Exist on Earth-like Planet, Scientists Say'.
[17] Wall, 'Is Planet Gliese 581g Really the "First Potentially Habitable" Alien World?'
[18] Moseman, 'The Estimated Number of Stars in the Universe Just Tripled'.
[19] European Southern Observatory, 'Ultracool Dwarf and the Seven Planets'.
[20] Davies, *The Mind of God*, 205.
[21] e.g. Duff, Okun and Veneziano, 'Trialogue on the Number of Fundamental Constants'.
[22] Uzan and Leclercq, *The Natural Laws of the Universe*, 38.
[23] Ibid., 25.
[24] Miller, *137: Jung, Pauli, and the Pursuit of a Scientific Obsession*, 34–35, 40, 247–248.
[25] Ibid., 41.
[26] Ibid., 248.
[27] Ibid., xviii.
[28] Ibid., 253.
[29] Ibid., 250–251.
[30] Ibid., 253–254.
[31] Gieser, *The Innermost Kernel*, 333.
[32] Meier, *Atom and Archetype*.
[33] Gieser, *The Innermost Kernel*, 333.
[34] Davies, *The Goldilocks Enigma*, 20–23; Spitzer, *New Proofs for the Existence of God*, 3.
[35] Banks, 'Planck Reveals "Almost Perfect" Universe'.
[36] Miller, *137: Jung, Pauli, and the Pursuit of a Scientific Obsession*, xv.
[37] Gilson, 'The Place of the Fine Structure Constant, *a* in Nature's Scheme'.
[38] Source for Fig. 3: by kind permission of the artist, Phil Disley.
[39] *The Economist*, 'Ye Cannae Change the Laws of Physics'.

40. Davies, *The Goldilocks Enigma*, 135-150.
41. Ibid., 58.
42. Hawking and Mlodinow, *The Grand Design*, 162.
43. Weinberg, 'Anthropic Bound on the Cosmological Constant', 2067.
44. Davies, *The Goldilocks Enigma*, 148-149.
45. Kaku, *Parallel Worlds*, 251.
46. Madrigal, 'Dark Energy Could Be Einstein's Cosmological Constant'.
47. Davies, *The Goldilocks Enigma*, 150.
48. Ibid., 281, n. 22.
49. Ibid., 146.
50. Spitzer, *New Proofs for the Existence of God*, 63-64.
51. Hoyle, 'The Universe: Past and Present Reflections', 12.
52. Ibid.
53. Ward, *Why There Almost Certainly Is a God*, 38-40.
54. Ibid., 40.
55. Hawking and Mlodinow, *The Grand Design*, 118-119.
56. Ibid., 180.
57. Stenger, 'The Grand Accident', 6.
58. Ibid., 'The Universe Shows No Evidence for Design', 3.
59. Penrose, *The Emperor's New Mind*, 342-344.
60. Ibid., 344.
61. Penrose, 'Is the Universe Fine-Tuned for Life and Mind?'
62. Ibid.
63. Penrose, *Cycles of Time*, 144-149.
64. Kuhn, 'Why This Universe?', 32.
65. Penrose, *Cycles of Time*, 167, 260n.
66. Kuhn, 'Why This Universe?', 32-35.
67. Mooney, 'The Evolution Polling Numbers Have Nudged a Little'; Newport, 'In U.S., 42% Believe Creationist View of Human Origins'.
68. Kuhn, 'Why This Universe?', 30.
69. Elgin, *The Living Universe*, 87.
70. Ibid., 83-91.
71. Mitchell, S., *Tao Te Ching*, 25; cf. Lau, *Lao Tzu: Tao Te Ching*, 78.
72. Kaku, *Parallel Worlds*, 241-252.
73. *Oxford English Dictionary Online*, s.v. 'supernatural'.
74. Thuan, *The Changing Universe*, 139.
75. Leslie, *Universes*, 79.
76. Hawking and Mlodinow, *The Grand Design*, 137.
77. Jung, *Synchronicity*, 112-117.
78. Lennox, *God's Undertaker*, 79.
79. Abrams and Primack, *The New Universe and the Human Future*, 79-89.
80. Krauss and Scherrer, 'The End of Cosmology?'
81. Abrams and Primack, *The New Universe and the Human Future*, 82.
82. Krauss and Scherrer, 'The End of Cosmology?', 50.
83. Abrams and Primack, *The View from the Center of the Universe*, 118, 271.
84. Ibid., 271-272.
85. Lovelock, *The Vanishing Face of Gaia*, 154.
86. Abrams and Primack, *The New Universe and the Human Future*, xii-xiii, 14.
87. Ibid., xiv.

88 Ibid., 33.
89 Ibid., 97.
90 Campbell, *Myths to Live By*, 243-244.
91 Source for Fig. 4: http://nssdc.gsfc.nasa.gov/photo_gallery/photogallery-earthmoon.html
92 Mitchell, J., *Woodstock*.
93 Abrams and Primack, *The New Universe and the Human Future*, 39-43.
94 Ibid., 48-50.
95 Ibid., 56.
96 Krauss and Scherrer, 'The End of Cosmology?', 48.
97 Gribbin, *The Reason Why*, ii.
98 Than, 'An Answer to the "Cosmic Coincidence"?'
99 Nerlich, 'Astronomy without a Telescope—Cosmic Coincidence'.
100 Abrams and Primack, *The View from the Center of the Universe*, 271.
101 Kuhn, 'Why This Universe?'
102 Ibid., 33-34.
103 Dawkins, *The God Delusion*, 40.
104 Ibid., p. 39.
105 Merton, *The Way of Chuang Tzu*, 125.
106 Carter, R., *The Nothingness Beyond God*, 99.
107 Gribbin, *The Reason Why*, xv.
108 Richo, *The Power of Coincidence*, 102.
109 Elgin, *The Living Universe*, 83.
110 Abrams and Primack, *The New Universe and the Human Future*, 100-101.

Chapter Four

Enigma Variations

In 1974, Arthur Koestler, that inveterate collector of coincidence stories, received a letter from Dr Tom Leonard, then a lecturer in the Department of Statistics at the University of Warwick. As is common with statisticians, Leonard was a staunch advocate for probabilistic explanations of unusual coincidences and the anecdote he related to Koestler, which he described as 'the best coincidence yarn I know',[1] can be readily accounted for by mathematical analysis. The story concerns a new statistics lecturer at the University, who in his very first lecture took out a coin from his pocket to illustrate the laws of probability. He tossed the coin in the air and then, in Leonard's graphic description: 'It landed on a polished floor, spun around a few times, and to a thunderous applause came to rest — vertically!'[2]

Obviously, any coin landing on its edge on a flat surface without eventually falling one way or another is an extremely unusual event, with odds against this happening estimated by Warren Weaver as a billion to one.[3] But whatever the statistical analysis, and with seven billion people on the planet it should in theory at least be a reasonably regular occurrence, it is not its low probability that makes this incident exceptional. It is the fact that it happened to a new statistics lecturer in his first lecture standing in front of a roomful of students he was no doubt keen to impress. Added to that, he tossed the coin not so much to see whether it would come down heads or tails but with the express purpose of illustrating the laws of probability. As a statistician he would have been ably equipped to dismiss the episode as 'mere coincidence'. However, as a human being he would almost certainly have been shaken, and perhaps even stirred.

Although the problem of watertight authentication is always present with such anecdotes, their very profusion suggests that most likely a good proportion of them are true. For example, those presented by Koestler in *The Challenge of Chance*, however they might ultimately be interpreted, do have a ring of authenticity about them that would be difficult to dismiss as the figment of a fertile imagination. And as odd and uncanny as such coincidences may appear to be, and indeed *any* anomalous activity that currently comes under the broad umbrella of ESP or parapsychology, they are in Koestler's view neither odder nor uncannier than the coincidences and anomalies associated with quantum physics.

Just as the previous chapter dealt with the coincidences within cosmology, this one addresses those to be found in quantum physics. Though far fewer, these 'quantum coincidences' are no less significant in their possible implications. Indeed, much of Koestler's popular *The Roots of Coincidence* is about the mind-boggling nature of microphysics, and his justification for writing about this fascinating field, as he does again in *The Challenge of Chance*, is to draw certain parallels between physics and parapsychology.

Koestler is, however, too canny a polymath to fall into the enticing trap of suggesting that the anomalies of physics provide evidence for parapsychology. His point, rather, is that far from being positively aligned, what the two fields have in common are their *negative* attributes: 'both defy common sense, and both defy laws previously considered as sacrosanct. Both are provocative and iconoclastic. And... the baffling paradoxa produced by one make the baffling paradoxa of the other appear a little less preposterous.'[4] This was also the reason, according to Koestler, why 'a number of eminent physicists, from Einstein downward'[5] have taken an interest in the possible affinity between these realms; and none more so than Wolfgang Pauli, whose 'revolutionary proposal was to extend the principle of non-causal events from microphysics (where its legitimacy was recognised) to macrophysics (where it was not)'.[6]

Pauli's revolutionary proposal was the serious consideration of Jung's hypothesis of synchronicity, which he had a significant hand in helping formulate, as has been revealed by the publication of their correspondence, in German in 1992 and nine years later in English, edited by Jung's colleague C.A. Meier.[7] Since then, a number of books have been published about this famous interdisciplinary collaboration: not that it would have been a particularly easy one for Pauli given Jung's propensity to expound intuitively and at length in public on subjects outside his speciality. In a letter to his assistant and close associate Markus Fierz in 1949, Pauli writes: 'I *dream* about physics as Herr Jung (and other non-physicists) *think* about physics. The danger of this situation lies in Herr Jung publishing nonsense about physics and could moreover quote me in the process.'[8]

It should not be forgotten that Jung was twenty-five years Pauli's senior and had helped him psychologically through a very stressful period during the 1930s, so it is almost inconceivable that, despite a marked tendency towards the acerbic, Pauli would ever have been less than circumspect in his dealings with Jung. It does, however, show some of the frustration he obviously had with Jung as regards conceptual precision, and this is evident from their correspondence. For example, after reading Jung's draft manuscript for his essay on synchronicity, Pauli writes:

> ...although microphysics allows for an acausal form of observation, it actually has no use for the concept of 'meaning'. So I have grave misgivings about placing physical discontinuities and synchronicity on the same level, which is what you do on p. 58. If you do not share my misgivings, I shall be most interested to hear what your arguments are [an editorial note by Meier links p. 58 of the draft to a specific passage towards the end of Jung's essay].[9]

Jung made a number of changes to his manuscript as a result of Pauli's suggestions and criticisms, though it is not clear from Meier's editorial reference whether he made any adjustments to the passage referred to by Pauli. But as the following response testifies, he obviously took Pauli's concerns on board: 'I fully agree with you that the synchronicity of the psychic sphere must be conceptually separated from the discontinuities of microphysics.'[10] Still, Pauli's disquiet as a physicist is understandable, and for evidence of this one need only look at the passage over which (according to the editorial note) he expressed 'grave misgivings'. This begins with the following assertion by Jung: 'The modern discovery of discontinuity (e.g. the orderedness of energy quanta, of radium decay, etc.) has put an end to the sovereign rule of causality...'[11]

Obviously, for Pauli, and he explains this carefully to Jung,[12] the discovery of discontinuity, as displayed in the sudden 'quantum leap' of electrons around an atomic nucleus from one orbit to another, does *not* put an end to the rule of causality. It is true that at the quantum level *specific* measurements cannot be individually predicted, and therefore have acausal characteristics. But when a continuing *series* of quantum measurements are made, they display immense precision. In addition, as Victor Mansfield puts it: '...the predictive power, wide scope of application, and accuracy of quantum theory are far superior to anything from classical physics.'[13]

At the start of the next paragraph Jung writes: 'Synchronicity is no more baffling or mysterious than the discontinuities of physics.'[14] This is actually very similar to the point Koestler makes about the negative affinities between quantum physics and parapsychology. In other words, if the apparent anomalies of microphysics are accepted by the scientific community, then those of synchronicity or parapsychology should not occasion outright rejection and disbelief. Jung himself bemoaned the 'exaggerated scepticism in regard to ESP',[15] a valid point, and one that is yet to be resolved within mainstream scientific orthodoxy. Indeed, there has been a long-running battle between proponents and sceptics over the status of psychic research,[16] though the whole notion of 'scepticism' seems to have become increasingly associated with ideological denial rather than genuine scientific doubt.[17]

Perhaps an appreciation of the possible implications of some of the startling anomalies of quantum physics could help bring some resolution to this rather nasty spat, or at least accommodation; though for those with dogmatically hardened views it may be that no evidence or argument is sufficient. For instance, the Apollo landings on the Moon have been consistently denied by certain Hindus who insist that the whole thing must have been a hoax because any such landing is contrary to what has been stated in the Vedic scriptures.[18] And while such views are generally regarded as completely unworthy of serious consideration, much less derision is afforded equivalent or near-equivalent pronouncements by eminent establishment figures, epitomised perhaps by the nineteenth-century scientist and philosopher Hermann von Helmholtz, whose views on telepathy appear to have been unequivocal:

> Neither the testimony of all the fellows of the Royal Society, nor even the evidence of my own sense would lead me to believe in the transmission of thought from one person to another independently of the recognised channels of sense. It is clearly impossible.[19]

The Double-Slit Experiment

It is likely, however, that for Helmholtz such a statement would largely have been rhetorical and an attack on the surprising number of his colleagues and peers who were interested in psychic research.[20] Had he, for example, lived well on into the next century and been shown the quantum version of the double-slit experiment, he might well have said, initially at least, that what he had observed was impossible. This double-slit experiment is not to be confused with the original one performed by Thomas Young in 1801, in which the wave-like nature of light was demonstrated by the placement of a light source in front of a screen with two slits. The result of this is that an *interference pattern* appears on a second screen. In Fig. 5 the light source comes from the left of the diagram and passes through the two slits:

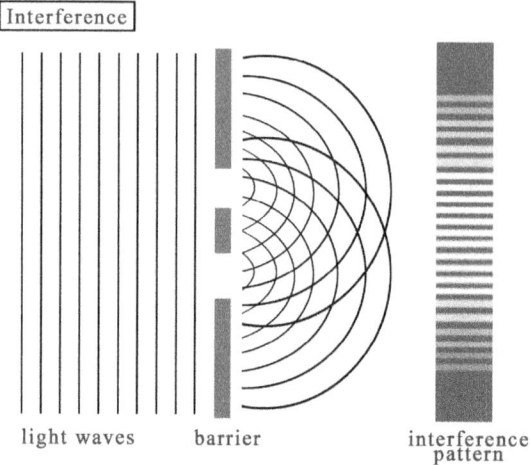

Fig. 5: Interference Pattern[21]

The interference pattern is to be expected if the nature of light is wave-like. The peaks and troughs of the competing waves coming through each slit collide and *interfere* with each other. Light waves behave just like water, and a variation of the experiment could employ a wave machine which pushes water towards a barrier with two openings. The waves coming through each opening would create a similar interference pattern from their interaction with one another. David Peat provides a clear explanation for what occurs in a standard double-slit experiment: 'As with the case of water, waves of light spread out after passing through each slit, then meet and interfere with each other. The result is a complex pattern of light and dark regions where crests meet crests, troughs meet troughs, and crests meet troughs. The overall interference pattern is displayed by allowing this light to fall on a screen.'[22]

On the screen are alternating light and dark strips, with a concentration of light towards the centre of the screen in the area where light from the two slits overlap. Young's experiment was an important one at the time, especially as it was widely believed, including by Newton, that light was made up of tiny bullet-like corpuscles. With the advent of quantum theory, however, the corpuscular theory of light made a strong comeback when it was hypothesised by Einstein in 1905, and a decade later confirmed, that as well as being a wave, light also manifests itself as particles, each one a discrete 'packet' or 'quantum' of light that came later to be referred to as a *photon*.

In a previous paragraph, mention was made of the sudden quantum leap of electrons from one orbit around the nucleus of an atom to another, an instantaneous jump that occurs when an atom is sufficiently exposed to a stimulus such as heat. Each of these jumps is classified as a *discontinuity* because there is *no path* taken by the electron from one position to the next and there is *no time* taken between its departure from one orbit and its arrival at the next. And whenever an electron makes a jump, it emits a finite quantity of electromagnetic energy as light, and each of these light particles constitutes a photon.[23] To get some perspective on both their abundance and size, it is worth reflecting that even a faint one-watt night-light emits a phenomenal 10^{18} photons per second.[24] So when it comes to performing a quantum-level double-slit experiment using photons, the light source needs to be made so faint that it is able to emit a single photon at a time, and the recording screen so sensitive that it can pick up where each photon lands and so determine the overall pattern.

When one of the slits is closed in Young's experiment, a simple strip of light is visible on the second screen, and an equivalent pattern emerges when individual photons are shot through a single slit during a quantum-level experiment. However, if the other slit is opened and the photons (which we should recall are *particles* of light) are fired indiscriminately through *both* slits, an interference pattern emerges just as it does in the standard experiment. This means that though photons are discrete and measurable particles or quanta of light, they also have a wave nature, which becomes apparent when they are provided with more than one route by which to travel in a double-slit experiment.

The same goes for electrons, which are also quantum particles, though of *matter* rather than light. When they are shot through a single slit, they behave as bullets from a machine gun would and those that get through the slit display a single stream, as bullets would. With both slits open they show an interference pattern, which indicates that at the quantum level matter, like light, has a dual nature, at once particle and wave. In addition, the photons or electrons *always* appear on the recording screen in particle form, which means that they start *and* end as discrete entities whatever the slit configuration: it is what goes on in between, when a choice of slits is provided, that is of particular interest.

At the next level of experiment, particles are emitted one at a time, the implication being that in this way they would not be able to interact with each other on the way through and should therefore remain in particle form, which is what they would do if only one slit were open. But this is *not* what occurs: even when particles are released in ordered sequence and have no chance of interfering with one another, they display an interference pattern. It is as if the particles somehow 'know' whether the second slit is open or closed. Peat reflects on this intriguing process:

> A photon is indivisible; it can only go through one of two slits. If it passes through slit A, for example, why should it matter if slit B is open or closed? Nevertheless, it does matter. When slit B is closed, the quantum-interference pattern vanishes; when slit B is open, this pattern reappears. But how can this be? How can a photon passing through slit A know whether slit B is open or closed? In passing though one part of the screen, how could it know what is happening in some other part?[25]

Not only does the quantum interference pattern disappear when one of the slits is closed, it *also* disappears when an attempt is made to observe which slit the photon or electron is travelling through. This is related to Heisenberg's uncertainty principle, which says that we cannot pin down both the position and the momentum of a particle at the same time. As Paul Davies and Julian Brown explain it:

> In order for the position of each electron to be measured accurately enough to discern the hole it is approaching, the electron's motion is so disturbed that the interference pattern defiantly vanishes! The very act of investigating where the electron is going ensures that the two-hole operation fails. Only if we decide not to trace the electron's route will its 'knowledge' of both routes be displayed.[26]

Double-Slit Variations

Furthermore, even if a slit is suddenly closed *after* the particle has travelled through the slits but *before* it has hit the recording screen, the formation of the interference pattern immediately ceases and the particle responds as if there had only been one slit open all the time. This is known as a 'delayed choice' experiment and was first proposed by the physicist John Wheeler. In the set-up two small telescopes are concealed behind a very flexible recording screen which can be removed at ultra-high speed *after* a photon travels through the slits but *before* it reaches the screen.

The telescopes, one pointed at slit A and the other at slit B, are capable of determining which slit the photon comes through, while the recording screen is only able to display where the photon lands. In theory, when the screen is removed, either one telescope will detect a flash or the other will, or each will detect a fainter flash as the photon splits and comes through both slits.

In practice, however, the third option does not materialise: the photon is detected either by one telescope or the other; it either comes through slit A or through slit B. The possibility of the photon coming through *both* slits only occurs if the screen is *not* removed and there no attempt at detection.[27] When that occurs, an interference pattern is recorded, indicating that a photon, whenever unobserved, remains in an undetermined or potential state.

This apparent ability by subatomic particles to outmanoeuvre scientists who wish to catch them in the act of functioning as waves is really an *extraordinary* outcome from the point of view of our standard procedures for obtaining knowledge from the world, far more outrageous than any weird or amazing coincidence. No wonder both Jung and Koestler felt justified in appealing to the anomalies of physics, for whatever the explanations and implications might be for psychic phenomena such as telepathy, they are no more improbable or unpalatable than those raised by the spectre of the double-slit experiment. It is as if it is a door to the quantum realm, where the usual subject–object dichotomies of classical physics and the world of our everyday interactions simply do not operate.

The photon in the experiment could be described as a borderline phenomenon: when it is treated as a microscopic object, that is how it reveals itself; when it is *not* subjected to classical techniques of measurement and observation, it 'reverts' to its natural state which, as can be inferred from the interference pattern it helps form, is a wave. And not *just* a wave, as the physicist Fred Alan Wolf (aka 'Dr Quantum') explains: 'Even though a particle seems to have a definite position and a definite location in space and time, when it's not being observed, it acts very strangely, like a field of waves spread out all over space and time and out to infinity.'[28]

The double-slit experiment has evolved over time to become a highly refined procedure, and such is the capacity for fine-tuning of the instruments involved that it is now possible to make the light needed to observe the direction taken by particles *so* faint that not all the particles emitted in a particular experiment are exposed to it. Nevertheless, the results are the same: the subset of particles that do not interact with the light form an interference pattern, while the subset that are exposed to it form a single stream in accord with whichever slit they came through.[29] In a further advance, using a process called 'weak measurement' a team was able to plot accurately the average trajectory of photons *without* disturbing the interference pattern created by the photon ensemble. For this they won first place in *Physics World's* top ten breakthroughs for 2011, not the least for having the courage to ask about the location of a photon before it is detected.[30]

Yet another development in regard to the double-slit experiment concerns the *size* of the particles that can be shown to function as waves. In addition to photons and electrons, both neutrons and whole atoms have been used as particles in the experiments, and even gigantic molecules made up of sixty carbon atoms. These molecules are known as 'fullerenes' after Buckminster Fuller, the inventor of the geodesic dome, whose shape they resemble, and they are also sometimes called 'buckyballs'.³¹ But the bar was raised again in 2012 when molecules with as many as 114 atoms were found to show an interference pattern, which leads inexorably to the fascinating if elusive question of a size limit at which the laws of classical physics must take over. Markus Arndt, a co-leader of the research team involved, had this to say following the experiment:

> We're still in the strange situation that if you believe that quantum physics is everything, then all of us are somehow quantum-connected, which is hard to believe. But it's also hard to believe that quantum physics ends at some point. That's why groups like us are trying to increase the complexity [of our molecules] to see if there is a threshold at some point.³²

In 2013, another team, also involving Arndt, was able to observe interference patterns in a double-slit experiment with molecules containing 810 atoms, a very significant increase in just a year.³³ Certainly, the idea that we are all quantum-connected, no matter how hard that might be for us to believe, makes logical sense when one considers that the physical world, which inevitably includes our bodies, is ultimately composed of the very same particles that show such paradoxical behaviour when subjected to the double-slit experiment. And, in principle, it does not matter how large or complex an object might be for it to be able to demonstrate an interference pattern, as the physicist Bruce Rosenblum affirms: 'The objects actually used have been photons, atoms, big molecules, large collections of atoms, etc. It gets harder with bigger things. But quantum mechanics supposedly applies in principle to anything—baseballs, the universe. To be general, we talk of "objects". We leave open whether they are hard, compact things or fuzzy clumps of cloudy stuff.'³⁴

The Collapse of the Wave Function

But whatever objects are involved in the double-slit experiment, the central mystery remains: why does the interference pattern disappear when an observation is made? This phenomenon is frequently, though not universally, referred to as the *collapse of the wave function*; and to highlight both the role of the observer and the part played by human choice in this collapse, Rosenblum and his colleague Fred Kuttner have proposed a double-slit variation, which they call a 'box-pair' experiment.³⁵

As illustrated in Fig. 6 (below), a particle of some sort, whose wave function is shown at t_1 in the diagram, is projected towards a semi-transparent mirror at t_2, where it splits into two halves. Each half is guided to a box, one directly and one via a fully reflective mirror. They enter through slits that are then immediately closed, trapping the wave-packets inside the boxes at t₃.

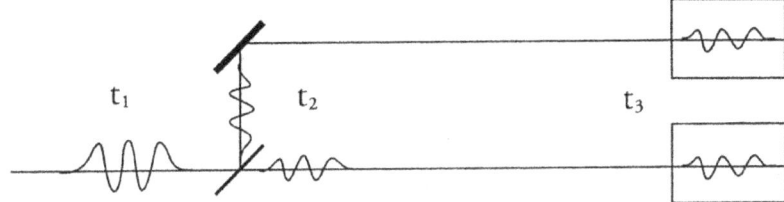

Fig. 6: Box-pair Experiment[36]

The reason why the boxes are arranged in a parallel position is because at the far end of each box is *another* slit. These slits need to stay closed for the wave-packets to remain trapped but can be opened, either in tandem or separately. Not pictured in the diagram but directly to the right of the boxes there is a recording screen that can display where the wave/particle lands, if either one or both slits are opened. As it turns out, when the procedure is repeated and both slits are opened a sufficient number of times an interference pattern appears on the screen, just as in the usual quantum double-slit experiment. But in a subtle twist that brings out the starkness of this version of the experiment, when only *one* of the slits is opened, one of two results is possible: either the *whole* particle shoots out and lands on the recording screen, though in 'bullet' formation rather than as part of an interference pattern; or *nothing* emerges from the box, meaning that the particle — for instance, an atom — is now wholly in the box *not* selected.

In other words, when only one of the boxes is opened, the wave function of the atom collapses: one box has the entire atom; the other is empty. Before that, the wave function of the atom was present in both boxes, even though the boxes are in distinct locations and interaction between them is out of the question. So we have a three-card trick of the highest order, and it is *impossible* to guess which box will contain the atom. The probability for each box is exactly half, but unlike the sleight of hand of even the most skilful magician, the whereabouts of the atom can never be known before one of the boxes is inspected.[37]

In terms of the actual experiment, the boxes do not physically need to be opened to ascertain which one contains the atom. Just by shining a beam, the gleam of the atom can be discerned.[38] The introduction of the beam itself is sufficient to collapse the wave function and cause the atom to emerge from its indeterminate 'superposition' state and coalesce in one of the boxes, leaving the other vacant. The point here is that the observer has a *choice* of whether to open one of the boxes, a procedure Rosenblum and Kuttner call a 'which-box?' experiment, or to open the slits of both boxes simultaneously and so perform an interference experiment. One outcome of this choice is that the experimenter's decision in the *present* seems to be able to determine what has already occurred in the *past*. If the experimenter chooses to conduct an interference experiment, it means that the atom travelled into both boxes in wave form; but if a 'which-box?' experiment is selected, it means that the atom did *not* divide and instead went directly and fully into the box in which it was found. Rosenblum and Kuttner explain:

> Finding an atom in a single box means that the whole atom came to the box on a particular *single* path after its earlier encounter with the semi-transparent mirror. Choosing an interference experiment would establish a *different* history: that aspects of the atom came on *two* paths to *both* boxes after its earlier encounter with the semi-transparent mirror.[39]

This is essentially a variation on Wheeler's delayed choice experiment referred to in the previous section. The two photon-detecting telescopes are hidden behind a retractable screen and one or the other will record the photon depending on which slit it comes through. But this only occurs if the screen is removed; so it is the *choice of the experimenter*, even if a random program is used, that determines whether the photon came through one or both of the slits. The important point here is that the decision to remove the screen is only made *after* the photon has passed the slits, which means that the choice of whether or not the screen is raised *retrospectively* determines the path of the photon.

This does not, however, mean that the past can be altered, which might be the impression arising from such an experiment, but that its trajectory only really comes into being when an observation is made. Before that, the photon remains in a superposition state and is not therefore a fixed entity: *it is the observation that solidifies its history*.[40] Even though at the quantum level we are dealing with nanoseconds, the same principle potentially applies on a much grander scale, as proposed by Wheeler in a cosmological thought experiment he describes as 'delayed choice with a vengeance'.[41] In this fascinating scenario, depicted in Fig. 7, light from a distant quasar is deflected by the gravitational pull of one or two massive galaxies that lie between the quasar and an observer on Earth:

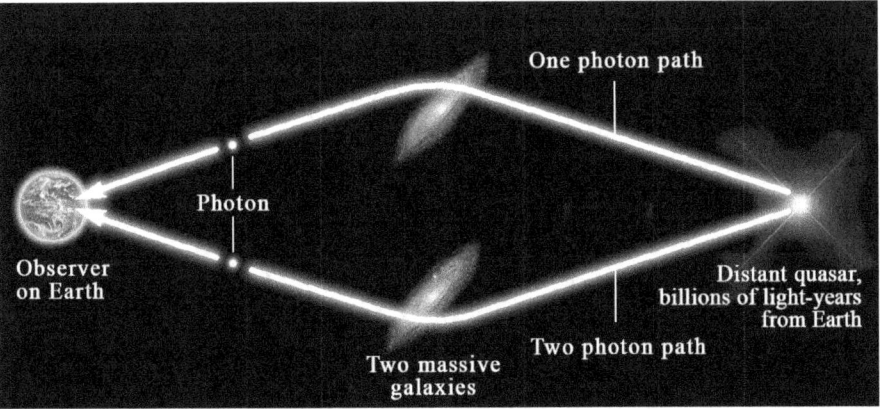

Fig. 7: Delayed Choice with a Vengeance[42]

If photons from the quasar are collected unobserved on photographic film they will show an interference pattern, suggesting that the same light is coming by both routes at once, just as in a double-slit experiment, with the galaxies substituting as slits. This would be made possible by the careful arrangement of mirrors so that the light from each of the galaxies is collected simultaneously on the film.[43] But it is not just the same *light* that comes through both routes: the interference pattern suggests that each *individual photon* takes both routes if it is unobserved, even though the routes may be separated by millions or even billions of light years.[44] That this is so could be demonstrated by a very distant and faint quasar whose photons arrive one at a time but *still* create an interference pattern, as in a regular double-slit experiment.[45]

However, if astronomers decide to point a telescope past one or other of the galaxies at the quasar, the photons they would see streaming from the quasar would then be confined to *that* particular route, just as when a detection device is suddenly introduced in a quantum delayed choice experiment. Unlike the photon in the experiment, an individual photon coming from the quasar will have been travelling for billions of years. Even so, it is not by any means predetermined whether it will end up taking one route or the other, or both. It all depends on whether the movements of the photon are observed, whether electronically or optically, or ignored, as Fred Alan Wolf makes abundantly clear: 'Thus it is we who decide by our choice of setup in the present moment whether the photon shall have travelled by "either path" or by "both paths". And we make this decision at the very last minute of the photon's existence, even though that photon left its source... [many billions of] years before we walked the planet.'[46]

This is a fascinating paradox and suggests that the *past itself* may not be fixed until it has been identified as such; as Wheeler puts it, 'the past has no meaning unless it exists as a record in the present.'[47] Thus we inhabit, according to Wheeler, a *participatory universe* that is shaped not only by physical forces but also by observations in a kind of loop effect, where the universe shapes observers, and observers shape the universe.[48] To what extent this is *actually* the case remains a matter for speculation. It is, however, a logical consequence arising from the unresolved enigma that remains at the heart of quantum mechanics, despite the many theories and interpretations that abound.[49]

This enigma, also known as the 'measurement problem', can be readily stated as a simple and straightforward question: why does the wave function or superposition state of an object collapse when an observer attempts to look at it or know about it directly? This is *the* central question that arises from the double-slit experiment and its numerous variations, some of which have been described in the preceding paragraphs. In addition, reflecting on the 'which-box?' experiment introduced by Rosenblum and Kuttner, there is the very odd circumstance of the collapsed particle ending up entirely randomly in one or another of the boxes.[50] Why is this so? Is God, as Einstein famously asked, really playing dice? This is another unanswered enigma, whether one views 'God' as a transcendent intelligence that has deliberately set this extraordinary universe in motion or, as the more atheistically inclined would prefer, as a highly complex physical process arising, virtually if not absolutely *ex nihilo*, from perturbations in a quantum vacuum.

Although the anomalies of quantum physics directly challenge our classical conception of the world and are therefore of fundamental significance, when their possible implications are raised, they are often done so in a distorted and exaggerated manner. A search for book titles on *amazon.com* containing the word 'quantum' brings up, in addition to the many authentic introductory explanations of quantum theory, as well a number of novels, such titles as *Quantum Success; Quantum Living; Quantum Healing; Quantum Leadership; Quantum Affirmations; Quantum Prophesy; Quantum Golf; Quantum Touch;* and *Quantum Wellness Cleanse*. This has meant that the profound, if rhetorical, question asked by Einstein as to whether the Moon exists if no one is looking at it comes to be misconstrued in a chain of dubious logic as 'you create your own reality', perhaps involving some form of 'quantum consciousness'.

What has occurred here no doubt involves an enthusiastic excess of extrapolation beyond the available data, which is precisely what Pauli was concerned about with Jung and the claims he made about the similarities between physics and synchronicity. The similarities themselves are not the issue: only if they are taken too literally. In his last major work, published a few years after his collaboration with Pauli on the synchronicity hypothesis, Jung made the following observation which, albeit pertinent, should not be used as an excuse for identifying analogy with actuality:

> All that *is* is not encompassed by our knowledge, so that we are not in a position to make any statements about its total nature. Microphysics is feeling its way into the unknown side of matter, just as complex psychology is pushing forward into the unknown side of the psyche. Both lines of investigation have yielded findings which can be conceived only by antinomies, and both have developed concepts which display remarkable analogies.[51]

Entanglement

One very remarkable source of analogy, not so far discussed, concerns quantum-level coincidences that do much to confirm the widely held intuition that everything is profoundly interconnected. The coincidences occur with particles whose properties have become fused or linked with one another so that even if they are physically separated they remain correlated. This state is known as *entanglement*, and it can be readily accomplished in a suitably equipped laboratory. All particles have a direction of 'spin' (somewhat analogous to rotation) and entangled particles may spin the same way or they may spin in opposite directions, no matter where they are physically located in relation to one another. A non-quantum example might be with two sets of coins, one a 'twin' pair and the other 'anti-twins'. Imagine there are two coin tossing devices in different buildings. The paired coins are tossed independently, one coin in each of the devices, and their results always correlate. The twins always come out the same way and the anti-twins always come out opposite.

While this is simply inconceivable in the everyday world of classical physics, it is the way things are in the world of quantum physics, also an 'everyday world' but hidden from us by its scale. Several experiments have shown that this is the case. In 1997, Nicolas Gisin and colleagues from the University of Geneva took a pair of entangled photons and on fibre-optic cables sent one to the north of the city and the other to the south, a distance apart of about 10 km. Along the way the photons were given random choices, for example, whether to take longer or shorter alternative routes. On every occasion the photons took the same routes, even though the choice of longer or shorter routes was entirely random. It was calculated that the difference in their response times was under three tenths of a billionth of a second, during which time light would only have been able to travel about 5.5 cm of the 10 km separating the photons.[52]

A decade later, Gisin and his team performed another experiment with a pair of entangled photons, this time separated by 18 km. The photons were again perfectly coordinated in their movements and had they been able to communicate physically, any information shared would have had to travel at 100,000 times the speed of light. As Gisin put it, not unreasonably: 'There is just no time for these two photons to communicate.'[53] So if the photons are not directly communicating, why then do they move in tandem with such coordinated precision? Perhaps there is some as yet undetected 'hidden variable' which makes this apparently instantaneous communication possible. Or perhaps there is a quantum reality *more* fundamental than the classical world of our senses that allows entangled particles to maintain their connection and correlation whatever their separation in space and time.

As a concrete illustration that is quite likely to be realised in the not too distant future, if one of a pair of twin photons were taken to Mars while the other remained on Earth, the mirroring of their movements would *still* be instantaneous. On the other hand, any external signal travelling at the speed of light between the two locations would take several minutes, the actual time depending on the relative orbital positions of the planets. Thus, it may well be that at the quantum level there exists an omnipresent indivisibility in which all physical structures and substances are embedded, where space and time are transcended and 'nonlocality' reigns. With reference to the implications of this 'nonseparability', Mansfield makes the following comments:

> We can no longer consider objects as independently existing entities that can be localised in well-defined regions of spacetime. They are interconnected in ways not even conceivable using ideas from classical physics... These are instantaneous interconnections. These quantum correlations reveal that nature is *noncausally* unified in ways we only dimly understand... It will take time for this view of nature to be fully understood and to penetrate the collective psyche. Nevertheless, it certainly provides a much more congenial world within which to understand synchronicity than the Newtonian world of independently and separately existing entities acting causally upon each other within an absolute space and time.[54]

A Conceptually Loaded Gun

A potential difficulty, for scientists at least, with this 'more congenial world' is that it is open to all manner of analogy and conjecture. This is no doubt why, when Bruce Rosenblum informed his physics faculty colleagues at the University of California at Santa Cruz of his intention to develop an introductory physics course for liberal arts students that included the mysteries of quantum theory, he was told by one staff member that to present this material to non-scientists would be 'the intellectual equivalent of allowing children to play with loaded guns'.[55] This somewhat dramatic warning is clearly a consequence of the momentous blow that has been dealt our notion of a 'real' world 'out there' by some of the findings of quantum mechanics, in particular the negation of the primacy of space and time: if not in practice in the macroworld of everyday interaction, then certainly in the microworld of particle physics, out of which the macroworld is ultimately formed.

A good example of the use of analogy and conjecture arising from such discoveries comes from the parapsychologist Dean Radin, whose book *Entangled Minds* speculates on the possibility that 'psi is the human experience of the entangled universe'.[56] Radin admits that there is insufficient evidence for such a conjecture but, he says, 'the ontological parallels implied by entanglement and psi are so compelling that they'd be foolish to ignore.'[57] Presumably, similar sentiments as those expressed by Rosenblum's colleague were shared by the doctors of the Catholic Church, when Galileo challenged official doctrine by insisting on the Copernican view that the Earth revolved around the Sun. Such a dangerous idea if widely disseminated would undoubtedly do further damage to the authority of the Papacy, which had already been undermined by the Reformation. It may not have been that the Church authorities accepted traditional Aristotelian geocentrism *en masse*; many of them may indeed have been quite sympathetic to the heliocentric position. But the issue was essentially one of power, and when vested interests are threatened in any serious way, they inevitably strike back.

Similarly, many scientists may be sympathetic to parapsychology; but as with heliocentricity before Newton, uncontroversial proof of its existence remains lacking, despite the consistent efforts of researchers to demonstrate otherwise. But as already mentioned earlier in this chapter, the controversy seems to have more to do with predetermined beliefs than actual research results, as suggested in the *New Scientist*: 'Over and over again, reputable researchers have found strong evidence for the existence of ESP in tightly controlled experiments. Many would conclude the evidence is more consistent with the existence of ESP than any other explanation, such as sloppy methodology or fraud... Sceptics, on the other hand, claim that pretty much any explanation for the evidence is more plausible than ESP... So any fresh evidence actually reduces their belief in ESP.'[58] Hence the frustration of Stanislav Grof, a long-time researcher in the field of altered states of consciousness: 'There exists hardly any other realm where the expert testimony of so many witnesses of the highest calibre has been discounted as stupidity and gullibility and thus been written off.'⁵⁹ The prominent psychic researcher Rupert Sheldrake summarises the situation thus:

> For well over a century there have been strongly divided opinions about the existence of psychic phenomena such as telepathy. The passions aroused by this argument are quite out of proportion to the phenomena under dispute. They stem from deeply held world-views and belief systems. They also raise fundamental questions about the nature of science itself.⁶⁰

Very much like the Catholic Church in the seventeenth century, perhaps in more ways than one, establishment science in the twenty-first century has considerable vested interests. Funding sources are hugely important, as are prestigious positions and awards. There is, in addition, the subtle matter of ideological conformity about what science represents. Inevitably, this is where the waters become muddied, as the comparative religion scholar Huston Smith makes plain in a sharp critique of the extent to which both the practice of science and its conception as an enterprise are permeated by *scientism*.⁶¹ Science itself, as Smith rightly points out, is what separates the modern world from the traditional, and is based on the scientific method, at the heart of which is 'the controlled experiment and its capacity to winnow true from false hypotheses about the empirical world'.⁶²

This is without question the great accomplishment of the scientific enterprise. However, there is an addendum or item of baggage that science carries on its proverbial back, and this addendum, according to Smith, contains two corollaries that make up the basis of the scientistic attitude: 'first, that the scientific method is, if not the *only* reliable method at getting at truth, then at least the *most* reliable method; and second, that the things science deals with—material entities—are the most fundamental things that exist.'⁶³ These are for the most part unarticulated assumptions that could easily appear to a detached but observant outsider to be very much part and parcel of mainstream science. They are not invariably held opinions but they do seem to exert a fairly considerable influence on the discourse surrounding science, and are reflected in the following observation made by the biologist E.O. Wilson before the turn of the millennium: 'The choice between transcendentalism and empiricism will be the coming century's version of the struggle for men's minds.'⁶⁴

Of course, an either/or approach is not *de rigueur* for dealing with the dichotomy between transcendentalism and empiricism. One can easily envisage a both/and approach, and in doing so one would be in good scientific company, part of a list that includes some of the biggest names of twentieth-century physics: not only Einstein and Pauli, but also Planck, Bohr, Heisenberg, de Broglie, Schrödinger, Jeans, and

Eddington.⁶⁵ To emphasise the thrall of a scientism, the transpersonal psychologist Charles Tart has developed an exercise he calls 'The Western Creed', which is a take on the Nicene Creed from Christian liturgy.⁶⁶ The 'creed', which for this exercise is to be repeated out loud, starts with these sentences: 'I BELIEVE—in the material universe—as the only and ultimate reality—a universe controlled by fixed physical laws—and blind chance. I AFFIRM—that the universe has no creator—no objective purpose—and no objective meaning or destiny.' After these two sentences there are several longer sections, and then the exercise ends with the following: 'I MAINTAIN—that the death of the body—is the death of the mind.—There is no afterlife—and all hope of such is nonsense.'⁶⁷

Tart includes the exercise in his book *The End of Materialism* in order to demonstrate to the reader the actual nature and 'feel' of thoroughgoing materialism. He reports that about five percent of those who do the Western Creed really enjoy it as it affirms their beliefs, while for many more it can be a rather disturbing experience.⁶⁸ The point about this is that if someone does sincerely hold to the Western Creed, then it is very unlikely that they will be sympathetic to any perspective on the nature of reality other than a materialistic one. Perhaps this is why, like the heliocentric system for the Church in the seventeenth century, the analogies and implications that naturally spring from an appreciation of the anomalies of quantum physics are akin to a loaded gun: because the gun is firmly pointed at materialism itself.

A Subtle Matrix

In 2007 a group of scientists, which included the Austrian experimental physicist Anton Zeilinger, visited Dharamsala in India for talks with the Dalai Lama, who has long taken an interest in collaborative discussions between Buddhism and science. In his formal dialogue with the Dalai Lama, Zeilinger began by saying that he would like to address the conceptual foundations of quantum mechanics, which after nearly a century were still unresolved. He asked, rhetorically, 'Why is the world so strange? Why do we have quantum mechanics?' Then he suggested: 'Maybe knowing, knowledge, is as fundamental or maybe even *more* fundamental, than material reality.'⁶⁹ Following these and other introductory remarks, he proceeded to explain the double-slit experiment with great care, emphasising that *only* when there is *no information* present from *any* source about which path a particular photon takes will an interference pattern appear.

The Dalai Lama understood clearly and responded through his interpreter to say that the unobserved wave function sounded like the notion of *prakriti*, a concept from the Sankhya school of Indian philosophy, which is 'generally translated as "primal substance" — and the macroscopic world of experience is thought to be manifestations coming out of this primal substance'.[70] *Prakriti* is defined by the India scholar J.F.T. Jordens as 'the matrix of all physical and psychic being',[71] a description that has definite affinities with Jung's concept of an undifferentiated unity or *unus mundus* underlying both the mind and the empirical world. As Jung saw it: 'The common background of microphysics and depth-psychology is as much physical as psychic and therefore neither, but rather a third thing, a neutral nature that can at most be grasped in hints since its essence is transcendental.'[72]

Jung was very interested in the anomalies of quantum physics, not only because of their intrinsic mystery, but because he considered them to be acausal parallels to synchronistic events and therefore linked through the wider *principle* of synchronicity, his umbrella term for categorising phenomena which demonstrate genuine acausality.[73] A good example would be the unpredictable behaviour of the particles in Rosenblum and Kuttner's 'which-box?' experiment. While most of what we know about this world demonstrates the play of cause and effect in one form or another, according to Jung there are certain '*a priori* factors such as the properties of natural numbers [and] the discontinuities of physics'[74] which do not. These he considered to be 'acts of creation' in the sense of their not being causally determined, though whether this is the case for the discontinuities of physics is yet to be resolved: there may be a deeper causality at the subatomic level that explains the apparent acausality at the observable level.[75]

The same goes for the results of ESP experiments. Granted that these may be 'unthinkable' from a strictly materialist causal position, and therefore 'acausal' from Jung's standpoint, they may in fact be evidence of a paranormal causality that is yet to be satisfactorily explained.[76] Still, even if specific examples of acausality proffered by Jung turn out not to be so, it does not mean that the notion of acausality itself is undermined. Clearly, when a meaning-connection is involved in a coincidental event, it is the *meaning* itself that stands out, and whatever form this meaning may take, it can never be a causal factor. The circumstances leading up to a specific coincidence will necessarily display chains of cause and effect, but not the fact of the coincidence itself. Take, for instance, the following anecdote, as reported in the anthology *Beyond Coincidence*:

> A golfer watched his perfect drive collide mid-flight with another ball — a recovery shot by another player in the opposite direction. Astounded by the coincidence, O'Brien and the other player ran to the collision point to introduce themselves. They were both called Kevin O'Brien.[77]

As with the example of the coin landing on its side, this unlikely occurrence can be explained by the laws of probability as a rare event though not an inconceivable one. While from this short report there is no indication as to whether either of the O'Briens experienced the coincidence as meaningful, one can safely assume that it could easily have been a factor for both men, in addition to the natural astonishment they would surely have felt. From a reading of the literature surrounding Jung's development of the synchronicity hypothesis, there appear to be three key ingredients in a synchronistic occurrence that distinguishes it from a chance coincidence (see Ch. 1). These are: an *equivalence of meaning* between an external event and deep psychological processes in the individual involved; an accompanying feeling of *numinosity* experienced as an emotional charge; and a *flash of total insight* or, as Jung called it, 'absolute knowledge'. He called it this, according to von Franz, because he wanted to emphasise how this form of sudden and immediate knowing 'differs completely from our conscious knowledge'.[78]

We do not know if this occurred for either, both or neither of the O'Briens, and whether it did or not is not particularly significant. What *is* significant and also important, however, is whether synchronistic experiences are able to provide clues as to the underlying nature of the reality we inhabit, and in particular whether or not that nature is psychophysical, a conception which is in marked contrast to the widely held view of a fundamentally physical universe, out of which life and consciousness have evolved, at least in one small pocket of the cosmic vastness. If the universe does turn out to be fundamentally physical — and that is a big if given the anomalies of quantum mechanics — it may be difficult to provide an adequate account of synchronistic occurrences, however numinous or meaningful, in any way other than as the subjective perception of meaning in conjunction with a chance coincidence.

The postulation of a psychophysical *unus mundus* would then be a lot more problematic because a physicalist conception by definition denies the existence of any realm *but* the physical. In such an interpretation consciousness is necessarily conceived of as fundamentally dependant on the brain and therefore limited to its confines, which makes the possibility of psychic phenomena a very doubtful proposition, if not ruled out *a priori*. Certainly ESP is less of an issue within a psychophysical model such as David Bohm's implicate order — to be touched on further in the final chapter — in which consciousness and matter, both living and non-living, are potentially united within an unbroken wholeness.[79] And although a hard-nosed physicist, Bohm himself was not averse to speculations concerning the paranormal.[80]

However, it may be that the implications of the actuality of synchronistic events, with all their puzzling and quirky nature, are of more significance than the debate over the existence or otherwise of ESP, a point made with some strength by Robert Anton Wilson in his book *Coincidance*:

> For over 100 years, various heretical scientists have been studying the so-called paranormal—strange events that are attributed to extrasensory perception, precognition or telekinesis. And every step of the way, this research has been attacked by critics who explain the positive results as 'mere coincidence' or (even worse) 'sheer coincidence'. Now there appears to be a possibility that coincidence may be more important scientifically—and may change our scientific paradigm much more radically—than telepathy would. Coincidence may be more earth-shaking than telekinesis. There have been coincidences so dramatic, so symbolic or so wildly improbable that they have aroused feelings of the uncanny in scientists and laymen alike for generations. Could such things happen by chance alone?[81]

As a writer, Wilson is well known for hyperbole, yet here he makes a very good point: coincidence may indeed be more earthshattering in its implications than ESP. The above paragraph opens a chapter entitled 'The Physics of Synchronicity', and the physics Wilson refers to is essentially the discovery that entangled particles remain precisely correlated with one another even when they are separated physically.[82] He posits this as a clue to answering the enigma of meaningful coincidences, though like many others he simply points out the parallels without showing any substantial connection between synchronicity and entanglement. But it is not the rather misleading chapter title that is of interest here, nor the tentative speculation about how coincidences on the macro level might be linked to those on the micro; it is his suggestion that 'coincidence may be more important scientifically—and may change our scientific paradigm much more radically—than telepathy would'.

Because if Jung is right and there really *is* a *unus mundus* underlying our manifest existence, and if synchronicities really *do* constitute moments when the *unus mundus* breaks through into our awareness, then we are faced with a paradigm that requires subjective and objective reality to be in fundamental alignment, not with the former as an epiphenomenon of the latter but with both as dual aspects of an underlying unity. This does not mean that the scientific account of our origins is negated, by no means: it is still the scientific consensus that our universe began around 13.8 billion years ago with the Big Bang, and through a series of highly fortuitous cosmic coincidences and chance evolutionary turns, we find ourselves awake and aware on this beautiful blue planet.

The important issue here, however, is not so much the creation or even the sustenance of the universe but what *exactly* it is that constitutes our awakeness and our awareness, and whether there *is* an underlying field which involves consciousness.

And of the unresolved enigmas of quantum physics, it is in particular the measurement problem that adds considerable weight to the possibility that a *unus mundus* conception of an underlying psychophysical reality, one that incorporates both mind and matter on an equal footing. This is already so at the quantum level, for as Niels Bohr put it, and which Zeilinger quoted more than once in his talk with the Dalai Lama, 'No phenomenon is a phenomenon unless it is an observed phenomenon.'[83] To which might be added the oft quoted line from Pascual Jordan, one of the participants in the founding of quantum theory: 'Observations not only *disturb* what is to be measured, they *produce* it.'[84] Mansfield, however, has a softer approach: 'Unobserved objects in quantum mechanics... do not have well-defined, pre-existent properties prior to measurement.'[85] Whichever quote one prefers, the point is well-made: at the quantum level there is no independent, physical object without an act of measurement, and that, necessarily, requires an observer, for as Erwin Schrödinger makes all too clear in this statement of the obvious:

> The observer is never entirely replaced by instruments; for if he were, he could obviously obtain no knowledge whatsoever... The most careful record, when not inspected, tells us nothing.[86]

The Play of Consciousness

But there is another possibility: at the other end of the spectrum from a physicalist interpretation of reality, in which the universe is 'out there', independent of the consciousness of any observer, are the various theoretical constructs that view consciousness itself as the 'ground of being', which by definition incorporates everything that exists, including physical objects. In such theories, which often come under the general heading of *panpsychism*, the entire universe is composed of some sort of 'mind-stuff' or pure consciousness, and it is this that distinguishes them from *dual aspect* theories, which postulate a psychophysically neutral realm underlying both mind and matter.[87]

There is much in common, however, in the arguments in support of these two general approaches, certainly when compared with the physicalist position, and proponents of both would take heart from authoritative pronouncements such as the following from the theoretical physicist Bernard d'Espagnat: 'The doctrine that the world is made up of objects whose existence is independent of human consciousness turns out to be in conflict with quantum mechanics and with facts established by experiment.'[88] D'Espagnat himself conceives of a 'veiled reality' behind the empirical world, one that exists at the interface of what can and cannot be known.[89] This may be in line with the glimpses that are provided of the *unus mundus* in synchronistic events, especially as d'Espagnat's proposal of a veiled reality also constitutes what the interdisciplinary researcher Harald Atmanspacher describes as a 'monist, psychophysically neutral reality', alongside Jung's *unus mundus* and Bohm's implicate order.[90]

As mentioned, these dual aspect models are to be differentiated from those that view mind or consciousness as the substratum from which matter emerges. The astrophysicist Richard Conn Henry, writing in *Nature*, makes clear his position when he states: 'The only reality is mind and observations, but observations are not of things... The 1925 discovery of quantum mechanics solved the problem of the Universe's nature. Bright physicists were again led to believe the unbelievable — this time, that the Universe is mental.'[91] The 'bright physicists' Henry refers to include James Jeans and Arthur Eddington, and it is from the latter that Henry selects the following no doubt pertinent quote: 'It is difficult for the matter-of-fact physicist to accept the view that the substratum of everything is of mental character.'[92] As for Jeans:

> ...the universe begins to look more like a great thought than like a great machine. Mind no longer appears as an accidental intruder into the realm of matter; we are beginning to suspect that we ought rather to hail it as the creator and governor of the realm of matter — not, of course, our individual minds, but the mind in which the atoms out of which our individual minds have grown exist as thoughts.[93]

Whether, according to the latest findings of neuroscience, the last line of this quote has salience or not is beside the point, which is that Jeans was convinced that the universe exists as 'a world of pure thought'.[94] One of the reasons he gives for this is the fact that it is only through pure mathematics, which 'are creations of pure thought, of reason operating solely within her own sphere',[95] that the physical world can be understood. He notes that these mathematical processes include imaginary numbers and other abstract systems that have been worked out almost completely independently of the outer world and yet it is only they that provide an accurate picture of the workings of nature.[96] He also seems to have had a deist or Platonic conception of the power or intelligence behind creation, asserting that 'the Great Architect of the Universe now begins to appear as a pure mathematician.'[97]

A more impersonal and perhaps more radical as well as simple conception of the place of consciousness within the universe is proposed by Menas Kafatos, Rudolph Tanzi and Deepak Chopra. They posit consciousness as a 'field phenomenon, analogous to but preceding the quantum field'.[98] If there is an ultimate source or origin of this universe, they argue, then that source must be *uncreated*, which means that it is self-sufficient and self-regulating, and also capable of developing complex systems at every level, both micro and macro:

> Nothing can exist outside its influence. Ultimately, the uncreated source must turn into the physical universe, not simply oversee it as God or the gods do in conventional religion. We feel that only consciousness fits the bill, for as a prima facie truth, no experience takes place outside consciousness, which means that if there is a reality existing beyond our awareness (counting mathematics and the laws of physics as one part of our conscious experience), we will never be able to know it.[99]

Kafatos, Tanzi and Chopra regard space and time as conceptual constructions arising, like mathematics, from primordial consciousness, and suggest that in the competition with physicalism and its various explanations, the playing field has now been levelled: for if ideas are not in themselves substantial, neither are elementary particles.[100] In support of this observation they quote Heisenberg from his 1932 Nobel Prize speech in which he stated that atoms have 'no immediate and direct physical properties at all'.[101] And what applies to elementary particles must therefore apply all the way up the size chain, a point which they elaborate on with a certain irony: 'The universe was doing a vanishing act in Heisenberg's day, and it certainly hasn't become more solid since.'[102]

A key mystery, therefore, is what occurs at the interface of micro and macro, and how the transformation from the one to the other takes place, for it is at this point, Kafatos, Tanzi and Chopra conjecture, that 'consciousness acquires the nature of a substance'.[103] And it could well be that at this interface, this 'mysterious edge' as they call it, that the idea of a psychophysical matrix is found to be a useful construct within a consciousness model, for it is here that the bifurcation between the apparently substantial and the apparently insubstantial occurs, and it would therefore be reasonable to assume that these two apparent realities arise from an ontologically prior unity. Since it is at this juncture that the ephemeral becomes solid, it is logical to suggest that there is a neutral place where the two realms remain undivided.

This is consistently alluded to in the various dual aspect theories, not least being Jung's postulation of an underlying *unus mundus*, glimpses of which may well be available, albeit sporadically and unpredictably, through the meaningful coincidences that can so unexpectedly touch our hearts and our lives. When this occurs, subject and object become temporarily united in a timeless epiphany which, although it may only last for a moment, provides an escape from what Marie-Louise von Franz describes as 'the stifling clutches of a one-sided view of life'.[104] This one-sided view is a consequence of the human condition, cut off as we are in our isolated subjectivity from the world that we are so patently a part. Our isolated subjectivity may in fact be but a macroworld illusion, one that is punctured and penetrated in small ways by such anomalies as synchronistic occurrences and the double-slit experiment, though they are as remote from each other as chalk and cheese. What they do have in common, however, is that both undermine the cohesion of the subject–object dichotomy, and also perhaps the mind–matter dichotomy as well. And as Wolfgang Pauli wrote in his essay on Kepler, first published in 1952 alongside Jung's main treatise on synchronicity:

> It would be most satisfactory of all if psyche and physis could be seen as complementary aspects of the same reality.[105]

Endnotes

1. Vaughan, *Incredible Coincidence*, 175.
2. Ibid., 175–176.
3. Weaver, *Lady Luck*, 222.
4. Hardy, Harvie and Koestler, *The Challenge of Chance*, 222.
5. Ibid.
6. Koestler, *The Roots of Coincidence*, 99.
7. Meier, *Atom and Archetype*.
8. Gieser, *The Innermost Kernel*, 283.
9. Meier, *Atom and Archetype*, 56; ref. Jung, *Synchronicity*, 140–141.
10. Meier, *Atom and Archetype*, 69.
11. Jung, *Synchronicity*, 140.
12. Meier, *Atom and Archetype*, 55–56.
13. Mansfield, *Synchronicity, Science and Soul-Making*, 9.
14. Jung, *Synchronicity*, 141.
15. Ibid.
16. Carter, C., *Parapsychology and the Skeptics*.
17. Sheldrake, *The Science Delusion*, 253–257.
18. Goswami, 'Man On The Moon — A Colossal Hoax that Cost Billions of Dollars'.
19. Sheldrake, *The Science Delusion*, 232.
20. Koestler, *The Roots of Coincidence*, 31–35.
21. Source for Fig. 5: http://abyss.uoregon.edu/~js/21st_century_science/lectures/lec13.html
22. Peat, *Einstein's Moon*, 6.
23. Davies and Brown, *The Ghost in the Atom*, 2–3.
24. Hawking and Mlodinow, *The Grand Design*, 70.

25 Peat, *Einstein's Moon*, 10.
26 Davies and Brown, *The Ghost in the Atom*, 9.
27 Rhodes, 'Wheeler's Classic Delayed Choice Experiment'.
28 Wolf, 'The Quantum Universe', 72.
29 Hawking and Mlodinow, *The Grand Design*, 80–81.
30 Johnston, '*Physics World* Reveals its Top 10 Breakthroughs for 2011'.
31 Hawking and Mlodinow, *The Grand Design*, 6; Fritzsch, *You are Wrong Mr Einstein!*, 40.
32 Moskowitz, 'Largest Molecules Yet Behave Like Waves in Quantum Double-Slit Experiment'.
33 Eibenberger et al., 'Matter-Wave Interference with Particles Selected from a Molecular Library with Masses Exceeding 10000 amu'.
34 Rosenblum, 'Quantum Physics Encounters Consciousness'.
35 Rosenblum and Kuttner, *Quantum Enigma*, 94–95.
36 Source for Fig. 6: Kuttner and Rosenblum, 'The Conscious Observer in the Quantum Experiment', used by kind permission of the authors.
37 Rosenblum and Kuttner, *Quantum Enigma*, 92–94.
38 Ibid., 94.
39 Ibid., 96.
40 Davies, *The Goldilocks Enigma*, 248.
41 Davies and Brown, *The Ghost in the Atom*, 67.
42 Source for Fig. 7: http://discovermagazine.com/2002/jun/featuniverse/universe_2.jpg
43 Folger, 'Does the Universe Exist if We're Not Looking?'
44 Wolf, *Time Loops and Space Twists*, 97–98.
45 Folger, 'Does the Universe Exist if We're Not Looking?'
46 Wolf, *Time Loops and Space Twists*, 98–99.
47 Davies and Brown, *The Ghost in the Atom*, 68.
48 Davies, *The Goldilocks Enigma*, 249.
49 Rosenblum and Kuttner, *Quantum Enigma*, 207–220.
50 Ibid., 247.
51 Jung, *Mysterium Conjunctionis*, 538.
52 Ricard and Thuan, *The Quantum and the Lotus*, 68.
53 Brumfiel, 'Physicists Spooked by Faster-than-Light Information Transfer'.
54 Mansfield, *Synchronicity, Science and Soul-Making*, 122.
55 Rosenblum and Kuttner, *Quantum Enigma*, 8.
56 Radin, *Entangled Minds*, 235.
57 Ibid.
58 Matthews, 'Opposites Detract'.
59 Hollick, *The Science of Oneness*, 287.
60 Sheldrake, foreword to Carter, C., *Parapsychology and the Skeptics*, i.
61 Smith, *Why Religion Matters*, 59–78.
62 Ibid., 59.
63 Ibid., 59–60.
64 Ibid., 193.
65 Wilber, *Quantum Questions*.
66 Tart, *The End of Materialism*, 22–32.
67 Ibid., 28.
68 Ibid., 29–30.

69. The Dalai Lama, 'Mind and Life XIV – Day 1, pm'.
70. Ibid.
71. Jordens, 'Prakriti and the Collective Unconscious', 146.
72. Jung, *Mysterium Conjunctionis*, 538.
73. Jung, *Synchronicity*, 139–140.
74. Ibid., 139.
75. Main, *The Rupture of Time*, 55.
76. Ibid., 54.
77. Plimmer and King, *Beyond Coincidence*, 225.
78. von Franz, *Psyche and Matter*, 254.
79. Bohm, *Wholeness and the Implicate Order*, 196–197.
80. Talbot, *The Holographic Universe*, 122, 212.
81. Wilson, *Coincidance*, 148.
82. Ibid., 153–154.
83. The Dalai Lama, 'Mind and Life XIV – Day 1 pm'.
84. Rosenblum and Kuttner, *Quantum Enigma*, 129.
85. Mansfield, *Synchronicity, Science and Soul-Making*, 97.
86. Ibid., 106.
87. Atmanspacher, 'Quantum Approaches to Consciousness'.
88. d'Espagnat, 'The Quantum Theory and Reality', 158.
89. d'Espagnat, *Reality and the Physicist*, 171.
90. Atmanspacher, 'Editorial', 3.
91. Henry, 'The Mental Universe', 29.
92. Ibid.
93. Jeans, 'A Universe of Pure Thought', 151.
94. Ibid., 149.
95. Jeans, 'In the Mind of Some Eternal Spirit', 137.
96. Ibid., 135–142.
97. Ibid., 147.
98. Kafatos, Tanzi and Chopra, 'How Consciousness Becomes the Physical Universe', 1125.
99. Ibid.
100. Ibid., 1126.
101. Ibid., 1121.
102. Ibid.
103. Ibid., 1126.
104. von Franz, *Number and Time*, 261.
105. Pauli, *Writings on Physics and Philosophy*, 260.

Chapter Five

Coincidence Explanations

The two previous chapters have had much more to do with the extraordinary coincidences to be found within cosmology and quantum physics than with possible explanations for their human-scale counterparts. Part of the purpose for this apparent diversion has been to demonstrate that the parameters of our existence on our isolated, life-giving planet are reliant on coincidences *far* more remarkable than can be found in any publication concerned with 'amazing' coincidences. Nevertheless, there is a fair amount of valuable material in such publications, a good example being Martin Plimmer and Brain King's *Beyond Coincidence*, which starts with a perceptive insight by Agatha Christie: '"Any coincidence," said Miss Marple to herself, "is always worth noting. You can throw it away later if it is only a coincidence".'[1]

When it comes to the stunning array of cosmic coincidences that have set the stage for life on Earth, their very intricacy and profusion, as outlined in Chapter Three, is for many simply too overwhelming to doubt the existence of a divine intelligence. On the other hand, for others, the available data do not warrant such a conclusion and they point instead to a vast but ultimately *physical* multiverse, with no need to invoke an intelligent Creator. But on whatever side of this long-running argument one falls, and that surely is influenced by personal preference and deeply held beliefs as much as any supporting evidence that can be marshalled, it cannot be denied that we are living in a universe that displays at its core a *profound* mystery, whatever the nature of that mystery might be. Plimmer and King, after presenting some two hundred and fifty coincidence stories in their book, many of them genuinely astounding, end with a short chapter entitled 'The Ultimate Coincidence', the opening paragraph of which reads as follows:

> Perhaps we should call it the First Coincidence. Or the Last Coincidence. Either would suit, but 'Ultimate' most fits its superlative significance. It's the most important coincidence in our life, in everybody's life, in the life of our planet, our Solar System and our Universe. To begin with, it brought us all together. It's the reason we are. And if ever its felicitous consonance should alter, we won't be around to speculate whether it

was a happy accident or part of a grand unified design. Nothing will be around.²

One area of speculation that seems to emerge naturally from the study of coincidences is whether they are in any way able to shed light on the 'Ultimate Coincidence'. Jung felt that they were, and hence the importance he gave to the articulation of his synchronicity hypothesis. But coincidences can be awkward and are not always easy to categorise: one person's profoundly meaningful synchronistic experience may be another's probability calculation, or a third's causal analysis. Yet fascination remains, perhaps because we are somehow *hardwired* in our sensitivity to coincidence. According to the cognitive scientist Joshua Tenenbaum, much of the way we learn is influenced by our perception of coincidences: 'Coincidences drive so many of the inferences our minds make. Our neural circuitry is set up to notice these anomalies and use them to drive new learning.'³

If a child learns the word 'dog', not just as a vocalisation but with appropriate attribution to dogs of all shapes and sizes, the child will need to be able to discern accurately those features, like barking and panting, which distinguish dogs from other furry animals that can run. Dachshunds, Labradors and Great Danes are very different from one another, but they all bark and pant and wag their tails, unlike cats, rabbits or Shetland ponies. It is these features, which are perceived as coincidences by the mind of the child, that allow for the word 'dog' to take its appropriate place in the child's vocabulary.⁴ This hardwiring is also evident in the place of coincidences in humour, especially puns and other forms of wordplay. For example, there is the famous line by the cricket commentator John Arlott, made during a match between Hampshire and Somerset. The bowler was Clive Rice, the batsman Viv Richards, and in the field was an Irishman, Andy Murtagh. Rice bowled to Richards who hit the ball to Murtagh, and Arlott dryly remarked: 'Rice bowls; Paddy fields.'⁵

Perhaps the search for meaning in coincidences is very much a natural aspect of our psychological makeup. It is not surprising, therefore, that in *all* traditional cultures some form of divination was regularly and widely practised. A pertinent example is the Roman Empire, a technologically and organisationally very advanced society but one that was deeply reliant on augury and other forms of divination for planning and decision making. And even though we are living in a high-tech society which has by and large dispensed with divination for decision making, life continues to present itself as *patterns* which we need to be able to interpret for our survival and personal advantage.⁶ This is inevitably the case, whether for a hunter in the Amazon rainforest trying to determine the significance of a rustling in the bushes fifty metres away, or a day trader using all the tools and information at his or her fingertips to make a quick decision about whether to buy or sell a particular stock. Then, there are complex social situations where nuances and subtle indications seem to operate at the edge of our conscious awareness. In a job interview, for example, the applicant needs very swiftly to be able to glean the character and unspoken expectations of the interview panel; while the panel will obviously look for much more than qualifications in order to make an appropriate selection. And it is very easy to misinterpret subtle signals.

Many a job applicant has emerged optimistic after what appears by all indications to have been a positive and favourable interview, only to learn later that they have been passed over. The same goes for employers: not uncommonly a particular applicant performs extremely well at an interview and so is hired, but later turns out to be a serious liability for the organisation. So, similarly, when faced with a genuinely arresting coincidence, and given that misinterpretation of *non-coincidental* everyday situations is so easy, it requires some finesse to arrive at a measured conclusion that neither too quickly embraces the coincidence as meaningful nor too quickly explains it away with probability calculations or common cause analysis. What sense, therefore, should one make of the following coincidence anecdote, as presented here by Plimmer and King?

> In June 2001, ten-year-old Laura Buxton of Burton in Staffordshire was at a party where she wrote her name and address on a luggage label, attached it to a helium balloon and released it into a clear blue sky.
> The balloon floated 140 miles until finally coming to rest in the garden of another Laura Buxton, aged ten, in Pewsey, Wiltshire.
> Laura in Wiltshire immediately got in touch with Laura in Staffordshire and the girls have since become friends. They've discovered that not only do they share the same name and are the same age, they are both fair-haired, and each owns a black labrador, a guinea-pig and a rabbit.[7] (For a fuller account see 'Whether Balloon', snopes.com)

Categorising Coincidences

In Chapter Two, four overarching explanatory categories for coincidences were suggested, and one of the main features of this categorisation is that a particular coincidence can have a number of possible explanations, as was explored with Frederick Forsyth's close encounter with a Nigerian sniper. In addition, the categories are not mutually exclusive and a particular coincidence might be best explained through a combination of categories. For example, the remarkable coincidences associated with the reunited identical twins described in Chapter Two might arguably be best understood through a combination of *all* the categories listed below:

Coincidence Categories

— Random chance explanations
— Conventional causal explanations
— Paranormal causal explanations
— Synchronicity explanations

In Chapter Three, the nomenclature was refined slightly to include the exceptional status of the cosmic coincidences, and so for the causal categories 'conventional' was changed to 'natural', and 'paranormal' to 'supernatural'. It would obviously be inappropriate to describe the creation of the universe by God as 'paranormal', as it would be to characterise the constants of nature underpinning the laws of physics as 'conventional'. The same problems do not arise with 'natural' and 'supernatural', which are broad enough terms to cover the main distinction that is required here: that between causal explanations which are readily accepted by science, and those which are not. And as 'supernatural' effectively includes 'paranormal', and 'conventional' can be subsumed under 'natural' without too much distortion of meaning, there is really no need to complicate the category headings by using an awkward expression such as 'natural and conventional causal explanations'.

Coincidence Categories

— Random chance explanations
— Natural causal explanations
— Supernatural causal explanations
— Synchronicity explanations

So, with reference to these broad categories, how might the coincidence of the two Laura Buxtons and the helium balloon be analysed? At one level, the entire episode can readily be attributed to chance and the laws of probability. After all, the balloon had to land somewhere, neither Laura nor Buxton is an unusual name, and there would no doubt have been thousands of such balloons released before and since without this sort of striking coincidence. As with the case, mentioned in the previous chapter, of the two Kevin O'Briens whose golf balls collided, we have an entirely unexpected encounter under exceptional circumstances between two people with the same name. In addition, there are some extra correspondences in the report: the two Lauras are the same age, are both fair-haired and each owns a black Labrador, a guinea-pig and a rabbit. These added elements can, of course, also be readily explained by the laws of probability, as essentially can *any* unlikely coincidence.

Doing so, however, has the effect, intended or otherwise, of sidelining the *qualitative* aspects of the coincidence and its impact on those involved, and thus its manifestation *as a totality* is lost. This is a point highlighted by Plimmer and King who on their acknowledgements page give 'thanks to our favourites—the two Laura Buxtons, whose balloon pops in the face of those who deny that coincidence, whatever its meaning, or lack of meaning, is charming, spooky, mischievous and endlessly entertaining'.[8] One thing that can be said for sure about this coincidence is that it does *not* appear to have been causally engineered, unless the invisible hand of God or some other beneficent power deliberately blew the balloon to its destination. Indeed, that might have been how it felt to the little girls, and no statistical explanation is likely to have been able to talk them out of the sense that each was somehow 'meant' to find the other Laura Buxton.

In regard to whether synchronicity was involved, once again we cannot be sure, as with Forsyth's narrow escape and the O'Briens' colliding golf balls. So let us assume for the sake of argument that neither of the Lauras, nor their family members, nor anyone else involved had a sense of the *meaning-equivalence* that is central to a synchronistic event: for everyone it was just a wonderful coincidence. Does that mean that chance is the only realistic explanation? On face value, that is very much how it might look; yet there is another possibility in the absence of a standard synchronicity explanation, and that is Kammerer's idea of *seriality*, which was briefly introduced in Chapter One.

The Coming Together of Affinities

The essence of this hypothesis, according to Koestler, is that 'coexistent with causality there is an a-causal principle active in the universe, which tends towards unity'.[9] This principle operates outside the laws of physics but 'intrudes into the causal order of things—both in dramatic and trivial ways'.[10] Koestler compares it with gravity, though 'unlike gravity which acts on all mass indiscriminately, this force acts selectively on *form* and *function* to bring similar configurations together in space and time; it correlates by *affinity*'.[11] The seriality explanation, then, is that for the coming together of the Laura Buxtons or the Kevin O'Briens, as well as the subject matter of so many of the coincidence stories in the various compilations, there is *an attractive force at play* which expresses itself through the coming together of affinities. Unlike Jung, Kammerer rejected ESP,[12] and so did not turn to the paranormal for support for his hypothesis. In his view, and in his own words, seriality can be conceived of as 'a world mosaic or cosmic kaleidoscope, which, in spite of constant shufflings and rearrangements, also takes care of bringing like and like together'.[13]

Koestler was particularly interested in Kammerer and wrote about him extensively in *The Case of the Midwife Toad*. He also believed that Jung borrowed liberally from his *Das Gesetz der Serie* in the development of his concept of synchronicity.[14] Even if that is so, there is between the two conceptualisations a crucial difference which revolves around the question of *acausality*. It is interesting to note that Koestler, presumably in line with Kammerer's thesis, describes seriality as a 'force' which both 'intrudes' and 'acts selectively'. It is akin to gravity, and if that is the case, it may be stretching the definition of acausality to describe it as such, and perhaps seriality would be best categorised as a 'supernatural causal explanation', though how it might actually function in practice is difficult to determine.

On the other hand, synchronistic occurrences do not appear to be active in the same sense; rather than having a 'tendency towards unity', they are, in Jung's conceptualisation, a manifestation *in* time of 'the transcendental *unus mundus*, the potential world outside of time',[15] which von Franz further describes as the 'cosmic background which is neither matter nor psyche... [where] all opposites are still unified'.[16] By definition, therefore, the *unus mundus* does *not* act selectively or intrude, rather it is *revealed* under the specific conditions of a synchronistic event. That said, there does seem to be more than a passing resemblance between Kammerer's seriality and Jung's principle of synchronicity, and this is because clearly they are both developments of the medieval notion of *correspondentia* which, as Jung points out, 'was propounded by the natural philosophers of the Middle Ages, and particularly the classical idea of the *sympathy of all things*'.[17] He goes on to quote Hippocrates:

> There is one common flow, one common breathing, all things are in sympathy. The whole organism and each one of its parts are working in conjunction for the same purpose... the great principle extends to the extremest part, and from the extremest part it returns to the great principle, to the one nature, being and not-being.[18]

This is very much in accord with certain descriptions of the *tao*, and in Jung's essay it follows directly on from his discussion of the *tao* as a precursor to the synchronicity principle.[19] As discussed in some detail in Chapter One, Jung did not restrict the notion of synchronicity to meaningful coincidences. He conceived of it, in addition, as an underlying principle behind *all* manifestations of acausality, into which category he specifically includes psychic phenomena and the anomalies of microphysics.[20] He also raised the interesting possibility that synchronicity, in its narrower, coincidental sense, 'might also occur without the participation of the human psyche' and, if this is the case, 'we should have to speak not of *meaning* but of equivalence or conformity'.[21] While this only appears as a speculative footnote in his essay, it in effect opens the door to provide a synchronistic explanation, with or without a direct experience of meaning-equivalence, for the coincidence of the two Laura Buxtons and the helium balloon, as well as the black Labradors, the guinea-pigs and the rabbits.

These 'affinities' are obviously manifestations of equivalence *without* its meaning aspect and as such may simply be a reworking of the ancient idea of the sympathy of all things. Jung thought there was more to it, though, and conjectured that through 'archetypal processes' synchronicity has had a part to play, alongside chance, in biological evolution,[22] a consideration that also exercised great fascination for Pauli during his later years.[23] This is a pertinent topic, and worthy of further investigation, especially in view of Jung's proposition of a psychophysically neutral *unus mundus* underlying both the phenomenal world and that of our subjective awareness. For if there actually *is* a latent realm where mind and matter are still undifferentiated, it is not unreasonable to take seriously the consideration that perhaps the psychic aspect of this realm has in some way had an influence on the evolutionary process alongside its physical counterpart.

Nevertheless, a categorisation difficulty arises with the suggestion that synchronistic events may not require the participation of observers, for although not explicitly stated, and perhaps contrary to some of Jung's speculations, the 'synchronicity explanation' category proposed in these pages requires that there be an *observer* who directly experiences the equivalence of meaning between the subjective and objective aspects of the coincidence. By deliberately leaving out this option in categorising the coincidence of the two Lauras and the helium balloon, we appear to be left with either a chance or a supernatural cause explanation. And the recurring problem with the latter, except where there is a strong case for ESP or psychokinesis, is the difficulty of substantiation, as with Kammerer's seriality or explanations invoking the hand of God. That said, if the world does indeed turn out to be fundamentally psychophysical, as entertained in the previous chapter, it may be that the coming together of affinities is not as far-fetched an idea as it undoubtedly is from a physicalist perspective. Certainly that would have been Jung's position and very likely that of Kammerer as well.

In contrast with the array of coincidences surrounding, for example, the Jim Twins,[24] the incident involving the Laura Buxtons is comparatively straightforward and can easily be ascribed solely to chance. However, to do so might be somewhat unsatisfactory, for labelling it as 'just a coincidence' does not, as already mentioned, take into account the full impact and ramifications of the event on those involved. Perhaps the coincidence, with all its inherent charm, could be categorised as *serendipitous*, a whimsical and fortuitous happenstance, operating in something of a grey area between chance and synchronicity, where there is a hint of meaning-equivalence but possibly not quite enough for a definitive categorisation of synchronicity. As the humourous poet Ogden Nash explains it:

> If your coat catches on a branch just as you are about
> to slip over a precipice precipitous,
> That's serendipitous.[25]

But if there is such a thing as serendipity, there is also surely its antithesis, as illustrated by the following rather macabre anecdote. Two sisters driving Jeeps in opposite directions, each on the way to visit the other, were involved in a head-on collision when the vehicle being driven by one of the sisters crossed the central partition and crashed into the vehicle being driven by the other, sadly killing both.[26] This is a very tragic coincidence—if that is what it was, for there is also a possible causal explanation. It is conceivable, though unlikely, that the driver who veered onto the opposite side of the highway had suddenly noticed her sister's Jeep, and with the unexpected shock of that recognition lost control for a split-second and for some unaccountable reason reacted by heading straight for her sister. As with the previous example, the actual analysis of the coincidence appears to raise more questions than it provides answers. While the explanatory categories seem on the surface to be straightforward and comprehensive, the actual designation of a particular coincidence into one or another category can be quite tricky, particularly given the perennial problem of a lack of sufficient detail in the reporting.

A good example of the difficulty of ascertaining facts is provided by Koestler in the following account. In 1971, a young architect, after suffering a nervous breakdown, threw himself in front of a train on the London Underground. Although he was severely injured, he was not killed and eventually recovered. This was not because the driver saw him in time but because a passenger had pulled the emergency brake handle a few moments earlier. There is *no way* the passenger could have known that someone had thrown themselves on the line, and when further investigations were made it was understood that London

Transport had considered suing the passenger for pulling the handle for no good reason. Koestler's informant was a relative of the victim who had read *The Roots of Coincidence* and so wrote to him about the intriguing circumstances of the case:

> This passenger's pulling the handle must have saved Harold's life. They had to jack up the train to get him out, therefore he must have been well under it. On the other hand a wheel cannot have passed over him or he would have been killed. Pulling the 'Emergency' handle applies the brakes automatically. The difference between life and death must have been measured in nanoseconds.
>
> If one had precise figures for the incidence of suicides by this method at this station, the incidence of 'false alarm' calls by passengers etc., etc., a calculation of statistical probability could be made, but one supposes the chances to be infinitesimally small.[27]

Koestler attempted to find out more about this case but London Transport would not reveal the passenger's name, and though they did provide him with the driver's, further enquiries petered out. He would have very much liked to have had the opportunity to interview the passenger and to ask him *why* he had pulled the emergency handle. Did he have some sort of premonition? Was he suddenly impelled to pull the handle? Or was it just a whim? According to Koestler, 'This is obviously a case which could be interpreted either in terms of telepathy combined with premonition, or as a "coincidental event". As already said [in an earlier passage], the two categories overlap.'[28] As with so many coincidence accounts there is more than one possible explanation, though that is by no means a bad thing as it keeps open the discussion and helps prevent the hegemonic predominance of a particular view. There are those who distrust anomalous explanations, and those who jump at them as evidence that there is more to life than the inexorable laws of probability and physical causation. If coincidences can be examined *without* the tinted glasses of metaphysical or ideological bias, as has so often been the case, then it might well turn out that this rather difficult field of study has much to say about the world we inhabit.

Underlying Coincidences

It is one thing to attempt to categorise coincidences of the sort described in the above paragraphs but quite another to do so when it comes to those that underpin our very existence. Chapters Three and Four dealt, respectively, with the vast and intricate cohesion of our universe, and with the perplexing anomalies that exist at the quantum level. In Chapter Three, three areas of cosmic coincidence were explored: firstly, those to do with the fundamental parameters and initial conditions at the Big Bang; secondly, the extraordinary confluence of Goldilocks conditions that have made possible the existence and fecundity of life on Earth; and thirdly, the *temporal* cosmic coincidences, including the fact that we now have an accurate conception of the physical universe, and that this *very* recent discovery coincides with the *very* real peril that now exists for the future of both humanity and biodiversity on this planet.

Indeed, if there was ever justification for the use of Jung's favoured expression 'unthinkable', then it is surely warranted when looking at the collective improbability of all these intricately entwined coincidences. And even though they are the least unlikely in terms of probability calculations, the temporal coincidences are arguably the most intriguing, and this is perhaps because they are directly associated with meaning. The Goldilocks conditions can potentially be explained by the play of chance in a vast multiverse, and obviously so can the temporal coincidences, but the latter have the flavour of a large-scale synchronicity which seems to be urging humanity in a particular direction, a nudge and a wake-up call: time for us to forget our differences and find a way to live together peacefully and sustainably on this magnificent planet, all alone as we are in a corner of the cosmos, for us the very heart of the boundless universe.

Then there is the argument over why the measurements underlying the structure of our universe appear so finely tuned; why, for instance, the fact that *no* stars could have formed if the ratio of the strong nuclear force to the electromagnetic force had been different by just *one* part in 10^{16}. This is but one example of the highly intricate fine-tuning that is found with such abundance in the fundamental laws of nature.[29] Taken together, the collective improbability of these measurements *exceeds* the probability resources of the 10^{500} universes that might exist within a possible multiverse,[30] with our universe being one of the supremely lucky ones, featuring as it does parameters that are 'just right' for life. And this is *without* taking into consideration the odds against the initial conditions at the Big Bang having a low entropy state consistent with the second law of thermodynamics, calculated at one in $10\exp(10^{124})$ by Roger Penrose, a probability calculation so mindboggling and outrageously tiny that, as Penrose has said, it makes all other fine-tuning considerations virtually irrelevant.[31] Therefore, given these absurdly low probability calculations, do we opt for a *natural* or a *supernatural* ultimate explanation of the cosmic coincidences, or do we compromise and opt for something in between? Again, this very much depends on the beliefs and predispositions of those entering into the fray, for as yet there is no definitive evidence that can tip the scales one way or the other.

As far as the quantum coincidences are concerned, it does seem that entanglement at least can be fairly easily classified. Although the movements of separated entangled particles correspond precisely with one another at speeds so much faster than light that our usual notions of time and space must be set aside, it is hard to conceive of any explanation for this phenomenon outside one involving natural causality. Nevertheless, it remains unclear what constitutes the causal mechanism behind the instantaneous correlation of the particles, irrespective of their location. It could be that the explanation is relatively straightforward in itself, and that the difficulty lies with our perceptual capacities and their operation within the space-time matrix.

The double-slit experiment, on the other hand, presents rather more of a conundrum because, as discussed in the previous chapter, the wave function of a particle only 'collapses', in other words, solidifies into an object, when an attempt is made to observe or measure it. This is the 'measurement problem' of quantum physics, and it raises the question as to whether, ultimately, the material world has any concrete form without the presence of observers. If not, it could well point to the possibility of a *unus mundus* conception of reality, in which mind and matter are complementary aspects of an underlying psychophysically neutral realm. As to how the measurement problem might contribute to such a view, we can consider the 'cosmic' version of John Wheeler's delayed-choice experiment, in which light from a distant quasar is deflected by the gravitational pull of one or two massive galaxies so that it travels to Earth by two routes (see Fig. 7). However, only when it is *observed* by an astronomer on Earth does a photon from that light become fixed to *one* particular route and *not* the other. Paul Davies explains the implications:

> The novel feature Wheeler introduced via his delayed-choice experiment was the possibility of observers today, and in the future, shaping the nature of physical reality *in the past*, including the far past where no observers existed. That is indeed a radical idea, for it gives life and mind a type of creative role in physics, making them an indispensable part of the entire cosmological story... Thus the universe explains observers and observers explain the universe. Wheeler thereby rejected the notion of the universe as a machine subject to fixed a priori laws and replaced it with a self-synthesising world he called the 'participatory universe'.[32]

A participatory universe gives us much more of a *unus mundus* conception of reality, in which both mind and matter become integral features of a psychophysical totality. If this is in fact how the world as we know it is constituted, then it may be that Jung's claim that synchronistic events provide direct evidence of a *unus mundus*[33] is worth serious consideration. For if genuine synchronicities really do constitute what Jung called a 'rupture of time' that 'closely resembles numinous experiences in which space, time and causality are abolished',[34] then the underlying reality they point to is surely an extraordinary one, as von Franz spells out in no uncertain term:

> The most essential and certainly the most impressive thing about synchronistic occurrences, the thing which really constitutes their numinosity, is the fact that in them the duality of soul and matter seems to be eliminated. They are therefore an *empirical* indication of an ultimate unity of all existence, which Jung, using the terminology of medieval natural philosophy, called the *unus mundus*.[35]

To that end, the remainder of this chapter will focus on clarifying what exactly is meant by synchronicity, not as the wider, acausal connecting principle envisaged by Jung in his treatise, but rather the *narrower* conception concerned with meaningful coincidences and what they represent. Because the synchronicity category is so crucial to an overall conception of how coincidence explanations might be organised, and because the term has been bandied about so freely in popular culture, to the extent that it has become synonymous with every sort of amazing or not-so-amazing coincidence, it is important to clarify to as great an extent as possible what actually it *is* that constitutes a synchronistic event. These are, of course, many and varied, and an excellent example of a synchronistic occurrence that has all the elements Jung was referring to when he spoke of the 'rupture of time' is provided by Roderick Main in his book *Revelations of Chance*.

On August 23, 1973, whilst on holiday with his wife in Cambridge, Stephen Jenkins, a schoolteacher from the south of England interested in unusual phenomena, saw from his hotel room something that left him both shaken and stirred. At the time, Jenkins was heavily immersed in a comparative study of Christian and Buddhist apocalyptic literature, and when he came out onto the balcony of his hotel room that evening, according to his records at precisely 7.15pm, he had just completed an exhaustive study of Zechariah, noting in particular that the colours of the horses in Zechariah's vision—red, black, white and dappled—reappear with the Four Horsemen of the Apocalypse.[36] And there before him, in 'the long field below the hotel were quietly grazing four horses: red, black, dapple, and white'.[37] This coincidence so astonished Jenkins that the next day he photographed the horses 'to prove to myself more than anyone else that they were really there. After all, there could have been five, or two black ones or a grey, or a piebald or a chestnut'.[38]

The coincidence of the horses and their colours, however, was not to end there. Eleven months later, Jenkins was with some of his school pupils on an outing to Oakhampton Common, near Yes Tor in Devon.

They were taking photos of a particular rock formation, and while they were engaged in this Jenkins looked towards Yes Tor and saw a small herd of Dartmoor ponies coming over its eastern shoulder: 'Ahead of them by a clear 100 yards was a group of four: red, black, dapple, and white. I could hardly believe my eyes and took care to photograph them too.'[39]

Unpacking Synchronicity

What makes this case stand out, and perhaps why Main uses it as an introduction to the idea of synchronicity in his book, is not only because it has all the hallmarks of a genuinely acausal meaningful coincidence, even without the second encounter, but also because of the highly unusual and idiosyncratic nature of the circumstances. Indeed, these almost appear to have been tailor-made for Jenkins. No doubt many guests at the hotel had looked out from their balconies and noticed the horses, and some of them may have even remarked on the variety of their colours. It is, however, unlikely that any would have made the association with Zechariah's vision, and even if a biblical scholar were amongst their number and did make the connection, the chances of it having the sort of impact that it had for Jenkins would be slight, though obviously not impossible. As for the sighting of the Dartmoor ponies, that would for Jenkins have been a confirmation for whatever conclusion he had come to regarding the significance of the first encounter.

Of course, a sceptic might argue that after his initial experience, Jenkins would quite likely have glanced at other horse-inhabited fields he happened to pass to see if the same configuration were present, and that sooner or later he would be bound to encounter a relatively isolated quartet of red, black, dapple and white horses. Be that as it may, the overall experience was obviously very moving for Jenkins and if we are to accept his account as authentic, it would certainly satisfy Jung's criteria for a synchronistic occurrence or meaningful coincidence in which there is no possible causal connection between the outer or physical circumstances and the inner or psychological state of the individual involved. Their only connection lies in the *equivalence of meaning* corresponding to both situations, and how that meaning is received by the person in question, for as von Franz puts it: 'Inner and outer events that are parallel can be perceived only if they have some relation to the ego-consciousness of an observer.'[40]

Nevertheless, say that our sceptic decides to persist, and at the same time has some passing familiarity with the Bible. She or he might have noted that only *three* of the horses mentioned in Revelations concur with Zechariah: the fourth horseman rides a *pale* rather than a dappled horse (in most translations; see BibleGateway.com for comparisons). Therefore, had the four horses in the field below the hotel contained, for instance, a cream-coloured horse instead of the dapple, it is not unreasonable to suggest that Jenkins would have been equally moved by the coincidence. His reaction, however, might well have taken a more ominous turn as there is a very different flavour in Zechariah's vision in which four teams of horses — red, black, white and dapple — pull four chariots in different directions, each chariot representing the spirit of heaven. In contrast, the Four Horsemen of the Apocalypse represent cataclysm and death. And one might wonder how Jenkins, given his predilection for apocalyptic scenarios, might have reacted had the fourth horse in Cambridge been a dapple and the fourth Dartmoor pony a cream. But all this is speculative: it does not describe what happened; only what might have happened, and any such speculation takes our attention from the actuality as well as impact of specific instances of synchronicity.

Another interesting anecdote comes from Kirby Surprise, the aptly named author of *Synchronicity: The Art of Coincidence, Choice, and Unlocking Your Mind*, and it is with this story that he begins his book. Surprise relates that he was sitting in his car waiting to pick up a friend and listening to the radio to pass the time. During a commercial break, there was an ad for the film *Carrie*, which Surprise had seen. The film is about a girl with the ability to move objects with her mind, and during its climax Carrie uses her power to crush her family home. Across the street from where Surprise was parked was an old cottage; spurred by the ad and recalling an article he had read in the *National Enquirer* about a house being turned over on its side by a psychic force, Surprise wondered how it would feel to be able to move a house with his mind. He was not, however, prepared for what then took place. As he stared at the cottage, it shuddered violently and began to move, and then rolled over onto its side. Naturally enough, this panicked Surprise and he started to wonder whether he had really caused this totally unexpected circumstance. Unfortunately, there is no corroboration for any of this, or for what occurred next, and we are obliged to take Surprise's word for it:

> 'OK,' I said to myself. 'If I just did that, then I want to see the house crushed like in the movie.'
>
> As I stared, awestruck, the house again began to shudder. The roof started to collapse inward as if the centre of the house were slowly imploding. Beams burst through walls and windows shattered as the house began to tear itself apart. A moment later, I saw the flash of yellow paint above the house and the largest bulldozer I had ever seen climbed lazily over the centre of the house, crushing the structure into

rubble in a few moments. It then started to load the debris into waiting dump trucks. The house had obscured the demolition equipment from sight. With the radio on and the windows up, I couldn't hear the tractor engine. My fantasy had come to pass, my wish fulfilled through a series of synchronistic events.[41]

In order to gain a clearer appreciation of the varied nature of meaningful coincidences, it might be instructive to contrast the two accounts presented above. As mentioned in the previous chapter, there appear from the Jungian perspective to be three key elements that are present in what might be described as classic or 'full-blown' instances of synchronicity. These are: an equivalence of meaning between the psychological processes of the person involved and the external event,[42] an accompanying flash of immediate insight or 'absolute knowledge',[43] and also a felt sense of numinosity.[44] All three elements seem to have been present in the double coincidence experienced by Jenkins, though one can never be quite sure just from reading an account. But if what he wrote accords with what occurred, he almost certainly experienced both meaning-equivalence and a split-second of sudden insight when he saw the four horses from his balcony window, and again on Dartmoor. And although there is no mention of any emotion beyond surprise and astonishment, it is not unreasonable to suggest that for Jenkins it was a profoundly numinous experience, especially given how closely associated numinosity is with synchronistic events.[45]

For Surprise, on the other hand, the coincidence was of a rather different nature. From the description of his reactions, it was neither numinosity nor a flash of insight that Surprise experienced when the house began to roll onto its side, to all appearances in response to the content of his thoughts; it was panic. But then, when the yellow paint of the tractor appeared, it was as if the curtain had been drawn and the illusion revealed for what it was, nothing more than a standard demolition of a building. Although he makes no mention of it in his book, it goes without saying that for Surprise it was not until *after* he had been able to discount the very unsettling possibility that it was his psychic power that had caused the house to collapse, that he would have been able fully to appreciate the episode as a synchronistic event. In other words, what looked like it might be an amazing feat of psychokinesis turned out to be 'just' a coincidence. But it was clearly a significant one for Surprise, and as he states in an interview, this incident helped fuel his fascination for synchronicity.[46]

In another interview Surprise claims that, while he was in college, he was having twenty to thirty synchronistic experiences a day.[47] This is very different from Jung's characterisation of synchronistic events as 'relatively rare acausal phenomena',[48] and so great is the discrepancy that it is more than possible that here we have two very different interpretations of synchronicity. This is not entirely unsurprising given how word meanings naturally change over time or are usurped for different purposes. As regards the latter, it is instructive to observe how the word has been adopted by academia. When one types 'synchronicity' into the *Google Scholar* academic search engine, the majority of citations that appear on the first two or three pages have nothing whatsoever to do with Jung or meaningful coincidences. Here, for example, is a novel definition from an information management journal: 'Media synchronicity theory (MST) focuses on the ability of media to support synchronicity, a shared pattern of coordinated behavior among individuals as they work together.'[49]

And in a medical journal article we find that when synchronicity is absent in an echocardiographic image, we need to be able to recognise the extent of *asynchronicity*: 'To quantify visual recognition of myocardial asynchronicity in echocardiographic images, computer-simulated delay phantom loops were generated from a 3.3 MHz digital image...'[50] So for the term that Jung coined to denote *both* meaningful coincidences *and* the acausal connecting principle underlying their occurrence to have migrated so far from its original meaning suggests that differences of definition amongst those concerned with the subject are to be expected.

To be getting twenty to thirty meaningful coincidences a day may point to active participation on the part of the person reporting them. According to the psychiatrist Bernard Beitman, who with colleagues has carried out research on the range and frequency of 'weird coincidences'[51] reported by university students: 'People create coincidences by matching their mental-emotional patterns with patterns that they perceive in the environment.'[52] This is very different to Jung's insistence that synchronistic events are *acausal*, as well as being both sporadic and unpredictable in their occurrence.[53] In the Jungian conception, during a synchronistic event psyche and matter are momentarily revealed as *one* reality, the *unus mundus*, which Jung describes as 'the latent unity of the world'.[54] The person experiencing the synchronicity gets a brief glimpse of this timeless realm, but soon returns to the world of everyday duality.[55]

However, it is not always the case that events that later turn out to be synchronistic are obviously so at the time of their occurrence. As Jean Shinoda Bolen points out in her popular introduction to synchronicity, *The Tao of Psychology*, it may take some time and a teasing out of a particular coincidental theme, as in the example Bolen gives of a woman having three car accidents in a row, none of which was her fault, and each time she was hit by a female driver. During this period she had been having emotional difficulties with a particular woman at her work, and it was not until the third accident that she was able to see a symbolic connection: 'On the same day as the last accident (in which she was hit by a woman whose brakes had failed), her co-worker's car brakes had also failed. After that, it was clearly time to accept the accidents as synchronistic events that were commenting on the situation... It was time to stop trying to be friends.'[56]

Tucked away amongst all that must have occurred for this woman, in both her strained relationship with her co-worker and with dealing with the practical as well as emotional consequences of having three separate car accidents in fairly quick succession, would have been the specific trigger that lifted the whole episode from the realm of 'ordinary' to that of 'meaningful' coincidence. And this, almost certainly, would have been when she heard that her co-worker's brakes had also failed on the day of the third accident: suddenly, an equivalence of meaning is directly intuited, very likely accompanied by a brief feeling of numinosity; and it is the combination of these effects, both cognitive and affective, that makes a coincidence, or series of coincidences, synchronistic. If there is a demarcation point between synchronistic events and coincidences that may be amusing or interesting but which are not particularly meaningful, then it is to do with the overall impact the meaning-equivalence has on the person who experiences it.

This is not to be confused with a possible *projection of meaning* onto a situation or set of circumstances, and thereby 'creating' a coincidence that was not realistically present. However, there exists something of a grey area here as some people are genuinely more sensitive to coincidences. In research undertaken by Beitman and his colleagues, it was found that those who see themselves as 'spiritual' and/or 'religious' tend to be more 'coincidence-prone' than those who do not.[57] Perhaps the spiritually or religiously inclined, by dint of their belief in a higher power, are more likely to be on the lookout for hints or messages of guidance and therefore read meaning into situations that do not necessarily warrant it. And there will be some who may not be particularly spiritual or religious but who nevertheless are coincidence-prone, and this might be because they have a strong tendency towards associative thinking and therefore see correspondences that most people would not pick up on.

It may well be that Surprise as a young man, with his twenty to thirty coincidences a day, fell into the category of a highly sensitive associative thinker, for as Beitman observes: 'People who associate ideas easily are more likely to make connections between mental patterns and contextual events.'[58] From the examples provided in his book, it is evident that Surprise is very adept at recognising external situations that resonate with his thought processes. One example he gives is being at the office waiting for someone and thinking about the space shuttle programme. There had been a news item the night before concerning a delay with the shuttle launch and he was wondering when it would fly again. Just then co-worker came up to him and said, 'The shuttle's going to be delayed. There's an accident somewhere.' Surprise felt stunned at this apparent concordance with his train of thought and when he registered his confusion, the co-worker explained that the office shuttle bus had been delayed by an accident on the freeway.[59]

This was certainly a coincidence, though apart from its astonishment value it does not appear *per se* to be particularly meaningful. Nevertheless, Surprise identifies such coincidences as synchronistic events, even where there is no obvious meaning beyond the correspondence itself. This is evident in the following example, which concerns a set of Gerber knives that he and his wife had recently bought. He was doing the washing up one day and listening to the news on the radio. As he washed one of the knives, he stopped for a moment to admire its shape: 'I turned it over and was looking at the Gerber name stamped into the steel handle. At that moment the news report ended with the correspondent identifying herself, "...Nancy Gerber reporting..."'[60]

Such coincidences would be good candidates for Kammerer's seriality, with its notion of the attraction of affinities. Jung, however, specifically identifies coincidences of the Nancy Gerber variety as no more than chance correlations, and thus essentially meaningless,[61] and this despite his speculation that in some circumstances synchronicity might demonstrate equivalence *without* meaning.[62] But to be fair to Surprise it should be mentioned that he reports, in addition to the moving house episode, several coincidences that would be considered synchronistic in the usual Jungian sense.[63]

The main problem with his approach is essentially one of nomenclature, in that he labels coincidences of just about every stripe as synchronistic events. This, incidentally, includes those he deliberately constructs by focusing on a particular theme or symbol and then waiting to see how his unconscious mind responds in its detection of patterns of meaning.[64] Thus, somewhat like the academic journals mentioned above, he borrows the term for his own purposes. Not that this is a bad thing, for it adds to the general discussion, and in any case it should be remembered that 'synchronicity' is not a copyrighted word with a fixed definition, like *Coca-Cola* or *Microsoft*. And while from a Jungian perspective there is no hard and fast rule determining which coincidences ought to be categorised as synchronistic and which ought not, a rule-ofthumb guideline for separating the wheat from the chaff is suggested by the author and therapist Robert Hopcke:

> Ordinary coincidences occur fairly often. I go to the movie theater and bump into a friend I have been meaning to call for a few weeks. I head to the store for a gallon of milk, and the tortellini on sale in the pasta aisle are just what your husband had been fantasizing aloud for dinner that night. I'm finishing a crossword puzzle, need the answer to a seven-letter word for 'singer from Hoboken', and a Frank Sinatra song comes on the radio. Such coincidences happen with regularity, and they are at times amusing to notice and usually delightful to experience. However, what Jung calls 'synchronistic' are not these simple and everyday coincidences but rather meaningful coincidences, i.e., rather unusual or striking co-occurrences that have either a profound emotional impact on one or have a discernible influence on one's life or attitude.[65]

The Shadow Side of Coincidence Interpretation

What Hopcke does not mention in the above quote, but of which as a therapist he would certainly be very aware—so too Surprise, who is also a therapist[66]—is that there is a great difference between the effect of 'unusual and striking co-occurrences' on those who are psychologically stable and those who are not. The latter are much more likely to engage in self-serving interpretations that are innately delusional, sometimes dangerously so. Beitman and his colleague Albert Shaw provide several graphic examples of such thinking.[67] The most troubling and indeed terrifying of these involves the twisted logic of Mark David Chapman, who on December 8, 1980, shot and killed John Lennon. Part of Chapman's justification or 'reasoning' for assassinating Lennon involved a convoluted series of correlations. At that time Lennon was living in the Dakota building in New York, where *Rosemary's Baby* was filmed. The film's director was Roman Polanski, the husband of Sharon Tate, who was pregnant when she was killed by the Manson gang in 1969. Charles Manson's favourite song, and also the title of his autobiography, was *Helter Skelter*, a Beatles song.

Chapman was reflecting on these connections on the morning of December 8, when something occurred that capped off this illusory run of far-fetched coincidences and in effect sealed Lennon's fate. In the words of the journalist Jack Jones, who interviewed Chapman in prison: 'As he stood outside the Dakota thinking these things, Mia Farrow, the actress who played "Rosemary", walked by. For Chapman, the coincidence of all these connected events meant that he should kill John Lennon today.'[68] Even amidst all this ghastliness there is a tragic irony, for Jones's description of the 'coincidences' described above includes the sentence, '*Helter Skelter* was written by John Lennon.'[69] This may have been what Chapman told Jones when he was describing his thought processes; however, the song was in fact written and sung by Paul McCartney.[70]

Beitman and Shaw also give less extreme examples of how coincidences are misinterpreted through projection. One of these concerns a woman who fell so completely in love that she felt it was destined by fate and that she and her lover would be together for eternity. As support for her conviction she noted that his sister's name was the same as her mother's and his father's name was the same as her brother's. She could sense his presence when he was in the same building and felt that they were able to communicate telepathically. But their relationship did not last and after it broke up she changed her interpretation of events: 'As it turns out, the coincidences were meaningful only for the time we were together. They did not mean forever.'[71] This woman interpreted the coincidences she experienced in a certain way when she was intoxicated by her love but in quite another way when the relationship had ended and she had come down to Earth. Beitman and Shaw comment on this case: 'Although heavily imbued with positive emotion, such self-referential meaningful coincidences can be mistaken. Love involves two people. The coincidences encouraged her to believe that their love stretched into eternity. Her lover felt differently.'[72]

A useful concept that can be used to help distinguish between healthy and unhealthy ways of interpreting coincidences is the *pre/post fallacy*, as suggested by the consciousness theorist Ken Wilber.[73] Wilber distinguishes between *pre-rational* and *post-rational* modes of cognition, which are completely different from one another, except in that they are both *non-rational*. To think in a pre-rational way suggests egocentric associative thinking and an immature capacity for reason, as is characteristically found in small children, as well as some adults. Post-rational cognition, on the other hand, can be found in established meditative states, such as that enjoyed by the South Indian sage, Ramana Maharshi, who also displayed a highly developed capacity for reason.[74] Pre-rational and post-rational are both natural states of cognition and are not in themselves deviations of rationality. Indeed, post-rationality necessarily *transcends and includes* rationality, in the same way that abstract reasoning transcends and includes concrete operations.

A problem occurs, however, when pre-rational and post-rational become conflated in the mind of an individual who may imagine that his post-rational intuitive faculties are functioning so well that he does not need to subject his insights to the scrutiny of reason. And this can all too easily occur with synchronicity, the very identification of which, as Richard Tarnas puts it, '...requires subtle judgements made in circumstances usually pervaded by ambiguity and open to multiple interpretations'.[75] This implies that if there is insufficient rationality in the approach to coincidences, magical thinking combined with delusions of self-reference can become the order of the day. Tarnas again: 'For synchronicities have a shadow side, as in the exaggeration of the trivial to discover a self-inflating meaning.'[76]

Jung's Personal Approach

But if there is an exemplar in how the delicate skill of recognising and interpreting synchronicity might be approached, it could well be Jung himself, especially in his later years. For even though Jung considered synchronicities to be rare, he was very much attuned to the possibility of their occurrence. An anecdote related by Heinrich Fierz, a Jungian analyst and the twin brother of Pauli's assistant Markus Fierz, illustrates this aspect of Jung's character. Fierz had come to see Jung concerning the possible publication of a book by a scientist who had recently died. The meeting was scheduled for five o'clock and when they met Jung voiced his opinion that the manuscript should not be published. Fierz disagreed and the discussion became rather sharp, at which point Jung looked at his watch with what Fierz felt was the intention to terminate the meeting. Then, entirely unexpectedly from Fierz's perspective, Jung asked him:

> 'When did you come?' I: 'At five, as agreed.' Jung: 'But that's queer. My watch came back from the watchmaker this morning after a complete revision, and now I have 5:05. But you must have been here much longer. What time do you have?' I: 'It's 5:35.' Whereon Jung said: 'So you have the right time, and I have the wrong one. Let us discuss the thing again.' This time I could convince Jung that the book should be published.[77]

Tarnas considers this episode to be of particular interest, not because of the outer circumstances of the synchronistic event, which for most people would not be at all obvious, but because of how the juxtaposition of otherwise unconnected incongruities was interpreted by Jung. He recognised the stopping of his watch as a parallel occurrence to a possible error in his thinking. As Tarnas explains, with reference both to Jung's ability to think symbolically and to his epistemological openness:

> For Jung, the symbolic connection between the two events was as transparently intelligible as if he were reading a newspaper, and he acted accordingly. What made the correlation between the inner and outer events intelligible was the presence of two factors: first, a developed capacity for thinking and perceiving symbolically, a cultivated sensitivity to metaphoric and analogical patterns that connect and

thereby illuminate diverse phenomena; and second, an epistemological openness to the possibility that such meaning can be carried by the outer world as well as the inner, by all of nature and one's surrounding environment, not just the human psyche.[78]

Like the peoples of the ancient world, Jung was sensitive to what the classical historian Robin Lane Fox describes as the 'rustling universe'.[79] The continual ebb and flow of the forces of nature, as well as the movements and moods of those he encountered, were for Jung potential mirrors for what was going on within his psyche. In other words, particularly in his later years when he was able to spend more time at his country retreat in Bollingen on the shores of Lake Zurich, Jung came to inhabit a synchronistic reality where the external and internal were in continual reflection of one another. As Jung himself put it: 'Sometimes I feel as if I am spread out over the landscape and inside things, and am myself living in every tree, in the splashing of the waves, in the clouds and the procession of the seasons.'[80] At Bollingen there was no external source of power or water and Jung was able to live like a peasant: 'I have done without electricity, and tend the fireplace and stove myself. Evenings, I light the old lamps. There is no running water or electricity, and I pump the water from the well. I chop the wood and cook the food. These simple acts make man simple, and how difficult it is to be simple!'[81] He continues: 'In Bollingen, silence surrounds me almost audibly, and I live "in modest harmony with nature".'[82]

The quoted expression is taken from a Chinese woodcut of 'a little old man in a heroic landscape'.[83] There is a resonance here with the story of the Rainmaker that Jung was so fond of, and Suzanne Gieser makes the point that for Jung there was another kind of *induced* synchronicity, in addition to divinatory methods such as the *I Ching*. This further type of synchronicity, according to Gieser, is exemplified by the Rainmaker story, of the 'man of *tao*' who is both balanced and ordered in relation to his inner being, and therefore, coincidentally and without deliberation, brings order to the world around him.[84] Perhaps in his old age, particularly after his wife died in 1955, Jung began to attain something of that equanimity. This is the view of David Rosen, author of *The Tao of Jung*, who considers that in his final years Jung genuinely achieved the 'actionless action' of *wu wei*,[85] and it is perhaps fitting that in the final paragraph of his autobiography Jung both refers and defers to Lao Tzu:

> When Lao-tzu says: 'All are clear, I alone am clouded,' he is expressing what I now feel in advanced old age. Lao-tzu is the example of a man with superior insight who has seen and experienced worth and worthlessness, and who at the end of his life desires to return to his own being. The archetype of the old man who has seen enough is eternally

true. At every level of intelligence this type appears, and its lineaments are always the same, whether it be an old peasant or a great philosopher like Lao-tzu. This is old age, and a limitation. Yet there is so much that fills me: plants, animals, clouds, day and night, and the eternal in man. The more uncertain I have felt about myself, the more there has grown up in me a kinship with all things. In fact it seems to me as if that alienation which so long separated me from the world has become transferred into my own inner world, and has revealed to me an unexpected unfamiliarity with myself.[86]

Synchronicity Stages

Tarnas speculates that personal experience of synchronicity naturally goes through stages.[87] The first of these is when odd and perhaps vaguely suggestive coincidences appear in one's life but which can fairly readily be dismissed as subjective interpretations or perhaps as probabilistically inevitable but essentially meaningless co-occurrences. The next stage is that of the classic or dramatic synchronistic event which can have a profound effect on the direction of a person's life. As Tarnas puts it, such synchronicities are 'unambiguous in their coincidental force and the precision of their patterning...' and not infrequently 'occur in association with births, deaths, crises, and other major turning points in life'.[88] Sometimes such compelling coincidences can occur in rapid succession or in combination, 'having the effect of an overpowering epiphany of new meaning and purpose in the life of the individual'.[89]

A final stage suggested by Tarnas comes into effect when synchronicities become a regular part of life and serve as hints and indications to be attentive to those aspects of the psyche that may be mirrored in the outer world at any particular moment. Coincidences of this sort are generally of a subtler nature than the dramatic instances of synchronicity, and may require a certain alertness to pick them up. Jung's reaction to his stopped watch would be an example of this more integrated stage, in contrast to Jenkins' stunned response at the correspondence of the horses' colour schemes with Zechariah's vision. This is a useful distinction, though it is not one that Jung himself made explicitly.[90] It does, however, account for Jung's thoroughly synchronistic way of viewing the events taking place around him, especially during his later years.

Another way of looking at synchronicity through a stage model is to use the famous Zen oxherding pictures, of which there are many versions, both ancient and modern.[91] In the traditional format, a young seeker, who is depicted as an oxherder, is looking for his Buddha-nature, which is symbolised by an ox (or bull). In the first picture, seen below, the oxherder sets out on his journey to find the ox, and we can see how easily he is distracted from his task; in the second, he sees the ox's footprints and runs to catch up with it; and in the third, he succeeds in finding the ox and prepares to capture it. The prints depicted here (Figs. 8–17) are by the twentieth-century Kyoto woodblock artist, Tomikichiro Tokuriki:[92]

Figs. 8–10: The Oxherder, 1–3

With regard to using these stages as analogies for approaching synchronicity, the first two prints might be seen as leading up to the first unequivocal encounter with a meaningful coincidence, symbolised by the oxherder observing the hindquarters of the ox in the third print. In the fourth (Fig. 11, below), the ox is caught and this stage involves a terrific struggle as the oxherder attempts to subdue the ox and not allow it to overwhelm him or get out of his control. As Robert Carter explains in regard to Zen practice at stages three and four: '[The ox] is unruly and ungovernable. The herder's senses are not yet in harmonious order: his empirical self is disordered and runs wild. The taming of the deep self requires focused concentration and diligent training. Practice and discipline alone will lead to success.'[93]

In terms of responding to meaningful coincidences, at stage four the experiencer must be careful not to be thrown by the beguiling and multifarious possibilities of synchronistic interpretation, and also not become overwhelmed by the experience, especially if coincidences, meaningful or otherwise, appear to come fast and furious. And although correspondences with the oxherding sequence should not be taken too literally, this is certainly a critical stage with respect to synchronicity: for if the experiencer *does* become destabilised by his or her perception of coincidences, the consequences, as we have seen, can be particularly disturbing. Fortunately, in the fifth print, the oxherder gains control over the ox, and in the sixth print he rides it and plays the flute in celebration of his victory and his sheer joy at being alive. The fifth and particularly the sixth stage effectively correspond to the third stage suggested by Tarnas, in which synchronicities become a regular part of life. The young man plays the flute riding on the ox: in the same way, one who has integrated synchronicities can 'ride' on them without disturbance to the tune or expressive theme of his or her life:

Figs. 11–13: The Oxherder, 4–6

Although the full oxherding sequence comprises ten pictures, the ox itself does not appear in the last four. This is because in the original Buddhist conception, with the seventh print the oxherder has returned home and rests in tranquillity (Fig. 14), and there is no sign of the ox. The interpretation here is that at this stage the Buddha-nature is no longer separate from the seeker's self-identification, that in reality there is no ox and there *never was* an ox, as is symbolised forcefully in the eighth print, an empty circle in which, as Carter puts it, 'All distinctions have vanished into the fullness of nothingness.'[94] In the ninth print the world returns again but there is no observer, only the beauty of nature infused with the realisation of emptiness.[95]

Although these stages go well beyond the realm of meaningful coincidence and could therefore be profitably described as *post-synchronistic*, they do point to what Jung considered was glimpsed momentarily in the equivalence of meaning that he identified as subsisting at the heart of synchronistic occurrences: the *unus mundus*, the unbroken unity of psyche and matter; and it is particularly in the ninth print that this unity is depicted, though it cannot be properly understood without the proceeding images. Carter elucidates it thus: 'One sees the same world of nature in the ninth stage as one did in the earlier stages, but now one sees it "as-it-is-by-itself", in its "thusness". One's no-mindedness has allowed nature to be "nature".'[96] This is very much in line with Jung's description of the Rainmaker and his ability to bring balance to the outer world by establishing his own harmony within.[97] Indeed, prints seven, eight and nine could be viewed as depicting symbolically the internal alchemy practised by the Rainmaker to bring himself into harmony with the *tao*. He quietens himself, finds his own inner emptiness and allows it to merge with the outer world of form:

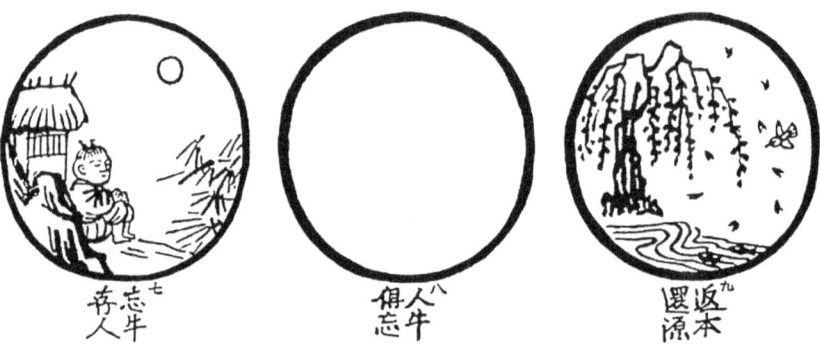

Figs. 14–16: The Oxherder, 7–9

The final oxherding picture has something of a resemblance to what occurs in a game of chess when a pawn succeeds in reaching the opponent's back row and is thereby transformed into a queen. Similarly, in the tenth print, the lowly oxherder becomes a Buddha and carries the beauty and unity of the world with him wherever he goes. Now, for him, every moment becomes infused with the primordial insight of the *unus mundus*, not passively as might be implied by the ninth print, but actively and in relation to the mass of humanity. Each of the oxherding pictures has a poem associated with it, and the tenth print comes with the following verse:

> Barefooted and naked of breast, I mingle with the people of the world.
> My clothes are ragged and dust-laden, and I am ever blissful.
> I use no magic to extend my life;
> Now, before me, the dead trees become alive.[98]

Fig. 17: The Oxherder, 10.

Endnotes

1. Plimmer and King, *Beyond Coincidence*, v.
2. Ibid., 303.
3. Neimark, 'Pattern and Circumstance: The Power of Coincidence', 50.
4. Ibid., 50.
5. Wijesinghe, 'Rice bowls… And Paddy fields'.
6. Surprise, *Synchronicity: The Art of Coincidence, Choice, and Unlocking Your Mind*, 18-19.
7. Plimmer and King, *Beyond Coincidence*, 130-131.
8. Ibid., iv.
9. Koestler, *The Roots of Coincidence*, 86.
10. Ibid., 85.
11. Ibid.
12. Ibid., 95.
13. Ibid., 86.
14. Koestler, *The Case of the Midwife Toad*, 141; Koestler, *The Roots of Coincidence*, 86.
15. Jung, *Mysterium Conjunctionis*, 505.
16. von Franz, *Psyche and Matter*, 217.
17. Jung, *Synchronicity*, 101.
18. Ibid.
19. Ibid., 95-101.
20. Ibid., 139.
21. Ibid., 118n.
22. Jung, *Letters Volume 2*, 494-495.
23. Gieser, *The Innermost Kernel*, 299-311.
24. Powell, *The ESP Enigma*, 50-51.
25. Merton and Barber, *The Travels and Adventures of Serendipity*, 95.
26. Plimmer and King, *Beyond Coincidence*, 141.
27. Hardy, Harvie and Koestler, *The Challenge of Chance*, 171.
28. Ibid., 172.
29. Lennox, *God's Undertaker*, 70-72.
30. Gordon, 'Inflationary Cosmology and the String Universe', 98.
31. Penrose, 'Is the Universe Fine-Tuned for Life and Mind?'
32. Davies, *The Goldilocks Enigma*, 249.
33. Jung, *Mysterium Conjunctionis*, 464.
34. McGuire and Hull, *C.G. Jung Speaking*, 223.
35. von Franz, *C.G. Jung: His Myth in Our Time*, 247.
36. Zechariah 6: 1-6; Revelation 6: 1-8.
37. Main, *Revelations of Chance*, 12.
38. Ibid.
39. Ibid.
40. von Franz, *Projection and Recollection in Jungian Psychology*, 193.
41. Surprise, *Synchronicity: The Art of Coincidence, Choice, and Unlocking Your Mind*, 14.
42. von Franz, *Psyche and Matter*, 41; Jung, *Synchronicity*, 51.
43. Jung, *Synchronicity*, 124.

44 Ibid., 29; Peat, 'Divine Contenders: Wolfgang Pauli and the Symmetry of the World', 20-21.
45 Main, *Revelations of Chance*, 39-43.
46 Jones, 'Synchronicity: The Art of Coincidence – An Interview with Dr Kirby Surprise'.
47 Anaya, 'Synchronicity as a Mirror of our Thoughts, Emotions, and Beliefs'.
48 Jung, *Synchronicity*, 11.
49 Dennis, Fuller and Valacich, 'Media, Tasks, and Communication Processes', p. 575.
50 Kvitting et al., 'How Accurate is Visual Assessment of Synchronicity?', p. 698.
51 Coleman, Beitman and Celebi, 'Weird Coincidences Commonly Occur'.
52 Beitman, 'Coincidence Studies', 567.
53 von Franz, *Psyche and Matter*, 28-29.
54 Jung, *Mysterium Conjunctionis*, 465.
55 von Franz, *Number and Time*, 261-264.
56 Bolen, *The Tao of Psychology*, 46.
57 Beitman, 'Coincidence Studies', 568.
58 Ibid., 568.
59 Surprise, *Synchronicity: The Art of Coincidence, Choice, and Unlocking Your Mind*, 194.
60 Ibid., 90.
61 Jung, *Synchronicity*, 13-15.
62 Ibid., 118n.
63 Surprise, e.g. 48-49.
64 Ibid., e.g. 227-228.
65 Hopcke, 'Synchronicity and Psychotherapy', 290.
66 Surprise, *Synchronicity: The Art of Coincidence, Choice, and Unlocking Your Mind*, 59-75.
67 Beitman and Shaw, 'Synchroners, High Emotion, and Coincidence Interpretation'.
68 Ibid., 3.
69 Ibid.
70 The Beatles Bible, 'Helter Skelter'.
71 Beitman and Shaw, 'Synchroners, High Emotion, and Coincidence Interpretation', 4.
72 Ibid., 4-5.
73 Wilber, *Integral Spirituality*, 51-53.
74 Maharshi, *Talks with Ramana Maharshi*.
75 Tarnas, *Cosmos and Psyche*, 55.
76 Ibid.
77 Ibid., 54.
78 Ibid., 54-55.
79 Karcher, 'Re-Enchanting the Mind', 210.
80 Jung, *Memories, Dreams, Reflections*, 252.
81 Ibid., 252-253.
82 Ibid., 253.
83 Ibid., 253n.
84 Gieser, *The Innermost Kernel*, 289n.

85 Rosen, *The Tao of Jung*, 159.
86 Jung, *Memories, Dreams, Reflections*, 393.
87 Tarnas, *Cosmos and Psyche*, 55-56.
88 Ibid., 55.
89 Ibid., 56.
90 Ibid.
91 e.g. Carter, R., *The Nothingness Beyond God*; Reps, *Zen Flesh, Zen Bones*; Wada, *The Oxherder*.
92 Source for Figs. 8-17: Reps, *Zen Flesh, Zen Bones*, 134-147.
93 Carter, R., *The Nothingness Beyond God*, 72.
94 Ibid., 74.
95 Ibid., 74-75.
96 Ibid., 75.
97 Jung, *Mysterium Conjunctionis*, 419-420n.
98 Reps, *Zen Flesh, Zen Bones*, 147.

Chapter Six
Exploring the Tao

There have been many references in these pages to the possibility of an underlying unity of mind and matter, and not without reason. For if synchronistic experiences are to be taken seriously as coherent in themselves and not ultimately reducible to subjective interpretations of random events, then they are in need of a credible theoretical explanation. Jung himself was only too aware of this, and very much following on from Leibniz's postulation of a 'pre-established harmony' underlying the apparent bifurcation of mind and matter, he thought it important to revive the medieval Scholastic notion of the *unus mundus*. His adoption of the term was no doubt inspired by his fascination with the medieval alchemists and the attempt of at least some of them to achieve union with 'the original non-differentiated unity of the world'.[1] Such a union, Jung emphasised, was not to be confused with 'a fusion of the individual with his environment, or even his adaptation to it, but a *unio mystica* with the potential world'.[2] Thus, the objective of these alchemists, in Jung's reading, was nothing less than mystical union with the *unus mundus* itself.

Jung held, in addition, that synchronistic occurrences constituted *empirical* evidence of the actuality of the *unus mundus* as the underlying condition of our existence.[3] This was quite a claim to make and not one that is at all easy to back up, especially as the sporadic and unpredictable nature of synchronistic events means that it is extremely problematic even to attempt to reproduce them at will. It may be more fruitful, therefore, to try to ascertain what precisely is implied by the term *unus mundus* and to determine whether there is any substantive evidence for its existence, evidence that does not depend on philosophical speculation. And this would include ideas and possibilities arising from the paradoxes of quantum physics. In other words, if the *unus mundus* can in some way be shown to be empirically viable, then the burden of 'proving' the validity of synchronistic occurrences — that they really do constitute fleeting glimpses of an underlying unity of psyche and matter — becomes considerably less onerous.

Interestingly, Jung makes no reference to the *unus mundus* in his principle essay on synchronicity, the foreword to which he wrote in 1950. He does, however, mention it in a letter to Pauli in 1952, where he describes it as 'a piece of alchemical philosophy'.[4] Jung's interest in the explanatory possibility of the *unus mundus* became evident during the 1950s, particularly with the publication of his last major work, *Mysterium Conjunctionis*, a treatise on alchemy. In it he describes the *unus mundus* as, 'a potential world, the eternal Ground of all empirical being'.[5] Furthermore, 'everything divided and different belongs to one and the same world, which is not the world of sense but a postulate whose probability is vouched for by the fact that until now no-one has been able to discover a world in which the known laws of nature are invalid."[6]

Jung was of course writing before the serious consideration of multiverse theories which, as discussed in Chapter Three, suggest that there may be other universes with other laws of nature. Even so, over half a century later, still no world has been found where the known laws of nature are invalid. He continues: 'That even the psychic world, which is so extraordinarily different from the physical world, does not have its roots outside one cosmos is evident from the undeniable fact that causal connections exist between the psyche and the body which point to their underlying unitary nature.'[7] The 'one cosmos' is not in Jung's view reducible to either matter or to mind, both positions involving what he felt were arbitrary hypotheses.[8] Jung appears therefore neither to have been a materialist nor an idealist, and he was certainly not a dualist in the Cartesian sense of a distinct division between mind and body. Indeed, he believed that at their most profound level psyche and matter are undivided, and that this fundamental unity is sporadically exposed in synchronistic events through the *equivalence of meaning* that is at their core.

Dual Aspect Approaches

Harald Atmanspacher, writing in the *Stanford Encyclopedia of Philosophy*, categorises Jung's theoretical position as embodying a *dual aspect* approach to consciousness. He defines a dual aspect approach or theory as one which considers 'mental and material domains of reality as aspects, or manifestations, of one underlying reality in which mind and matter are unseparated'.[9]

Another example given by Atmanspacher of a dual aspect theory is David Bohm's hypothesis of an *implicate order* underlying the classical world of space and time and everyday objects, which Bohm called the *explicate order*. The relationship between the two is explained by David Peat, Bohm's associate and biographer, who describes the quantum world of the implicate order as 'much vaster than the explicate. It is like a great ocean reaching below the surface… [which] has the capacity to embrace and contain the explicate, but not vice versa. This means that what appear to be separate objects in our everyday world have arisen out of the same common ground and thus contain connections and attractions for each other, correlations that remain outside the level of explicate causality'.[10] Despite arising from a very different context, there are some interesting resonances between Bohm's implicate order and Jung's articulation of the *unus mundus*, particularly the intimation of some kind of acausality within the implicate order.

There are a number of different philosophical positions that have in one way or another been identified as dual aspect theories, most famously Baruch Spinoza's conception of thought and spatial extension being 'two aspects of a single inclusive reality', which he identified interchangeably as 'God' or 'Nature'.[11] A contemporary dual aspect theory is that of *reflexive monism* proposed by the psychologist Max Velmans as an alternative to dualist and reductionist accounts of consciousness. Velmans argues that the world we experience through our senses is both 'out there' *and* in our brains. What we identify as the physical world is in fact 'a form of perceptual projection: a biologically evolved virtual reality' arising from the interaction between the external world as we perceive it and our preconscious *deeper* mind.[12]

This deeper mind is 'a vast set of mental and physical interconnected processes' that Velmans identifies as the unconscious ground of being upon which our conscious selves are metaphorically 'floating'. The dual aspects for Velmans are not so much mind and matter as such but rather the psychological and physical aspects of the psychophysical unity that gives rise to our subjective perceptions of the world around us, which naturally includes our bodies and the array of sensations associated with them. Although this is clearly not the same as Jung's conceptualisation of the psychophysical unity of the *unus mundus*, Velmans' postulation of an 'unconscious ground of being' in which our everyday consciousness is psychophysically embedded may well be a step in that direction.

In regard to Jung's proposition of a *unus mundus*, it is also important to consider the contribution of Wolfgang Pauli. As Atmanspacher points out, if Jung came to his *unus mundus* conception through extensive psychological research, Pauli came to the same conclusion not only by way of his sustained interaction with Jung but also through his profound understanding of quantum physics.[13] Atmanspacher also makes the interesting observation that many recent dual aspect approaches, including those of Bohm and Velmans, 'are, in one way or another, attached to ideas and notions that emerged during the development of quantum theory'.[14] Indeed, and no doubt precisely because the philosophical implications are so significant, Atmanspacher has coined the term 'the Pauli-Jung Conjecture' for the position arrived at by both Pauli and Jung from their radically different fields that psyche and matter should be conceived of as complementary aspects of the same reality.[15]

Defining the *Tao*

Jung regarded the classical Chinese concept of *tao* as the equivalent of the *unus mundus*[16] and it is probable that his enthusiasm for the latter arose because he saw it as an independently developed Western parallel. In other words, the idea of the *tao* was a more fundamental factor in Jung's thinking than the *unus mundus*, which he arrived at much later in life. Pauli too felt instinctively comfortable with idea of the *tao*,[17] as did his colleague and mentor Nils Bohr who, when awarded the Danish Order of the Elephant in 1947, included the yin-yang symbol in his coat of arms, along with the motto *contraria sunt complementa* (opposites are complementary). So when it comes to dual aspect approaches, we have with philosophical Taoism a fully formed one with an ancient and venerable tradition.

When Jung's close associate C.A. Meier was asked once whether he thought Jung was Taoist, Meier replied, 'Yes, he was Taoist, and today people don't realise that his psychology of opposites is virtually the same as Taoism.'[18] Indeed, it is highly unlikely that Jung would have been able to develop the idea of synchronicity with such clarity and conviction without his familiarity and affinity with the *tao*-based correlative thinking of the Chinese, especially as articulated in the *Tao Te Ching* and the *I Ching*. His friendship with the sinologist Richard Wilhelm was extremely significant in this regard and, during his memorial address for Wilhelm in 1930, Jung made clear his gratitude:

> He, as a Sinologue, and I, as a physician, would probably never have come into contact had we remained specialists. But we met in a field of humanity which begins beyond academic boundary posts. There lay our point of contact; there leaped across the spark that kindled the light destined to become for me one of the most meaningful events of my life.[19]

It is interesting to speculate as to what form, if any, Jung's exposition of synchronicity might have taken *without* his friendship with Wilhelm. Perhaps it would have been very much wound up with ESP and quantum physics in combination with his theory of archetypes, with much less of the quintessentially Chinese way of understanding coincidences that Jung so enthusiastically endorses in his foreword to

Wilhelm's translation of the *I Ching*. While Chinese thought may not be theoretically necessary for a coherent articulation of synchronicity, its inclusion opens the door to an extremely rich philosophical tradition: one that has no need to refer or defer to the latest findings in psychology or physics to make sense of coincidences.

It is easy enough to reflect on what might or might not have happened with the concept of synchronicity had Jung not met Wilhelm. However, that is not what occurred, and their meeting 'in a field of humanity which begins beyond academic boundary posts' was almost certainly the meaningful coincidence that spurred Jung in his endeavour to develop a non-reductive and convincing theoretical framework for the occurrence of genuinely meaningful coincidences. So, as it turns out, classical Chinese philosophy was for Jung crucial in this regard. And as the *tao* is such a significant element in Chinese thought and an unequivocally important background factor in Jung's espousal of the idea of the *unus mundus*, it is worthwhile attempting to understand what exactly the concept of *tao* represents.

Unlike the *unus mundus*, which refers solely to an underlying unity of existence, the *tao* has a considerable number of meaning-extensions. According to the eminent translator Arthur Waley, 'It means a road, path, way; and hence, the way in which one does something; method, principle, doctrine.'[20] Elaborating on these definitions, Waley writes, '*Tao* is the way that those must walk who would "achieve without doing". But *tao* is not only a means, a doctrine, principle. It is the ultimate reality in which all attributes are united, "it is heavy as stone, light as a feather"; it is the unity underlying plurality.'[21] The last sentence is clearly comparable to the *unus mundus*, and it is that aspect of its meaning Jung was undoubtedly referring to when he equated the two notions.

This is much more the Taoist rather than the Confucian understanding of *tao*, as can be seen from the two definitions provided by the *Oxford English Dictionary*: '1. In Taoism, an absolute entity which is the source of the universe; the way in which this absolute entity functions. 2. In Confucianism and in extended uses, the way to be followed, the right conduct; doctrine or method.'[22] But even with such precision, an adequate definition of the *tao* remains problematic, not least because of the warning given in the first line of the *Tao Te Ching* that, 'the *Tao* that can be spoken of is not the *Tao* itself.'[23] Another definitional issue is raised by D.C. Lau in the introduction to his translation of the *Tao Te Ching*. According to Lau, it is not the interpretation of the *tao* as the source of the universe that is the problem for finding an equivalent concept, but that any such concept must include a *concreteness* generally absent from accounts of a transcendent absolute:

> The difficulty in finding appropriate language to describe the *tao* lies in the fact that although the *tao* is conceived of as that which is responsible for the creation as well as the support of the universe, yet the description the Taoist aimed at was a description in terms of tangible qualities as though the *tao* were a concrete thing.[24]

This is a pertinent observation and suggests that the *tao* is substantial as well as insubstantial, at least as conceived of by the author(s) of the *Tao Te Ching*. To support his claim, Lau cites several descriptions of the *tao*, including this verse from Chapter 21:

> As a thing the way [*tao*] is
> Shadowy, indistinct.
> Indistinct and shadowy,
> Yet within it is an image;
> Shadowy and indistinct,
> Yet within it is a substance.
> Dim and dark,
> Yet within it is an essence.
> This essence is quite genuine
> And within it is something that can be tested.[25]

Although Lau's translation and commentary were not published until shortly after Jung's death, Jung would not have been surprised at the notion of the *tangibility* of the *tao*. Indeed, the above verse could easily be interpreted as an argument for the empirical replicability of direct contact with the *tao* as an introspective reality. This practical and experiential aspect of Taoism is also very much the focus of *The Secret of the Golden Flower*, for which Jung provided a detailed commentary as part of his collaboration with Wilhelm. In addition to its being a treatise for the practice of Taoist yoga, Jung considered *The Secret of the Golden Flower* to be an alchemical text comparable to the writings of the medieval alchemists of the West.[26]

He subsequently became particularly enthusiastic about Gerard Dorn, a sixteenth-century alchemist who wrote extensively about the stages of the alchemical 'work' and its final fruition or consummation, which could 'be expected only when the unity of spirit, soul, and body is made one with the original *unus mundus*'.[27] Dorn never claimed that he or any other alchemist had ever achieved this state, and as Jung notes, 'Naturally there were as many swindlers and dupes as ever who claimed the lapis or golden tincture, or to be able to make it. But the more honest alchemists readily admitted that they had not yet plumbed the final secret.'[28] Whatever his actual experience, Dorn clearly believed that the *unus mundus* was a reality, as did the ancient Taoists in regard to attaining the *tao*. But while alchemy, unless pursued *allegorically* as a vehicle for insight and personal transformation, seems to have been doomed from its inception, the same cannot be said as regards the rather more subtle aspirations of the Taoist sages.

The *Tao* is Silent

In 1977, a deceptively simple book by the logician Raymond Smullyan entitled *The Tao is Silent* was published. Although Smullyan's style is whimsical and chatty, there is a certain incisiveness in his philosophical logic that makes the case for the plausibility of the *tao* difficult to ignore. Since the *tao* is by definition vague and without sharp boundaries, it does not easily lend itself to the cut and thrust of propositional debate as regularly takes place between theists and atheists as to the existence of God. As Smullyan puts it: 'Since the Taoists make no claim that the Tao exists, it saves them a world of trouble trying to prove that the Tao exists.'[29]

He goes on to equate the Taoist with the Western logical positivist: any question concerning the existence or non-existence of the *tao* for either of them is essentially meaningless. Of course, the logical positivist's reason for declaring that such a question is meaningless differs from that of the Taoist. For the positivist, precision is required for verification so the very indefinability and vagueness of the term '*tao*' constitutes its meaninglessness. The Taoist, on the other hand, would be too busy contemplating and enjoying the *tao* to find the enquiry into its existence or non-existence anything other than meaningless.[30] In any case, particularly when faced with such a precisely dichotomous question, the Taoist may choose to remain silent, recalling the famous opening stanza from Chapter 56 of the *Tao Te Ching*: 'One who knows does not speak; one who speaks does not know.'[31] Fortunately, Smullyan is not overly bashful about his ignorance, and so provides a comprehensive response that incorporates both East and West:

> Suppose you actually cornered me in my study and said to me point blank: 'Smullyan! Stop equivocating! Do you or do you not believe the Tao exists?' What would I answer? This would depend on whether I happened to be in a more Western or more Eastern mood at the time I was asked. If I were in a more Western mood (and abided in the duality of existence versus nonexistence), then, since I tend to be a Platonist, I would probably answer, 'Yes, the Tao exists'. But suppose I were in an Eastern mood? Well now, if you asked a Zen-Master whether the Tao exists, he would probably give you a good blow with his stick. Now I, being of a somewhat more mild disposition, would probably just smile at you (perhaps in a somewhat condescending fashion) and offer you a cup of tea.[32]

Smullyan also provides a brief summary of the controversy within Scholasticism over the problem of *universals*, a problem that remains unresolved to this day. Do abstract qualities, or 'universals', such as *beauty* or *kindness* exist only as adjectives, as the medieval Nominalists held, or are they abstract entities in themselves, with an independent 'reality' in a Platonic world of Forms, as proposed by the Realists? Although he favours the existence of a Platonic realm, Smullyan accepts that it is quite conceivable that the idea of universals is a construct of the human mind and that the *tao* in reality exists only as an adjective. In other words, there are those who might 'refuse to believe in the existence of some "entity" called the Tao, but they would nevertheless accept as quite meaningful the adjective "Taoistic"'.[33]

This is certainly not a category into which Jung would have fitted: he regarded the *tao* as manifestly 'real', as he did the *unus mundus*, which he envisaged as 'a Platonic prior or primeval world'.[34] Lau, on the other hand, is uncomfortable with a Platonic categorisation for the *tao*, partly because in comparison with Plato's Form of the *Good*, which is not only the ultimate 'reality' but also totally *knowable*, the *tao* is both ineffable and unknowable. In addition, there is the status of the Form of the *Good* as the highest Form, transcending all others, while the *tao* is described far more often by *lower* rather than higher terms.[35] For the Taoist, Lau argues, 'whatever has existence cannot be real', so that it is better to describe the *tao* in terms of Nothing rather than Something, 'though, strictly speaking, the *tao* can be no more like Nothing than it is like Something'.[36] Lau's reference is to Chapter 40 of the *Tao Te Ching*:

> Turning back is how the way [*tao*] moves;
> Weakness is the means the way employs.
> The myriad creatures in the world are born from
> Something, and Something from Nothing.[37]

Since the *tao* by definition is vague, argues Smullyan, 'then it would follow that any precise notion of the Tao would be inaccurate *by virtue of its very precision*'.[38] So for the Taoist it is quite beside the point as to whether the *tao* is in fact 'real' in a Platonic sense, even whether it is *the* 'ultimate reality', the metaphysical equivalent of *Brahman* in Vedanta or the *One* of Plotinus, or whether it is simply a descriptive term to identify a cultural style and set of beliefs, as modern day nominalists might have it. Nevertheless, as Lau's translation of Chapter 21 the *Tao Te Ching* indicates, the *tao* itself may not be immune to replicable introspective investigation:

> Dim and dark,
> Yet within it is an essence.
> This essence is quite genuine
> And within it is something that can be tested.[39]

Permutations of the *Tao*

Perhaps more than any other major philosophical concept, the *tao* embodies the idea of the unification of opposites, and this is reflected in Jung's hypothesis that the incommensurable opposites of psyche and matter become psychophysically united during synchronistic events. The *unus mundus* is momentarily revealed, leaving a tantalising trace of numinosity and meaning-equivalence to be reflected on by the person involved. The *unus mundus* is clearly a narrower concept than the *tao*, though any differentiation between the two was never articulated by Jung. He did, however, make an explicit distinction between the more specific and therefore narrower category of synchronistic *events* and the wider *principle* of synchronicity which, as already mentioned in Chapter One, he postulated in his essay as an acausal ordering principle to complement the dominant Western principle of causality.

Jung considered these two 'principles' to represent the characteristic cognitive orientations of East and West, and concerning the relationship between them he wrote: 'Long experience with the products of the unconscious has taught me that there is a very remarkable parallelism between the specific character of the Western unconscious psyche and the "manifest" psyche of the East.'[40] In other words, according to Jung, in the East the style of thinking is *naturally* synchronistic, while in the West synchronicity occurs in association with the surfacing of unconscious contents, often in critical situations.[41] In the West, therefore, it is the *unconscious* that has the tendency towards wholeness, while in the East it is the *waking* consciousness that, in Jung's words, 'is characterised by an apperception of totality', in contrast to the waking consciousness of the West, which 'has developed a differentiated and therefore necessarily one-sided attention or awareness'. He continues:

> With it goes the Western concept of causality, a principle irreconcilably opposed to the principle of synchronicity which forms the basis and the source of Eastern 'incomprehensibility', and explains as well the 'strangeness' of the unconscious with which we in the West are confronted. The understanding of synchronicity is the key which unlocks the door to the Eastern apperception of totality that we find so mysterious.[42]

It should be remarked in passing that it is the traditional Eastern outlook, in particular that of the Far East, which Jung is commenting on, not the ubiquitous veneer of Western materialism and consumerism that has had such a powerful global impact since the end of World War II. And if the traditional thinking style of the East does have a fundamentally synchronistic orientation, as Jung asserts, it by no means implies that analytical thought must necessarily conflict with this orientation, despite the fact that this has been very much the case in the

West. Indeed, there is no intrinsic reason why the two cannot fruitfully coexist: one only has to look at the scientific and technological achievements of China and Japan prior to the seventeenth century, and again during the twentieth century, to appreciate this.

The sheer number of scientific inventions emerging out of China and later adopted in the West is staggering, and has been meticulously documented by Joseph Needham and his colleagues in the multi-volumed *Science and Civilisation in China*. Needham attributes this remarkable scientific fecundity in no small part to the Taoist attitude of *wu wei*, which translates literally as 'non-action' but has the deeper meaning of observing without conceptual interference.[43] According to Needham, 'The ability to practice *wu wei* implied learning from Nature by observation. This, in its turn, brought the Taoist to a scientific approach; by an almost imperceptible transition, it led him to experimentation, and was of capital importance for the whole development of science and technology in China.'[44] At its most pellucid and least superstitious, the synchronistic mindset of Taoist China was as affirming of scientific innovation as it later became in the West, though in China this innovatory attitude was not sustained.

As to why Chinese science failed to develop was for Needham the 'sixty-four thousand dollar question'.[45] One reason for this must surely have been the invasion of the Mongols during the thirteenth century and the devastating long-term effects this had on every region they plundered and pillaged. Another is that mathematics was never separated from religious and magical symbolism, and this was mirrored in the revered place of the *I Ching* as a classificatory system for all things under heaven, an enormously inhibiting factor for scientific progress, especially of the 'modern' kind. Needham contrasts the openness of the Taoist *wu wei* approach with the classificatory constraints of the *I Ching*, and suggests that early scholars would perhaps 'have been wiser to tie a millstone around the neck of the *I Ching* and cast it into the sea'.[46] Had the use of the *I Ching*, with its amalgamation of imagery and number, been restricted to divination, its effect on the development of Chinese science would have been much less pernicious.[47]

The *I Ching* was also incorporated into the bureaucratic structure of Chinese governance, but this in itself was of less significance than the sheer size and organisational complexity of China's vast feudal bureaucracy which as a result became far more stifling and moribund than the comparatively tiny baronial fiefdoms of the West. So while China stagnated, the social and political ferment of feudal Europe gave birth not only to the Scientific Revolution but also to Protestantism and entrepreneurial capitalism as well, in what Needham calls a 'package deal'.⁴⁸ This was in marked contrast to the contemporaneous situation in China, as Needham informs the reader in his 1985 introduction to Robert Temple's *The Genius of China*: 'Modern research is showing that the bureaucratic organisation of China in its earlier stages strongly helped science to grow; only in its later ones did it forcibly inhibit further growth, and in particular prevented a breakthrough which has occurred in Europe.'⁴⁹

But whatever the reasons for the demise of Chinese science, consideration must be taken of an inherent instability in the synchronistic mindset of the Far East, comparable to the instability underlying the one-sided analytical mindset of the West. History is replete with examples of the destructiveness of both, epitomised in the twentieth century by the horrors unleashed, respectively, by Japan and Germany prior to and during World War II.

In his article 'Zen and the Art of Divebombing, or The Dark Side of the Tao', the philosopher Kelley Ross considers the social ramifications arising from the incorporation of the *tao* into Chinese Ch'an Buddhism, later to become Japanese Zen. The appropriation of the *tao* itself was only part of the package: with it came Taoist aesthetics and the celebration of the beauty of nature through poetry, calligraphy and painting. As Ross puts it, 'The Taoist purpose of art is to perfect an art and achieve beauty. These are purposes *wholly alien* to Buddhism. Back in India, the idea that Buddhism might be used to achieve beauty in life would be absolutely farcical.'⁵⁰ The overriding purpose of Buddhism was to attain freedom from the suffering of the world, a very different goal from that of Taoism. As a religion, Buddhism in all its various forms has always been much more regimented and sharply defined than Taoism, and when the natural harmony of the *tao* was transmuted into the *satori* or sudden enlightenment of Zen, it was accompanied by a fierce authoritarian asceticism. Ross cites a teaching story from Paul Reps' *Zen Flesh, Zen Bones* which gives an indication of just how ruthless this tradition could be:

> Gutei raised his finger whenever he was asked a question about Zen. A boy attendant began to imitate him in this way. When anyone asked the boy what his master had preached about, the boy would raise his finger.
>
> Gutei heard about the boy's mischief. He seized him and cut off his finger. The boy cried and ran away. Gutei called and stopped him. When the boy turned his head to Gutei, Gutei raised up his own finger. In that instant the boy was enlightened.⁵¹

While the commentary on this story by the master Mumon is critical of Gutei, it is not an isolated example of gratuitous violence in the service of Zen enlightenment. Another story concerns the master Nansen cutting a cat in two to teach his monks a lesson, and yet another celebrates the ease with which Bodhidharma, the legendary figure who first brought Buddhism to China, was able to bring enlightenment to his only disciple when the latter offered him his severed arm with the request that he pacify his mind.[52] These stories are from a thirteenth-century Chinese collection and later became part of the Japanese Zen tradition, which was favoured not only by Buddhist monks but by much of the samurai elite. Ross argues that the brutal Japanese militarism of the first half of the twentieth century had its roots in the samurai warrior code and thereby in Zen. Evidence of this can be seen in the training manual given to Kamikaze pilots.[53] These young pilots were clearly engaged in the practice of a martial art or 'do' (meaning 'tao' as in *judo*, *kendo*, *aikido* and *taekwondo* in Korea), as can be seen from the following exhortation translated from the manual: 'In order that you can exert the highest possible capability, you must prepare well your inner self. Some people say that spirit must come first before skill, but they are wrong. Spirit and skill are one. The two elements must be mastered together. Spirit supports skill and skill supports spirit.'[54]

Ross also criticises the 'aestheticisation of violence' that is so central a feature of the martial arts. He considers it to be 'necessarily offensive to both Confucianism and Buddhism, and would be an unexpected and unwelcome possibility to Taoism'.[55] Ironically, however, the current popular conception of Taoism, as promoted in Kung Fu films and worldwide training academies, continues to engage in this aestheticisation of violence, a resonant echo of the catastrophic misappropriation of the *tao* of the *Tao Te Ching*, whose last words are, in Lau's translation:

> The way of heaven benefits and does not harm;
> The way of the sage is bountiful and does not contend.[56]

But the way of the sage and the myriad facets of human nature will inevitably clash: the history of Taoism is filled with all manner of ritualistic and magical practice, from the ceremonial worship of deities and divinatory methods like *feng-shui* to talismanic magic spells and the pursuit of both external and internal alchemy. External alchemy involved the ingestion of herbs and minerals, using the human body as a crucible to create the elixir of immortality, while internal alchemy pursued the same goal through the cultivation of *yin* and *yang* energies presumed to exist within the body.[57] A serious consequence of the practice of external alchemy was poisoning, resulting in extremely toxic effects on the spleen and liver and possible madness or death.[58]

Internal alchemy was a healthier choice and used meditational and yogic techniques to achieve its aims, including Taoist methods of sexual alchemy 'as a pragmatic way of gathering generative energy, especially for those who were no longer young and healthy'.[59] Taoist ideas were also used for politics and warfare, and much of the *Tao Te Ching* is concerned with such matters, as in these lines from Chapter 69: 'The strategists have a saying... "I will not advance an inch but retreat a foot instead"... There is no disaster greater than taking on an enemy too easily."[60] Since the *Tao Te Ching* was most likely written or compiled during the Warring States Period, between the fifth and third centuries BCE, this focus may not be entirely surprising, and shows how practical the application of Taoist principles and strategies could be. Chinese poetry and painting were also profoundly influenced by Taoism, as evident in this eighth-century commentary:

> When I sense the vigour of Chang Tsao's painting, I see no longer a painting—I see *Tao*. When painting, he leaves behind mere skills and measurements and his thoughts vanish into the creative night. The things brought out are not from the consciousness of the eye and the ear, but from the Spiritual Court. What he achieves in his heart is made known by his hand.[61]

Although Taoism is several centuries older than Christianity, it coalesced into a formal religion at around the same time, during the Eastern Han dynasty, which coincided with the first two centuries of the Christian era.[62] The start of the first millennium also marks the end of the period of philosophical Taoism, although there is serious doubt as to whether philosophical or classical Taoism, as represented in the *Tao Te Ching*, ever existed in any coherent form.[63] Nevertheless, it is generally held that during the second century BCE, the *tao* of the classical era became increasingly associated with alchemy and the pursuit of physical immortality, as evident in an influential Taoist text of that period, the *Huai Nan Tzu*.[64]

The sinologist and translator Lionel Giles, writing in the early years of the twentieth century, considered this period to be the start of what is sometimes described as the 'degeneration' of Taoism.[65] And employing a felicitous turn of phrase that might not be quite as acceptable in the twenty-first century, he wondered at the degree of despondency Lao Tzu would have felt 'could he have foreseen how his pure and idealistic teaching was destined to be dragged in the mire of degrading superstition, which for centuries has made Taoism a byword of reproach. Though frequently described as one of the "three religions of China", this cult is really little more than an inextricable mass of jugglery and fraud... conducted by a body of priests recruited from the very dregs of the Empire'.[66] Even if he had imbibed more than the normal portion of the heady imperialism of the era, for Giles to have been so scathing in the introduction to his translation of the *Tao Te Ching* shows how great the gulf between classical Taoism, in all its perceived purity, and popular religious Taoism had become. In contrast, Giles had only praise for the depth of vision bequeathed by Taoism over the centuries to Chinese literature and art, which, in his opinion, 'is hardly to be over-estimated', as is its historical importance of as a creative foil against 'the uncompromising stiffness of the Confucian ideal'.[67]

Accessing the *Tao*

According to Chang Chung-yuan, author of *Creativity and Taoism*, there have traditionally been two routes to enter into harmony with or 'attain' the *tao*.[68] One of these is through the practice of quiescence as advocated in various forms of Chinese yoga and meditation, allusions to which are evident in the *Tao Te Ching*.[69] Far more concrete and specific directions are to be found in later texts such as *The Secret of the Golden Flower*, first available in print during the eighteenth century.[70] By that time Taoist meditation had become thoroughly blended with internal alchemy and Buddhist practices, an unabashed syncretism that made active use of parallel ideas from different traditions to push a point home, as in the following excerpt from *The Secret of the Golden Flower*: 'All holy men have bequeathed this to one another: nothing is possible without contemplation. When Confucius says, "Perceiving brings one to the goal"; or when the Buddha calls it, "The vision of the heart"; or Lao-tse says, "Inner vision", it is all the same.'[71]

If one route to harmonising with the *tao* has been by way of focused contemplative practice, the other is through, as Chang puts it: 'direct, immediate, pre-ontological experience, which is intuitive, concrete and purposeless'.[72] This way of accessing the *tao* is very much in accord both with the flash of immediate insight or 'absolute knowledge' accompanying a synchronistic experience and Jung's characterisation of the *unus mundus* as 'the latent unity of the world'.[73] And it is this latent unity that breaks through in synchronistic events when, as von Franz puts it, 'everything happening in time is experienced as if gathered up into a timeless objective oneness'.[74]

The attainment and expression of the *tao* as a timeless and objective oneness was also the goal of traditional Chinese poetry and art, the empty spaces in landscape paintings symbolically infused with the 'living nothingness' of the *tao*.[75] Through pen and brush, artists and scholars, limited only by the depth of their personal attunement with the *tao* and the physical constraints of their craft, attempted to express the ineffable and inexpressible, despite the inevitable logical inconsistency associated with any such aspiration. This inconsistency had, however, already been foreseen by Chuang Tzu, for whom paradox was no stranger: 'Heaven and earth and I live together, and all things and I are One. Since we are all One, how can we express the One? If we express the One, our expression and the One become two.'[76]

Lau points out that 'the One' was very often used as another name for the *tao*,[77] and according to Chang, its direct intuition—the goal of those aspiring to attain the *tao*—is simultaneously 'the One' and yet not 'the One'; it is 'the One' *prior* to its formation as 'the One'. It is thus a *latent* oneness: in Chuang Tzu's words, 'It is where the One emerges before the One is formed.'[78] Zen Buddhism would later have little to do with such subtleties, and in a sixth-century Ch'an text we find such statements as: 'The truth has no distinctions; these come from our foolish clinging to this and that.' And even more enigmatically pertinent to the notion of 'the One', or indeed the *tao* itself: 'When both [this and that] cease to be, how can the unity subsist?'[79]

From an analytical perspective, however, Chuang Tzu's differentiation is an important one, particularly in relation to whether the *tao* is to be understood as *ontological*, in other words, as equivalent to 'existence itself', or as a *pre-ontological* 'backdrop' to existence and all that it entails, a conception that may well turn out to be of some relevance to the final questions of cosmology. Indeed, if such a thing were possible, the *tao* could be an ideal 'compromise candidate' for a conception of an ultimate origin that might actually be able to satisfy both theists and atheists, at least those whose views are not too intractable. As to whether the *tao* is conscious or intelligent, which seems to be the biggest bone of contention between theists and atheists as regards any ultimate explanation of the universe, philosophical Taoism appears to have little to say, and were it to pronounce on the topic, it would most likely do so through paradox.

What Taoism *does* say, however, is that the primordial intuition of the *tao* is both accessible and expressible, particularly for the genuine 'man of *tao*', archetypically portrayed in Chuang Tzu's stories of Prince Wen Hui's cook and Duke Hwan's wheelwright, and poetically recounted by Thomas Merton in his *The Way of Chuang Tzu*.[80] For whatever reason, the injunction to attain the *tao*, whether conceived of in those terms or as Buddhist enlightenment, became quintessentially important in the traditional arts of the Far East. So even though philosophical Taoism was largely subsumed during the Han dynasty into a wider Taoist syncretism of religion and magic, its core ideas reemerged, reinvigorated no doubt by the mutual exchange with early Chinese Buddhism, and found expression in many centuries of literary and artistic accomplishment. A stunning example of the latter is depicted in Fig. 18, though not in the original colour or size:

Fig. 18: *Fishermen's Evening Song* by Xu Daoning (970—1052).[81]

The ability to express the *tao* through brush and ink represents what the painter and writer Mai-mai Sze describes as the 'great unifying aim' of Chinese art.[82] This was never a theoretical hypothesis to be debated, nor a topic for speculative conjecture, but rather an artistically expressible objective attainment, immediately apparent to the discerning eye. Regarding the great Chinese poets such as Li Po and Wang Wei, both active during the Tang dynasty, the golden age of Chinese poetry, Chang writes: 'They owe a great debt to the ancient Taoists who taught that the contemplation of the utmost in quietude will lead to the hidden recesses of creative power and that it is from this realm that beauty is manifested to the objective world.'[83] The cultivation of this insight at the heart of Chinese aesthetics became extremely influential not only within Taoist and Buddhist circles but also for Confucianism, which is clearly evident in this brief poem by the Song dynasty Neo-Confucian scholar, Chu Hsi:

> The wide pond expands like a mirror,
> The heavenly light and cloud shadows play upon it.
> How does such clarity occur?
> It is because it contains the living stream from the Fountain.[84]

The living stream of creativity in nature is reflected in Chu Hsi's ability to mirror that stream in his own creative expression, attuned as he would have been as part of his self-cultivation to the primordial unity of both his own nature and that of the natural world. The cultural significance of such an understanding of aesthetics was far-reaching and profound. Chinese influence on Korea and Japan meant that they too were imbued with the subtleties of the Taoist approach to nature and art, although with their own idiosyncratic adaptations, understandably so in view of the fact that Taoism was never part of the direct heritage of either culture. Thus, in the northern Japanese prefecture of Yamagata, above the town of Yamadera, there is a statue of the celebrated poet Basho, with an inscription of a *haiku* poem he composed when staying at the mountain temple there during his famous journey to the north in 1689.[85] Basho's trip could be described as an aesthetic pilgrimage, a combination of an outer and an inner journey that he endeavoured to encapsulate in his *haiku*. The Yamadera *haiku* is a particularly well-known one in Japan and at the statue itself, for the benefit of foreign visitors, an English translation is provided:

> Silence.
> The voice of the cicada
> Penetrates the rocks.

Both this *haiku* and Chu Hsi's twelfth-century poem, with which Basho may well have been familiar, are examples of what might be described as *cultivated* synchronicity, a momentary fusion of subject and object achieved through a deliberate aesthetic attitude and an attunement with the *tao*, whether that would have been the term of choice for either the Confucian Chu Hsi or the Buddhist Basho. Both poems display an interpenetration or merging of the poet's subjective perception with the surrounding objective circumstances, which is very much what takes place during a synchronistic event. The main difference is that the poet *deliberately* pursues, or at least welcomes, any glimpse of epiphanic insight, while in a synchronistic experience the numinous moment of meaning-equivalence is entirely unexpected.

The West also has a literary tradition that cultivates the felt unity of mind and nature, though its manner of expression is naturally rooted in a very different type of discourse and conception of reality. A vivid example is Richard Jeffries' *The Story of my Heart*, first published in 1883, where in paragraph after breathtaking paragraph he describes in a rich and fluent prose his rapt wonder at the beauty of the English countryside. The way in which his subjective sense of self is intimately absorbed in his surroundings is in marked contrast to the *tao*-infused simplicity and restraint that characterises Far Eastern poetry, and distinctly more passionate and prayerful in its overt expression. With Jeffries the experience was not so much cultivated as an ecstasy in nature that came to him unbidden. If his experiences were to be described as synchronistic, then it would not be the usual type of meaningful coincidence as identified by Jung but more an opening to the vast and timeless cosmic coincidence that we are all embedded in and which, in theory, should fill us with unceasing wonder that life exists at all:

> I was aware of the grass blades, the flowers, the leaves on hawthorn and tree. I seemed to live more largely through them, as if each were a pore through which I drank. The grasshoppers called and leaped, the greenfinches sang, the blackbirds happily fluted, all the air hummed with life. I was plunged deep in existence and with all that existence I prayed.
>
> Through every grass blade in the thousand, thousand grasses; through the million leaves, veined edge-cut, on bush and tree; through the song-notes and the marked feathers of the birds; through the insects'

hum and the colour of the butterflies; through the soft warm air, the flecks of clouds dissolving — I used them all for prayer.[86]

The *Tao* Turns West

European fascination with China began in earnest during the seventeenth century, particularly as a result of the inroads made by the Jesuit missionary Mateo Ricci and later Jesuits including Leibnitz's correspondent Father Joachim Bouvet, mentioned in Chapter One. Both Leibniz and the French philosopher Nicolas Malebranche wrote on Chinese themes at the turn of the eighteenth century, and in subsequent decades there was a great deal of interest in Confucian philosophy, stimulated in particular by Christian Wolff in Germany and Voltaire in France.[87] A Latin translation of the *Tao Te Ching* was first presented in Europe in 1788, and in 1816 during a lecture in Heidelberg, Hegel was able to tell the audience he had actually seen a copy of the text when it was taken to Vienna. His conception of the *tao* was of a Platonic universal and he identified it, following the European tradition, as 'reason' or 'abstract Being'. But he also regarded Taoist philosophy as simplistic and at an elementary stage in comparison with the sophistication of European philosophical thinking.[88]

Such attitudes became increasingly common in the nineteenth century, particularly with the popularity and success of social Darwinism and associated theories, which meant that, as J.J. Clarke in his *The Tao of the West* puts it, '…the ossified religions of China could conveniently be allotted a place on the evolutionary ladder well below the Christian West.'[89] These attitudes, however, began to soften in the twentieth century with Lionel Giles in 1905 describing the *Tao Te Ching* as 'the well-defined though rudimentary outline of a great system of transcendental and ethical philosophy'.[90] In 1910, Richard Wilhelm published his translation of the text in German, and through his sensitive pen the *tao* was brought to life with an inspired freshness that helped lay the foundations for an ever-increasing interest in the *tao* as a philosophically and psychologically relevant conception. For instance, in his introduction Wilhelm gives a remarkable insight into the nature of the 'emptiness' of the *tao*, an interpretation that has no trace of the European chauvinism of the time, and one which more than a century later modern scholarship would find hard to better:

> Lao Zi's 'non-existence'… is not simply the same as nothingness, but something qualitatively different from existence. DAO is in all things but is not itself a thing. Its effectiveness is essentially qualitative. An analogy can be found in the laws of nature. The laws of physics are expressed in all phenomena, but are not something distinct and separable, capable of interfering with the course of events from the

> outside. In the same way Lao Zi's DAO is present in all that happens: it can be left or right [Chapter 34] but it is not exhausted in anything that happens. This non-exhaustion or, as Lao Zi puts it, this 'non filling-up', is the quality that makes it superior to all things, without this superiority ever expressing itself in any way. This non-expression of superiority, this 'weakness', can be called its smallness, while its all-pervading effectiveness in all things accounts for its 'greatness'.[91]

Wilhelm spent twenty years as a missionary in China and was very proud of the fact that during that time he never baptised a single Chinese.[92] Instead, he submerged himself in learning the language and cultural traditions and after a decade produced his translation of the *Tao Te Ching*. His great accomplishment, however, was not this but rather his meticulously prepared translation of the *I Ching*, which was much more for him than a scholarly project. Arthur Waley, who himself produced a highly acclaimed version of the *Tao Te Ching* in 1934, made an interesting distinction in regard to translations of sacred books: between those that he called historical, in other words translations of the original meaning of a text; and those that he called 'scriptural', which aim at conveying to the reader what the 'text means to those who use it today'. He also regarded Wilhelm's version of the *I Ching* as 'the most perfect example of scriptural translation',[93] and considering how wide the field of choice would have been by the 1930s, that is praise indeed.

Wilhelm had the good fortune in 1911 to meet and subsequently collaborate with Lao Nai-hsüan, a traditional scholar with considerable understanding of the *I Ching*. Their method of collaboration required first a detailed discussion of the meaning of the text. Wilhelm then translated it into German and then back into Chinese, and only when the full meaning emerged would they consider the translation complete. World War I proved to be a serious interruption, and Lao had to leave Qingdao, where Wilhelm was in charge of the Chinese Red Cross.[94] But he eventually returned, to Wilhelm's great joy, and they were able to finish the full translation. Of this last phase Wilhelm wrote: 'Those were rare hours of inspiration I spent with my aged master. When the work in its essential features was almost finished, fate called me back to Germany. In the meantime my venerable master departed this world.'[95]

Wilhelm was thus able to render the *I Ching* into German as a living document, unlike the partial Latin translation of the Jesuit Jean-Baptiste Régis, with which Leibniz was acquainted, or the various scholarly versions of the late nineteenth century, which included the first English translation, that of the Scottish missionary James Legge, who considered much of the text 'grotesque'.[96] And it was with Legge's translation that Jung in 1920 spent the whole of the summer holidays experimenting with the *I Ching* to see whether its answers were genuinely meaningful. In his memoir he recalls again and again experiencing amazing coincidences in this intense personal enquiry, which suggested to him that an acausal parallelism was at play, an idea that he was later to identify as synchronicity.[97] It may well be that had he *not* engaged with the *I Ching* in this way, Jung might never have arrived at the idea of synchronicity. Indeed, the religion writer Harold Coward has gone so far as to suggest that the whole notion of synchronicity is directly dependent on the *I Ching*.[98]

Whether that is the case or not, in terms of his ongoing theoretical clarification it was certainly fortuitous for Jung to meet Wilhelm in the early twenties on the latter's return from China. Not only did Wilhelm concur with Jung's perspective on meaningful connections,[99] his newly available translation of the *I Ching* was for Jung both a revelation and a confirmation of his growing sense of the reality of an acausal factor underpinning meaningful coincidences: 'Before I came to know Wilhelm's translation, I had for years worked with Legge's inadequate rendering, and was therefore in a position to recognise fully the extraordinary difference between the two. Wilhelm has succeeded in bringing to life again, in a new and vital form, this ancient work...'[100]

What was particularly brought to life for Jung and others who had access to Wilhelm's version was the *tao* itself. No longer simply an interesting and perhaps useful philosophical notion, readily compartmentalised as an analogous Chinese equivalent of various religious and philosophical conceptions of an absolute, the *tao* could be intuited *directly* as the connecting principle between the objective physical world and the subjective psychological world. Jung saw the *I Ching* as a way of *generating* an experience of the *tao* and considered Wilhelm's achievement to be of the utmost significance: '...he has transmitted to us the living germ of the Chinese spirit, capable of working an essential change in our view of life.'[101]

This essential change is the realisation that at the interface of the inner and outer worlds there is a still point that can be accessed at any time. This generally requires attentiveness and training, and almost certainly would have been a major element of what Wilhelm learned from Lao, with whom he appears to have had the benefit of a traditional student-master relationship. Far from being a superstitious or pathological regression, such disciplined attunement is at the very pinnacle of self-cultivation for philosophical Taoism; and, under the direction of an experienced practitioner, the *I Ching* could be of enormous benefit in helping consolidate the intuited presence of the *tao*. Jung was very aware of this and that is why he was so grateful to Wilhelm:

> Anyone who, like myself, has had the rare good fortune to experience in a spiritual exchange with Wilhelm the divinatory power of the *I Ching*, cannot for long remain ignorant of the fact that we have touched here an Archimedean point from which our Western attitude of mind could be shaken to its foundations.[102]

New Ways of Thinking

Another major Western intellectual figure profoundly shaken by the Archimedean point of the *tao*, though through the *Tao Te Ching* rather than the *I Ching*, was the German philosopher Martin Heidegger, whose reputation was seriously dented by revelations of Nazi sympathies during the 1930s, to the extent that after the war he was barred from teaching for a number of years.[103] Unsurprisingly, 1946 was a particularly difficult year for Heidegger, with probing questions raised publically concerning the extent of his involvement with the Nazi Party and therefore his future fitness as a university professor in post-war Germany.[104] But it was in this year that he met with the Chinese scholar Paul Hsaio Shih-yi to collaborate on a possible translation of the *Tao Te Ching* into German, and even though the project never came to fruition, both Hsaio and Heidegger's student Otto Pöggeler considered that this involvement marked a fundamental shift in Heidegger's thinking.[105] The upshot of this new direction in Heidegger's thought was his call for a *completely different* type of thinking, 'more sober than the irresistible race of rationalisation… outside of the distinction of rational and irrational… without effect and yet having its own necessity'.[106]

The way of thinking Heidegger consistently points towards in his later writings is meditative in character and has the distinct quality of a pulling back from abstract conceptualisation into a contemplative dwelling, as indicated in this sentence from one of his poems: 'To think is to confine yourself to a single thought that one day stands still like a star in the world's sky.'[107] In the introduction to his translation of the *Tao Te Ching*, published shortly before Heidegger's death, Chang Chung-yuan pays homage to Heidegger, whom he describes as 'the only Western philosopher who not only intellectually understands *tao*, but has intuitively experienced the essence of it as well'.[108] It would, of course, have been very difficult for Chang to back up this assertion in any kind of realistic way. Still, for him as a respected Chinese scholar even to suggest such a possibility is both remarkable and significant, and also indicates how close in actual substance Heidegger's later philosophy was to the core insights of the Far East. And it may well be that Heidegger was much more indebted to the philosophical traditions of East Asia than he realized—or was at least prepared publically to acknowledge.[109]

In a poignant account of his many years' association with Heidegger, Hsiao describes an unusual event which occurred in the beautiful Black Forest city of Freiburg, where Heidegger resided, during the bombing of late 1944. As a civilian centre Freiburg had been considered exempt, so it was all the more devastating when, unexpectedly, Allied bombs fell for the first time on November 27. In those days, there also resided in Freiburg an enormous duck, well known to regular visitors to the city park. On the day of the air-raid the duck started to quack and flap around frantically, continuing non-stop for twelve hours, thus warning the inhabitants that danger was afoot. The duck was sadly killed in the raid but its incessant quacking had been taken seriously and apparently saved many lives. A decade later a monument was erected to its memory, with the inscription 'God's creature laments, accuses and warns'.[110] Hsiao considers this incident significant because it demonstrates a fundamental difference in the thinking styles between Europe and China: the European would ask why the duck was so animated at that particular time and then perhaps even look for parapsychological answers, while for the Chinese 'the duck does not need any paranormal powers: everything is connected to everything else and in each moment there is concealed the entire past and also the open future.'[111]

This is a marvellous example of synchronistic thinking, and as Hsiao gently points out, '...temporality has always been understood differently in China than in the West.'[112] Despite a certain circumspect modesty in his writing, Hsiao gives the impression that Heidegger, with whom he was already personally acquainted, was profoundly touched during the course of their first encounter after the war. In December 1945, Heidegger had suffered a breakdown and so had to spend three weeks in a sanatorium.[113] At that time he was undergoing very stressful questioning in the course of de-Nazification proceedings and remained deeply affected when in 1946 he met Hsaio in the centre of a still devastated Freiberg. Heidegger spoke to him of the personal torment he was experiencing, to which Hsiao responded, finishing with the following quotation from Mencius:

> Mencius said: 'If heaven wants to impose a difficult task on someone, it first fills his heart and will with bitterness, rots his sinew and bones, starves his frame, imposes great poverty on his body, and confounds his undertakings, so that his heart will be inspired, his nature stimulated and his deficiencies remedied… From all these things we learn that life

arises out of anxiety and care, misery and privation; and that death on the other hand is the product of comforts and pleasure.'

Heidegger appeared to be quite moved by this quotation. We did not subsequently talk further about this topic. It was at this same meeting that he proposed translating the *Lao-tzu* together. I agreed to the proposal with joy.[114]

They completed only eight chapters of the translation and it was in fact Hsiao rather than Heidegger who pulled out because of other commitments, though he also admits to a fear that Heidegger's interpretation might go beyond the essential requirements of a translation.[115] Nevertheless, Hsiao had the impression that even these few chapters had a significant influence on Heidegger, and at a subsequent lecture in Freiburg Hsiao recalls him stating something to the effect of: 'If you want to prove God's existence by way of any of the traditional proofs, whether ontological, cosmological, teleological, ethical, and so on, you thereby belittle Him, since God is something like the *tao*, which is ineffable.'[116]

Heidegger was to go on to develop his own conceptual parallel to the *tao* in language more amenable to Western academic discourse. The word he coined was 'Appropriation', which Chang identifies directly with the *tao*[117] and also with the 'aesthetic feeling and preontological experience maintained by Chinese artists and philosophers'.[118] Unlike Jung, who was not shy to make cross-cultural correspondences, Heidegger himself was much more hesitant to do so. Thus, his explanation of Appropriation is very subtle and not so easy for the non-specialist to grasp. It would be out of place to try to summarise it here; nevertheless, there is perhaps something rather Taoist in the following attempt by Heidegger to express what Appropriation is *not*: 'Appropriation neither *is*, nor *is* Appropriation *there*. To say the one or to say the other is equally a distortion of the matter, just as if we wanted to derive the source from the river.'[119]

Heidegger took a very different route to that of Jung in the development of his understanding and appreciation of the *tao*, but no doubt a major attraction for both was the conceptual ability of the *tao* to unite the psychological and physical realms of human experience, an organising principle historically absent in the West, as Jung pointed out: 'Unfortunately our Western mind, lacking all culture in this respect, has never yet devised a concept, nor even a name, for the *union of opposites through the middle path*, that most fundamental item of inward experience, which could respectably be set against the Chinese concept of Tao.'[120]

Thus, the *tao* is available as an intermediary or balance point from which mental and material realities can be observed, akin to the head of

Janus looking simultaneously in opposite directions. Janus is also an apt metaphor for what occurs during a synchronistic event, when for the experiencer inner and outer worlds become temporarily fused in a fleeting glimpse of meaning-equivalence. One face gazes at psyche, the other at matter, and it is in the *mind* of Janus that the two visions become united in meaningful correspondence, as with a 3D film or stereogram. The analogy, however, is misleading because the *unus mundus* perception of Janus is not an illusion like the 3D film but rather a *clearing* of illusion. And within every human being there is an unfocused Janus, distractedly looking now to the outer world and now to the inner, rejoicing in those brief moments when the two coincide.

For most this occurs through unexpected epiphanies, moments of unsought oneness triggered perhaps by the ecstasies of love or the beauty of nature, perhaps by a series of remarkable coincidences, and for a few perhaps the fruit of an aesthetic or meditative discipline. Another metaphor is the 'window into eternity', the *fenestra aeternitatis* of the alchemists,[121] symbolically depicted in the *Flammarion Woodcut* (and explored further in the Appendix). While such a vision within medieval alchemy may be considered speculative and unsubstantiated, perception of the *unus mundus* as the *tao* in the profound insights of East Asian arts and philosophy, augmented by centuries of self-cultivation and contemplative practice, simply cannot be dismissed as conjecture.

It is an odd anomaly in our modern and sophisticated age that while the physical sciences are eager to go to very considerable lengths to discover how the physical world is constructed, the mind sciences seem to be just as eager to *avoid* making an equivalent effort to investigate the inner world of the psyche. As with the images in Plato's cave, the mind sciences focus on neural correlates in the brain rather than metaphorically stepping out of the cave and entering into the daylight of direct exploration of mental phenomena. Alan Wallace, author of the provocatively titled *The Taboo of Subjectivity*, sees this as an essentially ideologically motivated refusal to take seriously any description of reality *but* the physical, despite the existence of viable and empirically reproducible project proposals for investigation, by means of direct introspection, into the psyche and its hidden depths.[122] Thus, while there have been the Copernican and Darwinian revolutions in the physical and life sciences, for the mind sciences this is yet to occur. And just as in the Copernican and Darwinian revolutions the Earth's and then man's position became relativised so, according to Wallace, when a revolution in the mind sciences does occur, it will

…relativise the human mind by displacing it from a physical function of the brain to an emergent process arising from a dimension of reality more fundamental than the duality of mind and matter.[123]

Such a revolution within the mainstream mind sciences is yet to take place, and this means that the *tao*, for now, cannot as yet be subjected to the same forensic scrutiny as, for example, the human genome. It must remain within the provenance of philosophy and poetry, inferred rather than directly investigated, despite the invitation by Lao Tzu to put its genuineness to the test. Nevertheless, the *tao*, scientifically proven or not, remains an ineffable stillness around which the worlds turn in both inner and outer space. T.S. Eliot understood this well, as is evident in the following extract from *Burnt Norton*, quoted by Mai-mai Sze in 1954 in her highly acclaimed book on traditional Chinese art, *The Tao of Painting*:

> At the still point of the turning world. Neither flesh nor fleshless;
> Neither from nor towards; at the still point, there the dance is,
> But neither arrest nor movement. And do not call it fixity,
> Where past and future are gathered. Neither movement from nor towards,
> Neither ascent nor decline. Except for the point, the still point,
> There would be no dance, and there is only the dance.[124]

Endnotes

1. Jung, *Mysterium Conjunctionis*, 462.
2. Ibid., 538.
3. Ibid., 464; von Franz, *Psyche and Matter*, 41.
4. Meier, *Atom and Archetype*, 83.
5. Jung, *Mysterium Conjunctionis*, 534.
6. Ibid., 538.
7. Ibid.
8. Ibid., 537.
9. Atmanspacher, 'Quantum Approaches to Consciousness'.
10. Peat, *From Certainty to Uncertainty*, 65.
11. Hampshire, *Spinoza*, 63, 44.
12. Velmans, 'The Unconscious Ground of Being'.
13. Atmanspacher, '20th Century Variants of Dual-Aspect Thinking', 251–253.
14. Atmanspacher, 'Dual-Aspect Monism à la Pauli and Jung', 99.
15. Ibid.; Atmanspacher and Fuchs, *The Pauli-Jung Conjecture*.
16. Jung, *Mysterium Conjunctionis*, 464–465.
17. Gieser, *The Innermost Kernel*, 289n; Meier, *Atom and Archetype*, 75.
18. Rosen, *The Tao of Jung*, xxi.
19. Wilhelm and Jung, *The Secret of the Golden Flower*, 138.
20. Waley, *The Way and its Power*, 30.
21. Ibid., 50.
22. *Oxford English Dictionary Online*, s.v. 'tao'.

23 Chang, *Tao: A New Way of Thinking*, 3.
24 Lau, *Lao Tzu: Tao Te Ching*, 16.
25 Ibid., 17–18.
26 Wilhelm and Jung, *The Secret of the Golden Flower*, xiv.
27 Jung, *Mysterium Conjunctionis*, 465.
28 Ibid., 467–468.
29 Smullyan, *The Tao is Silent*, 5.
30 Ibid., 6–7.
31 Lau, *Lao Tzu: Tao Te Ching*, 177.
32 Smullyan, *The Tao is Silent*, 10.
33 Ibid., 9.
34 Meier, *Atom and Archetype*, 129.
35 Lau, *Lao Tzu: Tao Te Ching*, 20–21.
36 Ibid., 22.
37 Ibid., 101.
38 Smullyan, *The Tao is Silent*, 11.
39 Lau, *Lao Tzu: Tao Te Ching*, 78.
40 Jung, *Psychology and the East*, 211.
41 von Franz, *Projection and Recollection in Jungian Psychology*, 197.
42 Jung, *Psychology and the East*, 212.
43 Chang, *Tao: A New Way of Thinking*, 10.
44 Needham and Ronan, *The Shorter Science and Civilisation in China*, Vol. 1, 98.
45 Needham, introduction to Temple, *The Genius of China*, 7.
46 Needham and Ronan, *The Shorter Science and Civilisation in China*, Vol. 1, 184.
47 Ibid., 183.
48 Needham, introduction to Temple, *The Genius of China*, 7.
49 Ibid., 8.
50 Ross, 'Zen and the Art of Divebombing'.
51 Reps, *Zen Flesh, Zen Bones*, 98.
52 Ibid., 105–106, 125.
53 Axell, 'Notes from a Suicide Manual'.
54 Ibid.
55 Ross, 'Zen and the Art of Divebombing'.
56 Lau, *Lao Tzu: Tao Te Ching*, 143.
57 Wong, *The Shambhala Guide to Taoism*, 66.
58 Ibid., 75.
59 Ibid., 186.
60 Lau, *Lao Tzu: Tao Te Ching*, 131.
61 Chang, *Creativity and Taoism*, 207.
62 Wong, *The Shambhala Guide to Taoism*, 33–36.
63 Welch, *Taoism: The Parting of the Way*, 105; Kirkland, *Taoism: The Enduring Tradition*, 20–22.
64 Welch, *Taoism: The Parting of the Way*, 104–105; Wong, *The Shambhala Guide to Taoism*, 31–33.
65 Giles, *Taoist Teachings from the Book of Lieh Tzu*, 15.
66 Giles, *The Sayings of Lao-Tzu*, 19.
67 Giles, *Taoist Teachings from the Book of Lieh Tzu*, 15.
68 Chang, *Creativity and Taoism*, 123.

69 Ibid., 126; cf. Lau, *Lao Tzu: Tao Te Ching*, 72.
70 Wilhelm and Jung, *The Secret of the Golden Flower*, 3.
71 Ibid., 34.
72 Chang, *Tao: A New Way of Thinking*, xvii.
73 Jung, *Mysterium Conjunctionis*, 465.
74 von Franz, *C.G. Jung: His Myth in Our Time*, 252.
75 Sze, *The Way of Chinese Painting*, 18; Chang, *Tao: A New Way of Thinking*, xvii.
76 Chang, *Tao: A New Way of Thinking*, xvii.
77 Lau, *Lao Tzu: Tao Te Ching*, 16.
78 Chang, *Tao: A New Way of Thinking*, xvii.
79 Blyth, *Zen and Zen Classics, Volume One*, 83, 89.
80 Merton, *The Way of Chuang Tzu*, 25–29, 45–47, 82–83.
81 Source for Fig. 18: by kind permission of Nelson-Atkins Museum of Art, Kansas City, Missouri.
82 Sze, *The Way of Chinese Painting*, 5.
83 Chang, *Creativity and Taoism*, 184.
84 Ibid., 182.
85 Britton, *A Haiku Journey: Basho's 'Narrow Road to a Far Province'*.
86 Jeffries, *The Story of My Heart*, 35–36.
87 Mungello, 'Malebranche and Chinese Philosophy'; Lach, 'The Sinophilism of Christian Wolff'; Guy, 'Voltaire, Sinophile'.
88 Chang, *Tao: A New Way of Thinking*, vii–viii; Clarke, *The Tao of the West*, 42–43.
89 Clarke, *The Tao of the West*, 43.
90 Giles, *The Sayings of Lao-Tzu*, 12.
91 Wilhelm, R., *Tao Te Ching: The book of meaning and life*, 19.
92 Jung, *Memories, Dreams, Reflections*, 409.
93 Waley, *The Way and its Power*, 13.
94 Wilhelm, R., *I Ching or Book of Changes*, xlv.
95 Ibid., xlvi.
96 Clarke, *The Tao of the West*, 60–61.
97 Jung, *Memories, Dreams, Reflections*, 407–408.
98 Coward, 'Taoism and Jung: Synchronicity and the Self', 279.
99 Jung, *Memories, Dreams, Reflections*, 408.
100 Wilhelm and Jung, *The Secret of the Golden Flower*, 140.
101 Ibid.
102 Ibid.
103 Ott, *Martin Heidegger: A Political Life*, 336–348.
104 Ibid., 124–151.
105 Clarke, *The Tao of the West*, 174.
106 Heidegger, *On Time and Being*, 72.
107 Heidegger, *Poetry, Language, Thought*, 4.
108 Chang, *Tao: A New Way of Thinking*, ix.
109 May, *Heidegger's Hidden Sources*, 51–57.
110 Hsiao, 'Heidegger and Our Translation of the Tao Te Ching', 93–94.
111 Ibid., 94.
112 Ibid.
113 Pöggeler, 'West-East Dialogue: Heidegger and Lao-tzu', 51.
114 Hsiao, 'Heidegger and Our Translation of the Tao Te Ching', 96.

115 Ibid., 98.
116 Ibid.
117 Chang, *Tao: A New Way of Thinking*, xii–xiii.
118 Ibid., xxii.
119 Heidegger, *On Time and Being*, 24.
120 Jung, 'The Relations between the Ego and the Unconscious', 205.
121 von Franz, *Number and Time*, 260.
122 Wilber, *The Marriage of Sense and Soul*, 228–233; Wallace, *Hidden Dimensions*, 58–69.
123 Wallace, *Hidden Dimensions*, 12.
124 Sze, *The Tao of Painting*, 29.

Appendix

The *Flammarion Woodcut*

Un missionnaire du moyen âge raconte qu'il avait trouvé le point
où le ciel et la Terre se touchent...

Fig. 19: The original image and caption from page 163 of *L'atmosphère: météorologie populaire*, by Camille Flammarion, 1888.[1]

This widely reproduced image has long captured the popular imagination. Although at one time thought to have been created during the Renaissance, the origin of the woodcut (or more accurately a wood engraving, according to Wikipedia) has been traced to the above work by the astronomer and science writer, Camille Flammarion, whose reason for including this illustration appears have been in order to emphasise the absurdity of the medieval conception of the Earth as the centre of the cosmos. Despite the fact that Flammarion provides no attribution for the woodcut, it is thought that it was specifically commissioned by him.[2] In the text accompanying the picture, he wrote:

> Previous to the knowledge that the Earth was moving in space, and that space is everywhere, theologians had installed the Trinity in the empyrean, the angelic hierarchy, the saints, and all the heavenly host… A missionary of the Middle Ages even tells us that, in one of his voyages in search of the terrestrial paradise, he reached the horizon where the earth and the heavens met, and that he discovered a certain point where they were not joined together, and where, by stooping, he passed under the roof of the heavens… And yet this vault has, in fact, no real existence! I have myself risen higher in a balloon than the Greek Olympus was supposed to be situated, without being able to reach this limit, which, of course, recedes in proportion as one travels in pursuit of it — like the apples of Tantalus.[3]

The woodcut has been very widely reproduced and adapted, especially since the late sixties, when it represented the counter-cultural quest of young 'pilgrims' in search of the secrets of the universe far beyond the 'flat earth' perspective of materialistic society. For example, it was used on the inner sleeve of Donovan's 1973 album, *Cosmic Wheels*. Over the years, the illustration, in various guises, has appeared on cards and posters, in books and brochures, and is widely available on the internet. The details of the woodcut have been interpreted in many different ways, usually with the theme of a transition from ignorance to knowledge, and often with alternative captions. For instance, in *The Mathematical Experience* by Davis and Hersh, accompanying the illustration there is the following caption: 'The astronomer reaches for truth. He is depicted as breaking through the shell of appearances to arrive at an understanding of the fundamental mechanism that lies behind appearances.'[4]

Although, as the science historian Kerry Magruder suggests, Flammarion may have used the picture to ridicule the flat-earth position, it is also known that he was very interested in the paranormal. In 1900, he published a book called *L'inconnu et les problèmes psychiques*, in which featured the superb synchronicity story of M. de Fortgibu and the plum-pudding, as well as the following personal coincidence that occurred when he was writing *L'atmosphère: météorologie populaire*. He had been writing about 'the stange doings of the wind', when a sudden gust blew his papers off the table and out of the window, 'carrying them off in a sort of whirlwind among the trees'.[5] It then started to rain so Flammarion decided it would it would be a waste of time to go and look for them. But a few days later the printer delivered that particular chapter, without a page missing, to an astounded Flammarion.

It turned out that the porter from the printing office, who lived nearby and regularly delivered Flammarion's proof-sheets, had passed by sometime later and found the sodden papers. Thinking he must have dropped them himself, he picked them up carefully and took them to the printing office without telling anyone. Flammarion's general explanation for such meaningful coincidences was that they were due to telepathy, and in reference to this interpretation, Jung makes the following comment: 'The fact that he mentions these coincidences at all in connection with the problem of telepathy shows that Flammarion had a distinct intuition, albeit an unconscious one, of a far more comprehensive principle.'[6]

Jung includes the woodcut as an illustration in his 1958 essay, *Flying Saucers: A Modern Myth of Things Seen in the Skies*. He equates the disc-like shape of flying saucers, as UFOs were known in the 1950s, with the projection of *mandalas* from the unconscious, and one can see why he would have included a picture of someone with his head in another world looking at various unusual circular objects. He makes no reference to Flammarion's *L'atmosphère: météorologie populaire* as the source, and perhaps he was not aware of the connection. Marie-Louise von Franz, who reproduces the image in her *Number and Time: Reflections Leading toward a Unification of Depth Psychology and Physics*, also appears to be uncertain of its origin. This does not prevent her from making good use of the illustration as a pictorial metaphor for synchronicity, and she points out the symbolic significance of two features in particular: the open hole in the fabric of the known world and the functionally untenable double wheel.[7]

The caption under the illustration in *Number and Time* reads: 'The hole open to eternity: the spiritual pilgrim discovers another world.'[8] Such a conception, according to von Franz, comes from medieval alchemy wherein the Virgin Mary, who was identified with matter, was also called 'the window of eternity' or the 'window of escape'.[9] In addition, Gerard Dorn, the alchemist from whom Jung derived the concept of the *unus mundus*,[10] refers to the *spiraculum aeternitatis*, concerning which von Franz provides the following explanation: '*Spiraculum* is an air hole, through which eternity breathes into the temporal world.'[11] She brings these ideas together, with reference to synchronicity, in the text accompanying the illustration:

> In the picture the spiritual pilgrim leaves ordinary space-time behind and gazes through the 'window of eternity', into the world of timeless order, the collective unconscious. Through this 'window', man touches the eternal in himself and at the same time the eternal can reach into his

time-bound world in the form of synchronistic events. The double wheel, representing here Ezekiel's vision, should be noted.[12]

Double mandalas, or wheels, have traditionally been used as symbols for the intersection of linear time with the timeless, and were regularly employed in divinatory practices, usually with one wheel fixed, and the other over it, moving.[13] The double wheel from Ezekiel's vision[14] represents a common way of modelling the intersection of the wheels of time and eternal order. Even though the representation implies that one of the wheels is moving, in engineering terms this is impossible. Because we *cannot* imagine how they are functionally linked, we cannot therefore conceive of a rule or fixed law for their coordination. This, for von Franz, is a clue as to why regular laws for the occurrence of synchronistic events, which in Jung's theoretical model occur when there is a spontaneous and unpredictable coming together of the two realms, cannot be established. In her book, *On Divination and Synchronicity*, she provides a diagram to depict the intersection of the wheels,[15] as shown below; after that her commentary on the woodcut continues:

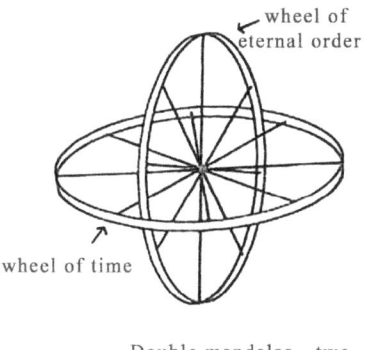

Double mandalas—two sorts of time.

Fig. 20: Double Mandalas[16]

This double wheel confronts us with one of the most difficult problems posed by the motif of the double (timeless and temporal) mandalas: Are the two systems in any way 'interlocked'? In other words, is it possible that synchronistic events may be *regular* manifestations? Certainly all the models of the timeless as well as the time-bound mandalas possess an internally ordered structure, but the manner in which they contact each other remains obscure. When they consist of wheels, for instance, they do not work in unison but are *contiguous at the centre*, which is a technical impossibility. *The two systems are incommensurable.* From this we can only conclude that the moments of contact occur when a spontaneous action emanates from their common centre. This conclusion agrees with the empirical evidence that synchronistic events occur, as far as we can see, only sporadically and irregularly.[17]

> The mysterious point of contact between the two systems appears to be the centre or a sort of pivot where psyche and matter meet. When an individual enters into relation with the forces of the pivot, he finds himself close to the source of 'miracles' which seemingly could not occur without a corresponding attitude on his part... When such a constellation exists and eternity breaks through momentarily into our temporal system, the primal unity actively manifests itself and temporarily unites the double structures into one, so to speak. This is how the *unus mundus* becomes revealed in the phenomenon of synchronicity. But immediately afterward the flow of events resumes its course on the track of the ordinary temporal pattern, and the timeless order falls back into the latent condition once more.[18]

Flammarion himself might have been bemused by this intricate interpretation, although considering the underlying conflict between his abiding fascination with the paranormal and his public reputation as a populariser of science (Magruder describes him as the 'Carl Sagan of the Nineteenth Century'), these opposing interests may have fortuitously come together in an illustrative masterpiece that has without question stood the test of time. A similar juxtaposition, and one of much greater artistic and historical significance, can be found in *The Karamazov Brothers*, which Freud described as 'the most magnificent novel ever written'.[19] Dostoevsky's primary aim was to explore the nature of goodness, particularly though his 'hero', Alyosha,[20] but the fascination of the work lies primarily in the portrayal of Alyosha's deeply flawed father and brothers. When conscious and unconscious energies are displayed in artistic harmony, the result, at its best, is an intrinsic completeness that is naturally able to communicate itself to the eye of the beholder.

Endnotes

1. Source for Fig. 19: http://johnsteins.com/is-the-flammarion-woodcut-medieval.html.
2. Magruder, 'Is this a Medieval Flat-Earth Woodcut?'
3. Ibid.
4. Davis, Hersh and Marchisotto, *The Mathematical Experience*, 77.
5. Inglis, *Coincidence*, 3.
6. Jung, *Synchronicity*, 21.
7. von Franz, *Number and Time*, 261–264.
8. Ibid., 262.
9. von Franz, *On Divination and Synchronicity*, 109.
10. Meier, *Atom and Archetype*, 128–129.
11. von Franz, *On Divination and Synchronicity*, 109.
12. von Franz, *Number and Time*, 261.
13. von Franz, *On Divination and Synchronicity*, 99.
14. Ezekiel 1: 16–17.

15 von Franz, *On Divination and Synchronicity*, 108.
16 Source for Fig. 20: Ibid.
17 von Franz, *Number and Time*, 261-262.
18 Ibid., 263.
19 Dostoevsky, *The Karamazov Brothers*, back cover.
20 Ibid., 5.

Afterword

One of the main aims of this book has been to try to develop an integrated approach to the study of coincidences. This would seem on first consideration to be a fairly straightforward task, and the four broad categories suggested—a) random chance; b) natural causality; c) supernatural causality; d) synchronicity—do genuinely represent the four main ways in which coincidences are customarily explained. At least, this is what I have tried to demonstrate, bearing in mind that there will obviously be differences of opinion regarding which category or combination of categories would be the most appropriate in specific instances. In fact, this latter point is potentially much more problematic than the actual classification, for the simple reason that the field of coincidence research, from the fine-tuning of the constants of nature to the veracity or otherwise of ESP, can so easily become an ideological battleground.

This is not made any easier by the implications of Jung's synchronicity hypothesis which, if taken at face value, suggests that there is a psychophysically neutral realm out of which both mind and matter have emerged. Not that Jung was alone in articulating a dual aspect conception of reality: in addition to his proposal of a *unus mundus*, there are, for example, Bernard d'Espagnat's notion of a veiled reality and also David Bohm's conception of an implicate order behind the explicate order of our apparently dualistic everyday existence.[1] And as was quoted at the end of Chapter Four, Wolfgang Pauli, Jung's chief collaborator in the development of his theory of synchronicity, was of the opinion that: 'It would be most satisfactory of all if psyche and physis could be seen as complementary aspects of the same reality.'[2]

Precisely because such a conception seems to be required for synchronicity to be considered as a genuine phenomenon in itself and not simply as an interpretive overlay resulting from the surprise factor associated with an unexpected coincidence, it could be difficult for those who tend towards a physicalist conception of existence to take Jung and Pauli's hypothesis seriously, or for that matter, any kind of dual aspect theory. But this does not automatically imply that the four-part categorisation proposed here should be rejected as inadequate, for there is no reason why it cannot be used fruitfully as a template for including all kinds of interpretations for coincidences, with questions of validity dealt with as a separate issue.

If the model is inadequate, it is not so much because of its conception but because it is so sparse. Combinations and sub-categories that could help distinguish different types of coincidences clearly need to be developed. For example, the extraordinary coincidences associated with separated identical twins, as discussed in Chapter Two, are extremely complex and need a lot of fine-toothed as well as open-minded analysis to come to a satisfactory determination of what exactly is going on. And if one takes seriously the wealth of anecdotal evidence concerning what appears to be telepathic communication between identical twins, all sorts of explanatory possibilities come into play. Many such instances are provided by Guy Lyon Playfair in his book *Twin Telepathy*. Are they to be dismissed simply as chance coincidences or delusory wishful thinking, or is there an as yet unexplained causal factor at work? Whatever the answer to that is, it would need to be able to account satisfactorily for the following incident, one that is not untypical of the genre, recounted from her childhood by Mrs Laura Hesler, an identical twin:

> When we were quite small, I was in the kitchen with Mother one day, and suddenly said, 'Hurry, Elizabeth has fallen off Jack's bicycle and hurt her knee!' Without doubting, Mother followed, and I ran down the street because I knew where she was. We found her still lying on the ground where she had fallen.[3]

Assuming for a moment that this is a genuine instance of twin telepathy, it could be that the explanation for it will turn out to be very natural and in accordance with the findings of particle physics, specifically quantum entanglement, some of the possible implications of which are discussed in Chapter Four. If this is the case, and it may well be shown to be so at some stage in the future, then the suggested coincidence category of 'natural causality' will acquire an added sub-category, while that of 'supernatural causality' will be reciprocally narrowed. Or there may be clear determination that the demarcation between meaningful coincidences and what we might now describe as 'paranormal' is far more fluid than has been suggested in these pages. As regards this very point, Harald Atmanspacher and his colleague Wolfgang Fach, using a psychophysical framework and backed by empirical data, have developed a typology of 'exceptional experiences', of which meaningful coincidences make up but one of a number of discrete categories.[4]

Such developments are certainly to be welcomed, for whenever new discoveries and determinations are made in any field, adjustments of classification and nomenclature must necessarily follow. Take, for example, the coincidence category of random chance, generally conceived of in terms of mathematically calculated probabilities and discussed at some length in Chapter Two. While it is this understanding of chance that is the one normally pitted against alternative coincidence explanations, it is *not* the only one there is. It ought, therefore, to be considered in our model as a sub-category—that of classical randomness. This distinction is made clear by the science writer Brian Clegg in his book *Dice World*, in which he differentiates between *three* kinds of randomness: classical, chaotic and quantum.[5] He argues that while chaotic random systems such as the weather, the stock market or being able to determine the next bestseller are more unpredictable than the statistical predictions of classical randomness, they are in theory calculable, unlike the utter randomness associated with the quantum realm:

> In chaotic randomness, we could in theory predict an outcome exactly, but in practice we get caught out time and time again because the complexity of the system means that shockingly large variations from anything that has happened previously can occur... But in principle, with a computer that was as big as the world, I could crunch the numbers and tell you what the next bestseller will be.
>
> However the real world continues to surprise us with the depth of its randomness. Because once we start to examine what is happening at the level of the individual particles that make up all matter, provide light and carry the forces that hold the universe together, we discover that there lies true randomness. Even perfect information and infinite computing power would not enable you to predict the outcome of a single quantum event. This is where true randomness rules.[6]

Before the twentieth century, neither chaotic nor quantum randomness had been conceived of and so classical randomness held sway. Presumably, as more scientific discoveries are made and further theoretical constructs are postulated, the ways in which chance and coincidence are viewed will change, though it would require the kind of computer Clegg describes above to determine what these changes might be. Perhaps synchronicity will be declared self-evident and a genuine indication of the presence of a psychophysical unity underlying the perceived split between mind and matter, or perhaps enough evidence will be produced to indicate that such a conception can in no way be substantiated. But we simply cannot know before the requisite discoveries are made, nor can we at present truly understand the implications of the absolute randomness that lies at the heart of quantum physics.

Meanwhile, it would be well to remember Elliott Sober's distinction in Chapter Two between the *naïve* and the *sophisticates*, the naïve representing those who look for causal connections of one sort or another to explain coincidences, and the sophisticates essentially doing the same with probabilistic reasoning.[7] Sober takes both camps to task for their doggedness and intractability, particularly the sophisticates, and a general point he appears to be making is that there is rather too much entrenched thinking on the subject of coincidences. This does seem to be the case, no doubt because how one thinks about coincidences is more often than not a reflection of deeper views about the essential nature of the universe we inhabit, which necessarily includes ideas about the nature of consciousness.

A pervasive, if muted, theme running through this enquiry into coincidences, especially in the middle chapters, has been the ideological standoff that exists between those who posit a divinity or intelligence of some sort behind the universe (or multiverse) and those who reject any such assumption. Although there is little point in once again going over this issue, perhaps the following brief account of a very minor synchronicity can go a little way towards envisioning circumstances in which some kind of rapprochement might be conceived, recalling in particular Richard Dawkins's remark, mentioned in Chapter Three, that 'Pantheism is sexed-up atheism.'[8] The coincidental event took place in Brisbane, Australia, towards the end of 2011, and I made a note of it shortly afterwards:

> A friend and I were having a light lunch in the outside area of a Chinese restaurant, the weather cloudy and with a pleasant breeze. In the course of our conversation, I mentioned Peter Cundall, the former presenter of *Gardening Australia*. In a recent television interview about his life, he had said that when it comes to believing in God, he was 'to the left of atheism', a phrase I had never heard before. Cundall also said that he didn't believe in God but that if you want to know the truth, go into the rainforest.
>
> The conversation continued and I found myself floating the idea that as atheists became increasingly fascinated with the beauty of the world, they would become more animistic. At that precise moment there was a peal of thunder and we both instantly recognised it as synchronistic confirmation. It was so obvious and was accompanied by a frisson of numinosity. Such was the clarity of the coincidental moment that we hardly needed to reflect on it and naturally allowed the conversation to move on.

Endnotes

1 Atmanspacher, 'Editorial', 3.
2 Pauli, *Writings on Physics and Philosophy*, 260.

3   Playfair, *Twin Telepathy*, 50.
4   Atmanspacher and Fach, 'A Structural-Phenomenological Typology of Mind-Matter Correlations'.
5   Clegg, *Dice World*, 18–31, 144–147.
6   Ibid., 145–146.
7   Sober, 'Coincidences and How to Reason About Them'.
8   Dawkins, *The God Delusion*, 40.

Bibliography

Abrams, Nancy, and Joel Primack. *The New Universe and the Human Future: How a Shared Cosmology could Transform the World*. New Haven: Yale University Press, 2011.

———. *The View from the Center of the Universe: Discovering our Extraordinary Place in the Cosmos*. New York: Riverhead Books, 2007.

Allen, Arthur. 'The Mystery of Twins.' *The Washington Post Magazine*, 11 January, 1998. http://www.washingtonpost.com/wp-srv/national/longterm/twins/twins2.htm.

Alleyne, Richard. 'The Perfect Hand; Stunned Whist Players are All Dealt a Complete Set of the Same Suit.' *The Daily Mail*, 27 January, 1998. http://findarticles.com/.

Anderson, Ken. *Coincidences: Accident or Design?* North Ryde, Sydney: Angus & Robertson, 1999.

Atmanspacher, Harald. 'Dual-Aspect Monism à la Pauli and Jung.' *Journal of Consciousness Studies* 19, nos. 9-10 (2012): 96–120.

———. Editorial to *Mind & Matter* 9, no. 1 (2011): 3–7.

———. 'Quantum Approaches to Consciousness.' *Stanford Encyclopedia of Philosophy*. Last Modified June 2, 2015. http://plato.stanford.edu/.

———. '20th Century Variants of Dual-Aspect Thinking.' *Mind & Matter* 12, no. 2 (2014): 245–288.

Atmanspacher, Harald, and Wolfgang Fach. 'A Structural-Phenomenological Typology of Mind-Matter Correlations.' *Journal of Analytical Psychology* 58 (2013): 219–244.

Atmanspacher, Harald, and Christopher Fuchs, eds. *The Pauli-Jung Conjecture and its Impact Today*. Exeter: Imprint Academic, 2014.

Atmanspacher, Harald, and Hans Primas. 'The Hidden Side of Wolfgang Pauli: An Eminent Physicist's Extraordinary Encounter with Depth Psychology.' *Journal of Scientific Exploration* 11, no. 3 (1997): 369–386.

———. 'Pauli's Ideas on Mind and Matter in the Context of Contemporary Science.' *Journal of Consciousness Studies* 13, no. 3 (2006): 5–50.

------------, eds. *Recasting Reality: Wolfgang Pauli's Philosophical Ideas and Contemporary Science*. Berlin: Springer, 2009.

Axell, Albert. 'Notes from a Suicide Manual.' *The Guardian*, 22 August, 2002. http://www.guardian.co.uk/world.

Baez, John. 'How Many Fundamental Constants Are There?' Last modified 22 April, 2011. http://math.ucr.edu/home/baez/constants.html.

Bailey, David. 'What are the Cosmic Coincidences, and What Do They Mean?' Last modified 1 January, 2016. http://www.sciencemeetsreligion.org/physics/cosmic.php.

Banks, Michael. 'Planck Reveals "Almost Perfect" Universe.' *Physics World*, 21 March, 2013. http://www.physicsworld.com.

Bann, Thomas. 'The Role of Serendipity in Drug Discovery.' *Dialogues in Clinical Neuroscience* 8, no. 3 (2006): 335–344.

Barrow, John. *The Artful Universe*. Oxford: Clarendon Press, 1995.

BBC News. 'Card Trick Defies the Odds.' 27 January, 1998. http://news.bbc.co.uk/.

Beitman, Bernard. 'Coincidence Studies.' *Psychiatric Annals* 41, no. 12 (2011): 561–571.

Beitman, Bernard and Albert Shaw. 2009, 'Synchroners, High Emotion, and Coincidence Interpretation.' *Psychiatric Annals* 39, no. 5 (2009): 280–286.

Beloff, John. *The Relentless Question: Reflections on the Paranormal*. Jefferson, NC: McFarland & Co., 1990.

BibleGateway.com. Accessed 11 February, 2013. https://www.biblegateway.com/.

Blake, Heidi. 'Alien Life Certain to Exist on Earth-like Planet, Scientists Say.' *The Daily Telegraph*, 30 September, 2010. http://www.telegraph.co.uk/.

Blyth, R.H. *Zen and Zen Classics, Volume One*. Rutland, VT: Charles E. Tuttle, 1988.

Bohm, David. *Wholeness and the Implicate Order*. London: Ark, 1983.

Bolen, Jean Shinoda. *The Tao of Psychology: Synchronicity and the Self*. New York: Harper & Row, 1982.

Britton, Dorothy. *A Haiku Journey: Basho's 'Narrow Road to a Far Province.'* Tokyo: Kodansha International, 1988.

Brumfiel, Geoff. 'Physicists Spooked by Faster-than-Light Information Transfer.' *Nature*, 13 August, 2008. http://www.nature.com/.

Cain, Fraser. 'How Many Galaxies Are There in the Universe.' *Universe Today*, 1 November, 2016. http://www.universetoday.com/30305/.

----------. 'How Many Stars Are in the Milky Way?' *Universe Today*, 11 December, 2016. http://www.universetoday.com/123225/.

----------. 2013, 'How Many Stars Are There in the Universe.' *Universe Today,* 16 October, 2016. http://www.universetoday.com/102630/.

Cambray, Joseph. 'The Place of the 17th Century in Jung's Encounter with China.' *Journal of Analytical Psychology* 50 (2005): 195-207.

----------. *Synchronicity: Nature and Psyche in an Interconnected Universe.* College Station, TX: Texas A & M University Press, 2009.

Campbell, Joseph. *Myths to Live By.* New York: Bantam, 1978.

----------. *The Power of Myth: With Bill Moyers.* New York: Doubleday, 1988.

Carter, Chris. *Parapsychology and the Skeptics: A Scientific Argument for the Existence of ESP.* Pittsburgh, PA: Paja Books, 2007.

Carter, Robert. *The Nothingness Beyond God: An Introduction to the Philosophy of Nishida Kitaro.* New York: Paragon House, 1989.

Chang, Chung-yuan. *Creativity and Taoism: A Study of Chinese Philosophy, Art and Poetry.* London: Wildwood House, 1975.

----------, trans. *Tao: a New Way of Thinking.* Taipei: Dunghuang Publications, 1975.

Chopra, Deepak. *Synchrodestiny: Harnessing the Infinite Power of Coincidence to Create Miracles.* London: Rider, 2005.

Clarke, J.J. *The Tao of the West: Western Transformations of Taoist Thought.* London: Routledge, 2000.

Clegg, Brian. *Dice World: Science and Life in a Random Universe.* London: Icon Books, 2013.

Coleman, Stephanie, Bernard Beitman, and Elif Celebi. 'Weird Coincidences Commonly Occur.' *Psychiatric Annals* 39, no 5 (2009): 265-270.

Combs, Allan, and Mark Holland. *Synchronicity: Science, Myth and the Trickster.* New York: Paragon House, 1990.

Cousineau, Phil. *Soul Moments: Marvelous Stories of Synchronicity — Meaningful Coincidences from a Seemingly Random World.* Berkeley, CA: Conari Press.

Coward, Harold. 'Taoism and Jung: Synchronicity and the Self.' In *Eastern Influences on Western Philosophy: A Reader,* edited by A.L. Macfie, 297-295. Edinburgh: Edinburgh University Press, 2003.

Davies, Paul. *The Goldilocks Enigma: Why is the Universe Just Right for Life?* Boston, MA: Mariner, 2008.

----------. *The Mind of God: Science and the Search for Ultimate Meaning.* London: Penguin, 1992.

Davies, Paul, and Julian Brown. *The Ghost in the Atom: A Discussion of the Mysteries of Quantum Physics.* Cambridge: Cambridge University Press, 1991.

Davis, Philip, Reuben Hersh, and Elena Anne Marchisotto. *The Mathematical Experience, Study Edition.* Boston, MA: Birkhäuser, 2011.

Dawkins, Richard. *The God Delusion*. London: Black Swan, 2007.

Dennis, Alan, Robert Fuller, and Joseph Valacich. 'Media, Tasks, and Communication Processes: A Theory of Media Synchronicity,' *MIS Quarterly* 32, no. 3 (2008): 575–600.

D'Espagnat, Bernard. 'The Quantum Theory and Reality.' *Scientific American*, November, 1979, 158-181. https://www.scientific american.com/media/pdf/197911_0158.pdf.

—————. *Reality and the Physicist: Knowledge, Duration and the Quantum World*. Translated by J.C. Whitehouse and Bernard D'Espagnat. Cambridge: Cambridge University Press, 1989.

Diaconis, Persi, and Frederick Mosteller. 'Methods for Studying Coincidences,' *Journal of the American Statistical Association* 84, no. 408 (1989): 853–861.

Donati, Marialuisa. 'Beyond Synchronicity: The Worldview of Carl Gustav Jung and Wolfgang Pauli.' In *Synchronicity: Multiple Perspectives on Meaningful Coincidence*, edited by Lance Storm, 42–63. Pari: Pari Publishing, 2008.

Dossey, Larry. *The Power of Premonitions: How Knowing the Future Can Shape our Lives*. London: Hay House, 2009.

Dostoevsky, Fyodor. *The Karamazov Brothers: Translated with an Introduction and Notes by Ignat Avsey*. Oxford: Oxford University Press, 1994.

Dowe, Phil. *Galileo, Darwin and Hawking: The Interplay of Science, Reason and Religion*, Grand Rapids, MI: Eerdmans, 2005.

Duff, Michael, Lev Okun, and Gabriele Veneziano. 'Trialogue on the Number of Fundamental Constants.' *Journal of High Energy Physics*, 03 (2002) 023.

Edeal, George. 'Why the Choir was Late,' *Life*, 27 March, 1950. http://books.google.com/.

Eibenberger, Sandra, Stefan Gerlich, Markus Arndt, Marcel Mayor, and Jens Tüxen. 'Matter-wave interference with particles selected from a molecular library with masses exceeding 10000 amu.' *Physical Chemistry Chemical Physics*, 30 October, 2013, 15: 14696–14700. http://arxiv.org/pdf/1310.8343v1.pdf

Elgin, Duane. *The Living Universe: Where are We? Who are We? Where are We Going?* San Francisco, CA: Berrett-Koehler Publishers, 2009.

Elliott, Christopher. 'Perfect Deal at Whist Drive Trumps the Odds.' *The Guardian*, 27 January, 1998. http://proquest.umi.com.

European Southern Observatory. 'Ultracool Dwarf and the Seven Planets.' 22 February, 2017. http://www.eso.org/public/news/eso1706/.

Everitt, Brian. *Chance Rules: An Informal Guide to Probability, Risk and Statistics*. New York: Copernicus, 1999.

Fisher, Len. 'Jung's Explosive Visit to Freud.' *Psychology Today*, 20 September, 2011. http://www.psychologytoday.com.

Fisher, R.A. *The Design of Experiments*. Edinburgh: Oliver & Boyd, 1966.

----------. *Statistical Methods and Scientific Inference*. New York: Hafner Press, 1973.

Flew, Antony. 'Coincidence and Synchronicity.' *Journal for the Society of Psychical Research* 37, no. 677 (1953): 198–201.

Folger, Tim. 'Does the Universe Exist if We're Not Looking?' *Discover*, 1 June, 2002. http://discovermagazine.com/2002/jun/featuniverse.

Fritzsch, Harald. *You are Wrong Mr Einstein! Newton, Einstein, Heisenberg and Feynman Discussing Quantum Mechanics*. Singapore: World Scientific.

Gieser, Suzanne. *The Innermost Kernel: Depth Psychology and Quantum Physics, Wolfgang Pauli's Dialogue with C.G. Jung*. Berlin: Springer, 2005.

Gigerenzer, Gerd, Zeno Swijtnk, Theodore Porter, Lorraine Daston, John Beatty, and Lorenz Krüger. *The Empire of Chance: How Probability has Changed Science and Everyday Life*. Cambridge: Cambridge University Press, 1989.

Giles, Lionel. *The Sayings of Lao-Tzu*. London: John Murray, 1972.

----------. *Taoist Teachings from the Book of Lieh Tzu*. London: John Murray, 1959.

Gilson, James. 'The Place of the Fine Structure Constant, α in Nature's scheme.' Last modified 9 November, 2003. http://www.fine-structure-constant.org/gil15.html.

Goswami, Satsvarupa-dasa. 'Man on the Moon—A Colossal Hoax that Cost Billions of Dollars.' Last modified May 8, 2014. http://krishna.org/?cat=10.

Grattan-Guinness, Ivor. 'Coincidences and Spontaneous Psychical Phenomena.' *Journal for the Society of Psychical Research* 52 (1983): 59–71.

----------. 'What are Coincidences?' *Journal for the Society of Psychical Research* 49 (1978): 949–955.

Gribbin, John. *The Reason Why: the Miracle of Life on Earth*. London: Allen Lane, 2011.

Guy, Basil. 'Voltaire, Sinophile.' In *Eastern Influences on Western Philosophy: A Reader*, edited by A.L. Macfie, 83–109. Edinburgh: Edinburgh University Press, 2003.

Hampshire, Stuart. *Spinoza*. Harmondsworth: Pelican, 1951.

Hanley, James. 'Jumping to Coincidence: Defying Odds in the Realm of the Preposterous.' *The American Statistician* 46, no. 3 (1992): 197–202.

Hardy, Alister, Robert Harvie, and Arthur Koestler. *The Challenge of Chance: Experiments and Speculations*. London: Hutchinson, 1973.

Hawking, Stephen, and Leonard Mlodinow. *The Grand Design*. London: Bantam Press, 2010.

Heidegger, Martin. *On Time and Being*. Translated by Joan Stambaugh. New York: Harper Torchbooks, 1972.

----------. *Poetry, Language, Thought*. Translated by Albert Hofstadter. New York: Harper Colophon Books, 1975.

Henry, Richard Conn. 'The Mental Universe.' *Nature*, 7 July, 2005. http://www.nature.com/.

Hill, Ray. 'Cot Death or Murder — Weighing the Probabilities.' *Developmental Psychology Conference*, June 2002. http://www.cse.salford.ac.uk/.

Holden, Constance. 'Identical Twins Reared Apart.' *Science*, 21 March, 1980, 1323-1328. http://www.sciencemag.org/content/207/4437/1323.extract.

Hollick, Malcolm. *The Science of Oneness: A Worldview for the Twenty-First Century*. Winchester: O Books, 2006.

Hopcke, Robert. 'Synchronicity and Psychotherapy: Jung's Concept and Its Use in Clinical Work.' *Psychiatric Annals* 39, no. 5 (2009): 287-293.

Hoyle, Fred. 'The Universe: Past and Present Reflections.' *Engineering and Science*, November, 1981, 8-12. http://calteches.library.caltech.edu/3312/1/Hoyle.pdf.

Hsiao, Paul. 'Heidegger and Our Translation of the Tao Te Ching.' In *Heidegger and Asian Thought*, edited by Graham Parkes, 93-104. Honolulu, HI: University of Hawaii Press, 1990.

Huxley, Aldous. *The Perennial Philosophy*, London, Triad, 1985.

Inglis, Brian. *Coincidence: A Matter of Chance – or Synchronicity?* London: Hutchinson, 1990.

----------. *The Hidden Power*. London: Jonathon Cape, 1986.

Jeans, James. 'In the Mind of Some Eternal Spirit.' In *Quantum Questions: Mystical Writings of the World's Greatest Physicists*, edited by Ken Wilber, 135-146. Boston, MA: Shambhala, 2001.

----------. 'A Universe of Pure Thought.' In *Quantum Questions: Mystical Writings of the World's Greatest Physicists*, edited by Ken Wilber, 147-52. Boston, MA: Shambhala, 2001.

Jeffries, Richard. *The Story of My Heart*. London: Quartet Books, 1979.

Jett, Stephen. 'Confessions of a Cultural Diffusionist.' *Yearbook. Conference of Latin Americanist Geographers* 26 (2000): 171-177.

----------. 'Further Information on the Geography of the Blowgun and Its Implications for Early Transoceanic Contacts.' *Annals of the Association of American Geographers* 81 (1991): 89-102.

Johnston, Hamish. '*Physics World* Reveals Its Top 10 Breakthroughs for 2011.' *Physics World*, 16 December, 2011. www.physicsworld.com.

Jones, David. 'Synchronicity: The Art of Coincidence — An Interview with Dr Kirby Surprise.' *New Dawn*, 8 September, 2012. http://www.newdawnmagazine.com/.

Jordens, J.F.T. 'Prakriti and the Collective Unconscious: Purusa and Self.' In *Jung and Eastern Thought*, by Harold Coward, 145–168. Albany, NY: State of New York University Press, 1985.

Jung, C.G. *Collected Works*, vol. 14, *Mysterium Conjunctionis: An Inquiry into the Separation and Synthesis of Psychic Opposites in Alchemy*. Translated and edited by Gerhard Adler and R.F.C. Hull. London: Routledge and Kegan Paul, 1970.

----------. *The Essential Jung: Selected Writings Introduced by Anthony Storr*. London: Fontana, 1986.

----------. *Flying Saucers: A Modern Myth of Things Seen in the Skies*. Translated by R.F.C. Hull. London: Ark, 1987.

----------. Foreword to *I Ching or Book of Changes*, xxi–xxxix. Translated by Richard Wilhelm and Cary F. Baynes. 3rd ed. London: Penguin, 2003.

----------. *Letters Volume 2 1951–1961: Selected and Edited by Gerhard Adler in collaboration with Anelia Jaffé*. Translated by R.F.C. Hull. London: Routledge, 1990.

----------, ed. *Man and His Symbols*. New York: Dell, 1979.

----------. *Memories, Dreams, Reflections: Recorded and Edited by Anelia Jaffé*. Translated by Richard and Clara Winston. New York: Vintage Books, 1989.

----------. 'On Synchronicity.' In *Collected Works*, vol. 8, *The Structure and Dynamics of the Psyche*. Translated by R.F.C. Hull. 2nd ed., 520–531. London: Routledge and Kegan Paul, 1981.

----------. *Psychology and the East*. Abingdon: Routledge, 2008.

----------. 'The Relations between the Ego and the Unconscious.' In *Collected Works*, vol. 7, *Two Essays on Analytical Philosophy*. Translated and edited by Gerhard Adler and R.F.C. Hull, 123–244. New York: Princeton University Press, 1972.

----------. *Synchronicity: An Acausal Connecting Principle*. Translated by R.F.C. Hull. London: Ark, 1991.

Kafatos, Menas, Rudolph Tanzi, and Deepak Chopra. 'How Consciousness Becomes the Physical Universe.' In *Consciousness and the Universe: Quantum Physics, Evolution, Brain and Mind*. Edited by Roger Penrose, Stuart Hameroff, and Subhash Kak, 1119–1128. Cambridge, MA: Cosmology Science Publishers, 2011.

Kaku, Michio. *Parallel Worlds: The Science of Alternative Universes and Our Future in the Cosmos*. London: Penguin, 2005.

Karcher, Stephen. 'Jung, the Tao, and the Classic of Change.' *Journal of Religion and Health* 38, no. 4 (1999): 287–304.

----------. 'Re-Enchanting the Mind: Oracles, Reading, Myth, and Mantics.' *Psychological Perspectives* 50, no. 2 (2007): 198–219.

Kelly, Kevin. 'The Technium: Progression of the Inevitable.' Last modified August 2009. http://kk.org/thetechnium/progression-of/.

Kennedy-Xypolitas, Emmanuel, ed. *The Fountain of the Love of Wisdom: An Homage to Marie-Louise von Franz*. Wilmette, IL: Chiron Publications, 2006.

Kirkland, Russell. *Taoism: The Enduring Tradition*. New York: Routledge, 2004.

Koestler, Arthur. *The Case of the Midwife Toad*. London: Picador, 1978.

----------. *The Roots of Coincidence*. London: Picador, 1974.

Kolata, Gina. '1-in-a-Trillion Coincidence, You Say? Not Really, Experts Find.' *New York Times*, 27 February, 1990. http://www.nytimes.com.

Krauss, Lawrence. 'A Universe from Nothing.' Filmed 3 October, 2009, 1:04:51. Posted on *YouTube* by Richard Dawkins Foundation for Reason and Science, October 21, 2009. http://www.youtube.com/watch?v=7ImvlS8PLIo.

Krauss, Lawrence, and Robert Scherrer. 'The End of Cosmology?' *Scientific American*, March, 2008: 46–53. http://www.scientificamerican.com/article/the-end-of-cosmology/.

Krohn, Paysach. *The Maggid Speaks*. New York: Mesorah Publishing, 1987.

Kuhn, Robert Lawrence. 'Why This Universe? Toward a Taxonomy of Possible Explanations.' *Skeptic* 13, no. 2 (2007): 28–39.

----------. 2008, 'Cosmos, Consciousness, God.' *CEO Magazine*, June, 2008: 22–24. http://chiefexecutive.net/cosmos-consciousness-god.

Kuttner, Fred, and Bruce Rosenblum. 'The Conscious Observer in the Quantum Experiment.' *The Journal of Cosmology* 14 (2011). http://journalofcosmology.com/Consciousness135.html.

Kvitting, John-Pedar, Lars Wigström, Jörg Strotmann, and George Sutherland. 'How Accurate is Visual Assessment of Synchronicity in Myocardial Motion?' *Journal of the American Society of Echocardiography* 12, no. 9 (2009): 698–705.

Lach, Donald. 'The Sinophilism of Christian Wolff (1679–1754).' In *Eastern Influences on Western Philosophy: A Reader*. Edited by A.L. Macfie, 60–82. Edinburgh: Edinburgh University Press, 2003.

Lanza, Robert, and Bob Berman. *Biocentrism: How Life and Consciousness are the Keys to Understanding the True Nature of the Universe*. Dallas, TX: BenBella Books, 2009.

Lau, D.C., trans. *Lao Tzu: Tao Te Ching*. Harmondsworth: Penguin, 1975.

Leal-Anaya, Jaime. 'Synchronicity as a Mirror of Our Thoughts, Emotions, and Beliefs.' *SuperConsciousness*, 23 April, 2012. http://www.superconsciousness.com/.

Lennox, John. *God and Stephen Hawking: Whose Design Is it Anyway?* Oxford: Lion.

----------. *God's Undertaker: Has Science Buried God?* Oxford: Lion, 2009.

Leslie, John. *Universes*. London: Routledge, 1989.

Lindorff, David. *Pauli and Jung: The Meeting of Two Great Minds.* Wheaton: Quest, 2004.

Lovelock, James. *The Revenge of Gaia*. New York: Basic Books, 2006.

----------. *The Vanishing Face of Gaia*. London: Penguin. 2010.

Macfie, A.L., ed. *Eastern Influences on Western Philosophy*. Edinburgh: Edinburgh University Press, 2003.

McGuire, William, and R.F.C. Hull, eds. *C.G. Jung Speaking: Interviews and Encounters*. London: Picador, 1980.

Mackey, J. Linn. 'The Collective Unconscious and the Akashic Field.' *Jung Journal: Culture and Psyche* 1, no. 2 (2007): 2–15.

Madrigal, Alexis. 'Dark Energy Could Be Einstein's Cosmological Constant.' *Wired Science*, 16 December, 2008. http://www.wired.com/2008/12/dark-energy-ein.

Magruder, Kerry. 'Is this a Medieval Flat-Earth Woodcut?' Last modified 28 July, 2003. http://kvmagruder.net/flatEarth/index.html.

Maharshi, Ramana. *Talks with Ramana Maharshi: On Realizing Abiding Peace and Happiness*. Carlsbad, CA: Inner Directions Publishing. 2001.

Main, Roderick. *Revelations of Chance: Synchronicity as Spiritual Experience*. Albany, NY: State University of New York Press, 2004.

----------. *The Rupture of Time: Synchronicity and Jung's Critique of Modern Western Culture*. Hove: Brunner-Routledge, 2004.

Mann, Adam. 'The Hunting of the Dark.' *Nature*, 23 March, 2011. http://www.nature.com/.

Mansfield, Victor. 'Distinguishing Synchronicity from Parapsychological Phenomena: An Essay in Honour of Marie-Louise von Franz.' Last modified 14 July, 2008. http://www.lightlink.com/vic/distinguishing.html.

----------. *Synchronicity, Science, and Soul-Making: Understanding Jungian Synchronicity through Physics, Buddhism and Philosophy*. Chicago and La Salle, IL: Open Court, 1999.

Mansfield, Victor, Sally Rhine-Feather, and James Hall. 'The Rhine Letters: Distinguishing Parapsychological from Synchronistic Events.' *The Journal of Parapsychology* 62, no. 1 (1998): 2–35.

Matthews, Robert. 'Opposites Detract.' *New Scientist*, 13 March, 2004. http://www.provingparanormal.com/New_Scientist_2004_Parapsychology_iv.pdf.

May, Reinhard. *Heidegger's Hidden Sources: East Asian Influences on His Work*. London: Routledge, 1996.

Meier, C.A., ed. *Atom and Archetype: The Jung/Pauli Letters, 1932–1958*. Translated by David Roscoe. London: Routledge, 2001.

Merton, Robert, and Elinor Barber. *The Travels and Adventures of Serendipity: A Study in Sociological Semantics and the Sociology of Science*. New York: Princeton University Press, 2004.

Merton, Thomas, trans. *The Way of Chuang Tzu*. London: Unwin Books, 1970.

Miller, Arthur I. *137: Jung, Pauli, and the Pursuit of a Scientific Obsession*. New York: Norton, 2010.

Mitchell, Joni. *Woodstock*. Accessed 16 September, 2011. http://jonimitchell.com/music/song.cfm?id=75.

Mitchell, Stephen, trans. *Tao Te Ching: An Illustrated Journey*. London: Frances Lincoln, 1999.

Mooney, Chris. 'The Evolution Polling Numbers Have Nudged a Little.' *Discover*, 21 December, 2010. http://discovermagazine.com/.

Moseman, Andrew. 'The Estimated Number of Stars in the Universe Just Tripled.' *Discover*, 1 December, 2010. http://discovermagazine.com/.

Moskowitz, Clara. 'Largest Molecules Yet Behave Like Waves in Quantum Double-Slit Experiment.' *Live Science*, 25 March, 2012. http://www.livescience.com.

Moss, Robert. *The Three 'Only' Things: Tapping the Power of Dreams, Coincidence and Imagination*. Novato, CA: New World Library, 2007.

Mungello, David. 'Malebranche and Chinese Philosophy.' In *Eastern Influences on Western Philosophy: A Reader*. Edited by A.L. Macfie, 29–54. Edinburgh: Edinburgh University Press, 2003.

Needham, Joseph. *Introduction to the Genius of China: 3,000 Years of Science, Discovery and Invention*, by Robert Temple, 6–8. London: Prion.

Needham, Joseph and Colin Ronan. *The Shorter Science and Civilisation in China, Vol. 1*. Cambridge: Cambridge University Press, 1978.

Neimark, Jill. 'Pattern and Circumstance: The Power of Coincidence.' *Psychology Today* 37, no. 4 (2004): 46–52, 87.

Nerlich, Steve. 'Astronomy Without A Telescope—Cosmic Coincidence.' *Universe Today*, 3 September, 2011. http://www.universetoday.com/88640/.

Newport, Frank. 'In U.S., 42% Believe Creationist View of Human Origins.' *Gallup*, 2 June, 2014. http://www.gallup.com/poll/170822/believe-creationist-view-human-origins.aspx.

Orzel, Chad. *How to Teach Quantum Physics to Your Dog*. Oxford: Oneworld, 2010.

----------. 'Watching Photons Interfere: "Observing the Average Trajectories of Single Photons in a Two-Slit Interferometer".' *ScienceBlogs*, 3 June, 2011. http://scienceblogs.com/principles/.

Ott, Hugo. *Martin Heidegger: A Political Life*. Translated by Allan Blunden. London: Fontana Press, 1994.

Parkes, Graham, ed. *Heidegger and Asian Thought*. Honolulu, HI: University of Hawaii Press, 1990.

Pauli, Wolfgang. *Writings on Physics and Philosophy*. Edited by Charles Enz and Karl von Meyenn. Translated by Robert Schlapp. Berlin: Springer-Verlag, 2010.

Paulos, John Allen. *Innumeracy: Mathematical Illiteracy and its Consequences*. London: Penguin, 2000.

----------. *Once Upon a Number: The Hidden Mathematical Logic of Stories*. Harmondsworth: Penguin, 1998.

Peat, F. David. 'Divine Contenders: Wolfgang Pauli and the Symmetry of the World.' In *Synchronicity: Multiple Perspectives on Meaningful Coincidence*. Edited by Lance Storm, 15–24. Pari: Pari Publishing, 2008.

----------. *Einstein's Moon: Bell's Theorem and the Curious Quest for Quantum Reality*. Chicago, IL: Contemporary Books, 1990.

----------. *From Certainty to Uncertainty: The Story of Science and Ideas in the Twentieth Century*. Washington, D.C.: Joseph Henry Press, 2002.

----------. *Pathways of Chance*. Pari: Pari Publishing.

----------. *Synchronicity: The Bridge between Mind and Matter*. New York: Bantam, 1987.

----------. *Synchronicity: The Marriage of Matter and Psyche*. Pari: Pari Publishing, 2014.

Pelton, Robert. *The Trickster in West Africa: A Study of Mythic Irony and Sacred Delight*. Berkeley, CA: University of California Press.

Penrose, Roger. *Cycles of Time: An Extraordinary New View of the Universe*. London: Vintage, 2011.

----------. *The Emperor's New Mind: Computers, Minds, and the Laws of Physics*. Oxford: Oxford University Press, 1990.

----------. 'Is the Universe Fine-Tuned for Life and Mind?' Interview with Robert Lawrence Kuhn. Filmed 2006/7. *Closer to Truth* video, 9:35. Last modified 2014. http://www.closertotruth.com/series/the-universe-fine-tuned-life-and-mind#video-2809.

Playfair, Guy Lyon. *Twin Telepathy*. Stroud: The History Press, 2009.

Plimmer, Martin, and Brian King. *Beyond Coincidence*. Thriplow, Cambridge: Icon Books, 2005.

Pöggeler, O., 1987. 'West-East Dialogue: Heidegger and Lao-tzu.' In *Heidegger and Asian Thought*. Edited by Graham Parkes, 47–78. Honolulu, HI: University of Hawaii Press, 1990.

Powell, Diane Hennacy. *The ESP Enigma: The Scientific Case for Psychic Phenomena*. New York: Walker & Co., 2009.

Price, H.H. Review of *Naturerklärung und Psyche*, by C.G. Jung and W. Pauli. *Journal for the Society of Psychical Research* 37 (1953): 26–35.

Progoff, Ira. *Jung, Synchronicity, and Human Destiny: Noncausal Dimensions of Human Experience*. New York: Delta, 1973.

Radin, Dean. *Entangled Minds: Extrasensory Experiences in a Quantum Reality*. New York: Paraview, 2006.

──────. *The Conscious Universe: The Scientific Truth of Psychic Phenomena*. San Francisco, CA: HarperEdge, 1999.

Reichenbach, Hans. *The Direction of Time*. Berkeley, CA: University of California Press, 1991.

Reps, Paul, ed. *Zen Flesh, Zen Bones*. London: Penguin, 2000.

Rhoades, B. Eric. 'Just Who Invented Radio and Which was the First Station?' Accessed 3 December, 2013. http://www.qsl.net/n7jy/radiohst.html.

Rhodes, Ross. 'Wheeler's Classic Delayed Choice Experiment.' Last modified 23 March, 2003. http://www.bottomlayer.com/bottom/basic_delayed_choice.htm.

Ricard, Matthieu, and Trinh Xuan Thuan. *The Quantum and the Lotus: A Journey to Where the Frontiers of Science and Buddhism Meet*. New York: Three Rivers Press, 2001.

Richo, David. *The Power of Coincidence: How Life Shows Us What We Need to Know*. Boston, MA: Shambhala, 2007.

Rosen, David. *The Tao of Jung: The Way of Integrity*. New York: Arkana, 1996.

Rosenblum, Bruce. 'Quantum Physics Encounters Consciousness: An Interview with Bruce Rosenblum.' *Holos* 4, no 1 (2008). http://www.holosforum.org/.

Rosenblum, Bruce, and Fred Kuttner, *Quantum Enigma: Physics Encounters Consciousness*. London: Duckworth Overlook, 2011.

Rosenthal, Jeffrey. *Struck by Lightning: The Curious World of Probabilities*. Washington, DC: Joseph Henry Press, 2006.

Ross, Kelley. 'Zen and the Art of Divebombing, or The Dark Side of the Tao.' Accessed 4 December, 2011. http://www.friesian.com/divebomb.htm#index.

Russell, Bertrand. *Mysticism and Logic and Other Essays*. Harmondsworth: Pelican, 1954.

Salsburg, David. *The Lady Tasting Tea: How Statistics Revolutionized Science in the Twentieth Century*. New York: Henry Holt & Co., 2002.

Segal, Nancy. *Entwined Lives: Twins and What They Tell Us about Human Behaviour*. New York: Plume, 2000.

----------. *Indivisible by Two: Lives of Extraordinary Twins*. Cambridge, MA: Harvard University Press, 2005.

Sheldrake, Rupert. Foreword to *Parapsychology and the Skeptics: A Scientific Argument for the Existence of ESP*, by Chris Carter, i-v. Pittsburgh, PA: Paja Books.

----------. *The Science Delusion: Freeing the Spirit of Enquiry*. London: Coronet, 2012.

Smith, Huston. *Why Religion Matters: The Fate of the Human Spirit in an Age of Disbelief*. San Francisco, CA: Harper, 2001.

Smoley, Richard. *The Dice Game of Shiva*. Novato, CA: New World Library, 2009.

Smullyan, Raymond. *The Tao is Silent*. New York: Harper and Row, 1977.

Snopes.com. 'Whether Balloon.' Last modified April 26, 2014. http://www.snopes.com/inboxer/trivia/buxton.asp.

Sober, Elliott. 'Coincidences and How to Reason about Them.' 2010 version of the essay from http://researchgate.net (originally available from http://philosophy.wisc.edu/sober/)..

----------. 'Reichenbach's Cubical Universe and the Problem of the External World.' *Synthese* 181 (2011): 3-21.

----------. 'Venetian Sea Levels, British Bread Prices, and the Principle of the Common Cause.' *The British Journal for the Philosophy of Science* 52 (2001): 341-346.

----------. 'Why Methodological Naturalism?' In *Biological Evolution Facts and Theories: A Critical Appraisal 150 Years After the Origin of Species*. Edited by Gennaro Aulette, Marc LeClerc, and Rafael A. Martinez, 359-378. Rome: Gregorian Biblical Press, 2011.

Spitzer, Robert. *New Proofs for the Existence of God: Contributions of Contemporary Physics and Philosophy*. Grand Rapids: Eerdmans, 2010.

Stenger, Victor. *The Fallacy of Fine-Tuning: Why the Universe is Not Designed for Us*. Amherst, MA: Prometheus Books, 2011.

----------. 'The Grand Accident.' Review of *The Grand Design* by Stephen Hawking and Leonard Mlodinow. *The Huffington Post*, 1 November, 2010. http://www.huffingtonpost.com/.

----------. 'The Universe Shows No Evidence for Design.' In *Debating Christian Theism*. Edited by J.P. Moreland, Chad Meister and Khaldoun A. Sweiss, 47-58. New York: Oxford University, 2013.

Storm, Lance, ed. *Synchronicity: Multiple Perspectives on Meaningful Coincidence*. Pari: Pari Publishing, 2008.

----------. 'Synchronicity, Causality, and Acausality.' In *Synchronicity: Multiple Perspectives on Meaningful Coincidence*. Edited by Lance Storm, 153–174. Pari: Pari Publishing, 2008.

Strogatz, Steven. *Sync: The Emerging Science of Spontaneous Order*. London: Penguin, 2004.

Sze, Mai-mai. *The Tao of Painting: A Study of the Ritual Disposition of Chinese Painting, Vol. 1*. London: Routledge and Kegan Paul, 1957.

----------. *The Way of Chinese Painting: Its Ideas and Technique*. New York: Vintage Books, 1959.

Talbot, Michael. *The Holographic Universe*. London: Harper Collins, 1996.

Taleb, Nassim Nicholas. *The Black Swan: The Impact of the Highly Improbable*. London: Penguin.

Tarnas, Richard. *Cosmos and Psyche: Intimations of a New World View*. New York: Plume, 2007.

Tart, Charles. 'Causality and Synchronicity: Steps Towards Clarification.' *Journal of the American*

----------. *The End of Materialism: How Evidence of the Paranormal is Bringing Science and Spirit Together*. Oakland: New Harbinger, 2009.

Temple, Robert. *The Genius of China: 3,000 Years of Science, Discovery and Invention*. London: Prion, 2005.

Than, Ker. 'An Answer to the "Cosmic Coincidence"?' *Cosmos Magazine*, 11 February, 2008. http://www.cosmosmagazine.com/news/1845/an-answer-cosmic-coincidence.

The Dalai Lama. 'Mind and Life XIV—Day 1 pm—with the Dalai Lama.' Filmed 9 April, 2007, 1:56:02. Posted on *YouTube* by Gyalwarinpoche, 22 June, 2010. http://www.youtube.com/watch?v=fO-K13cfJwo.

The Economist. 'Ye Cannae Change the Laws of Physics.' 2 September, 2010. http://www.economist.com/node/16941123.

Thuan, Trinh Xuan. *The Changing Universe: Big Bang and After*. London: Thames and Hudson, 1993.

Utts, Jessica. 'An Assessment of the Evidence for Psychic Functioning.' *Journal of Scientific Exploration* 10, no. 1 (1996): 3–30.

----------. 'Response to Ray Hyman's Report of September 11, 1995, "Evaluation of Program on Anomalous Mental Phenomena".' *Journal of Scientific Exploration* 10, no. 1 (1996): 59–61.

Uzan, Jean-Philippe, and Bénédicte Leclercq. *The Natural Laws of the Universe: Understanding Fundamental Constants*. Berlin: Springer, 2008.

Van der Post, Laurens. *A Mantis Carol*. London: Penguin, 1989.

Vaughan, Alan. *Incredible Coincidence: The Baffling World of Synchronicity*. New York: Ballantine, 1989.

Velmans, Max. 'Reflexive Monism.' *Journal of Consciousness Studies* 15, no. 2 (2008): 5–50.

----------. 'The Unconscious Ground of Being.' Filmed 9 July, 2009. *Cortona Week*, Tuscany, Italy. http://vimeo.com/9931520.

Villard, Ray. 'The Four Ages of Our Universe—What's Next?' *Discovery News*, 27 March, 2012. http://news.discovery.com/space/.

Von Franz, Marie-Louise. *C.G. Jung: His Myth in Our Time*. New York: Putnam, 1975.

-----------. *Number and Time: Reflections Leading Toward a Unification of Depth Psychology and Physics*. Boston, MA: Integral Books, 1974.

-----------. *On Divination and Synchronicity: The Psychology of Meaningful Chance*. Toronto: Inner City Books, 1980.

-----------. *Projection and Recollection in Jungian Psychology*. La Salle, IL: Open Court, 1990.

-----------. *Psyche and Matter*. Boston, MA: Shambhala, 1992.

Waley, Arthur, trans. *The Way and its Power: The Tao Te Ching and Its Place in Chinese Thought*. London: Unwin, 1977.

Wall, Mike. 'Is Planet Gliese 581g Really the "First Potentially Habitable" Alien World?' *SPACE.com*, July 23, 2012. http://www.space.com/.

----------. 'R.I.P. Possibly Habitable Planet Gliese 581g? Not So Fast, Co-Discoverer Says.' *SPACE.com*, February 19, 2011. http://www.space.com/.

Wallace, B. Alan. *Hidden Dimensions: The Unification of Physics and Consciousness*. New York: Colombia University Press, 2010.

Ward, Keith. *Why There Almost Certainly Is a God: Doubting Dawkins*. Oxford: Lion, 2008.

Ward, Peter and Donald Brownlee. *Rare Earth: Why Complex Life is Uncommon in the Universe*. New York: Copernicus, 2004.

Weaver, Warren. *Lady Luck: The Theory of Probability*. Harmondsworth: Pelican, 1977.

Weinberg, Steven. 'Anthropic Bound on the Cosmological Constant.' *Physical Review Letters* 59, no. 22 (1987): 2607–2610.

Welch, Holmes. *Taoism: The Parting of the Way*. Boston, MA: Beacon, 1966.

Wilber, Ken. *Collected Works*, vol. 8, *The Marriage of Sense and Soul*. Boston, MA: Shambhala, 2000.

----------. *Integral Spirituality: A Startling New Role for Religion in the Modern and Postmodern World*. Boston, MA: Integral Books, 2006.

----------, ed. *Quantum Questions: Mystical Writings of the World's Greatest Physicists*. Boston, MA: Shambhala, 2001.

Wilhelm, Hellmut. *Heaven, Earth and Man in the Book of Changes*. Seattle, WA: University of Washington Press, 1980.

Wilhelm, Richard, trans. *I Ching or Book of Changes*. Translated from the German by Cary F. Baynes. London: Penguin, 2003.

----------, trans. *Tao Te Ching: The Book of Meaning and Life*. Translated from the German by H.G. Ostwald. London: Arkana, 1989.

Wilhelm, Richard, and C.G. Jung. *The Secret of the Golden Flower: A Chinese Book of Life*. Translated by Cary F. Baynes. London: Routledge, 1972.

Wilson, Robert Anton. *Coincidance: A Head Test*. Reno, LV: New Falcon Publications, 2008.

Wolf, Fred Alan. 'The Quantum Universe: An Interview with Fred Alan Wolf.' In *Cosmic Conversations: Dialogues on the Nature of the Universe and the Search for Reality*. Edited by Stephan Martin, 71-83. Franklin Lakes, NJ: New Page Books.

----------. *Time Loops and Space Twists: How God Created the Universe*. San Antonio, TX: Hierophant Publishing, 2010.

Wong, Eva. *The Shambhala Guide to Taoism*. Boston, MA: Shambhala, 1997.

Wright, Lawrence. *Twins and What They Tell Us About Who We Are*. New York: John Wiley & Sons, 1997.

Yuasa, Yasuo. *Overcoming Modernity: Synchronicity and Image-Thinking*. Albany, NY: New York State University Press, 2008.

Zabriskie, Beverley. 'Jung and Pauli: A Meeting of Rare Minds.' In *Atom and Archetype: The Jung/Pauli Letters, 1932-1958*. Edited by C.A. Meier, xxvii-l. London: Routledge, 2001.

Index

Abrams, Nancy, 74-77, 79, 82
absolute knowledge, 12, 54, 105, 127, 155
acausal connecting principle, 1, 4, 14-15, 48, 124, 128
   Jung's treatise, 2-3, 14, 25, 30
acausality, 5, 15-16, 30, 49, 104, 118, 144
Adams, Evelyn, 39-41
affective charge, 17, 20, 22
affinities (coming together of), 117, 119-20, 130
Albertus Magnus, 24, 26
alchemy, alchemists, 137, 142-43, 147, 153-55, 165, 172
Alvarez, Al, 32
archetype(s), 17-18, 22, 134, 145
Arlott, John, 114
Arndt, Markus, 94
astrology, 22
Atmanspacher, Harald, 108, 143-45, 177

Basho, Matsuo, 157-58
Beatrice, Nebraska, 58, 61
Beitman, Bernard, 128-29, 131-32
Bell, Alexander Graham, 43
Beloff, John, 35
Bernoulli, Jacques, 38
Berry, Thomas, 82
Big Bang, 65, 69-70, 75, 79, 106, 122
birthday problem, 37
blowgun, 44-45, 52
Bohm, David (implicate order), 105, 108, 143-44, 176
Bohr, Nils, 10, 102, 107, 145
Bolen, Jean Shinoda, 128
Born, Max, 64
Bouvet, Father Joachim, 7, 159

box-pair experiment (Rosenblum and Kuttner), 94-95
Brown, Julian, 92
Brownlee, Donald, 60
Buddhism, 103, 152-53, 156
   and science, 103
   Ch'an, 152, 156
   Zen, 135-36, 148, 152-53, 156
Buxton, Laura(s), 115-17, 119-20

Campbell, Joseph, 23-24, 77-78
causality, xi, 1, 4-7, 12-15, 21-22, 30, 49, 51-54, 72, 88, 104, 116-17, 123-24, 144, 150, 176-77
   as coincidence category, 30, 51-54, 72, 80, 116, 176-77
   'historical' and 'scientific', 15
   law, principle of, 5-6, 14, 150
   magical, 7, 24
   paranormal, 39, 51-52, 54, 72, 104, 116, 163, 177
chance, ix, xi, 2, 4, 8, 19, 21-23, 30-31, 33f, 42, 47f, 59-62, 64, 67f, 79-82, 103, 105-7, 116-17, 119-22, 130, 176-78
   as coincidence category, 30, 51-54, 72, 80, 116, 176
   as 'mere coincidence', 41, 49, 87, 106
   as 'positivism's safety net', 37-39
Chang Chung-yuan, 155-57, 162, 164
Chapman, Mark David, 131
Chinese science, 151-52
Chopra, Deepak, 24, 109
Christie, Agatha, 113
Chu Hsi, 157-58
Chuang Tzu, 54, 81, 155-56
Clarke, J.J., 159
Clegg, Brian, 178
coincidence (in general), ix, 1f, 10-13, 16, 18f, 30-31, 36f, 58-59, 67, 71-74,

76, 79–80, 82, 86–87, 93, 99, 104–06, 109, 113f, 145–46, 158, 161, 165, 171–72, 176–78
   anecdotes, stories, 2–3, 12–13, 19, 48, 50, 52, 54, 58–59, 86, 113, 115, 120–21, 124f
   categories, 30, 51–54, 72–73, 80, 115–16, 119, 176–78
   causal (all types of), ix, x, 30, 37, 42f, 52–53, 55, 115, 118–21, 172
   chance, ix, 30, 32, 36f, 45, 49, 51, 53, 55, 59, 67, 86–87, 105–06, 116, 119, 124, 129–31, 177–78
   cosmic, x, 58, 65–67, 71–74, 76, 79–80, 82, 87, 106, 113, 116, 121–22, 158
   definition of, ix
   explanation(s), ix, x, 2–3, 5, 18, 25, 30, 32f, 42, 44, 47, 49f, 59, 80, 86, 113f, 142, 172, 176–78
   meaningful, ix, 1–3, 5, 10–13, 16, 18f, 30, 38, 48–51, 54, 73–74, 82, 105–06, 109, 115, 118, 124f, 131, 135–37, 145–46, 158, 161, 171–72, 177
   quantum, x, 87, 91, 99, 106, 113, 121, 123
   shadow side of, 18, 24, 131–33
   subjective projection of meaning, 18, 38, 105, 125, 128f
coincidence-prone, 129
Combs, Allan, 13, 22–23, 26
common cause, 42–43, 52, 115
   principle of, 42
Confucianism, 7, 20, 146, 153, 155, 157–59
constants of nature, 63, 79–80, 116, 176
Cosmic Wheels (Donovan album), 171
cosmological constant, 66, 79
creatio continua, 14
Cundall, Peter, 179

d'Espagnat, Bernard, 108, 176
Dalai Lama, 103, 107
dark energy, 66–67, 78–79, 82
dark matter, 70, 78–79
Darwin, Charles, 43
Davies, Paul, 63, 66–67, 92, 123
de Broglie, Louis, 102
deism, 67, 74, 108

delayed choice experiment, 92, 96–97, 123
Davis, Philip, 171
Descartes, Rene, 7
design argument, 68, 74
Diaconis, Persi, 38–40, 55
discontinuities of physics, 15, 88, 104
divination, 19f, 114, 151
Dorn, Gerard, 147, 172
Dostoevsky, Fyodor, 174
Dossey, Larry, 59
double mandalas, 173–74
double-slit experiment, 89f, 103, 110, 123
dual aspect theory, 106–09, 143–45, 176
Dyson, Freeman, 72

Eddington, Arthur, 64, 103, 108
Einstein, Albert, 4, 63, 66, 81, 87, 89, 98, 102
Elgin, Duane, 70–71
entanglement. *See* quantum entanglement
Enz, Charles, 65
equivalence of meaning, 11, 49, 51, 73, 105, 117, 119–20, 125, 127, 129, 137, 143, 150, 158, 165
equivalence (without meaning), 119, 130
Everitt, Brian, 31–32, 34
extra-sensory perception (ESP), 1, 9, 15–16, 22, 24, 48–50, 53, 72, 87–88, 101, 104–06, 117, 119, 145, 176

Fach, Wolfgang, 177
Feinberg, Gerald, 59
Feynman, Richard, 64
Fierz, Heinrich, 133
Fierz, Markus, 87, 133
fine structure constant (137), 63–66
fine-tuning, x, 67–69, 74, 80, 122, 176
Fisher, R.A., 41
Flammarion, Camille, 2, 36, 170f
   Flammarion Woodcut, 2, 165, 170f
Flew, Antony, 30
Forsyth, Frederick, 50f, 115, 117
Fox, Robin Lane, 134
Freud, Sigmund, 9–10, 174

Gay, John, 36

general acausal orderedness, 14
Gieser, Suzanne, 16–17, 64, 134
Giles, Lionel, 154–55, 159
Gilson, James, 65
Gisin, Nicolas, 99–100
Gliese 581g (exoplanet), 62
Goldilocks (parameters), 61–62, 65–66, 73, 76, 79, 81, 122
Gray, Elisha, 43
Gribbin, John, 81
Grof, Stanislav, 101

hand of God, 39, 61, 117, 119
Hall, James, 15–16
Hannah, Barbara, 26
Harrison, Edward, 74
Hart, Michael, 62
Hawking, Stephen, 68, 72
Hegel, G.W.F., 159
Heidegger, Martin, 162–64
Heisenberg, Werner, 10, 102, 109
  uncertainty principle, 92
Helmholtz, Hermann von, 89
Henry, Richard Conn, 108
Hersh, Reuben, 171
Hill, Ray, 33, 37
Hippocrates, 118
Holland, Mark, 13, 22–23, 26
Hopcke, Robert, 131
Hoyle, Fred, x, 67
Hsaio Shih-yi, Paul, 162–64
Hubble, Edwin, 66, 75
Hume, David, 6

I Ching, 8, 19f, 134, 145–46, 151, 160–62
Inglis, Brian, 36–37, 52, 54
interference pattern, 89f, 103

Jeans, James, 102, 108
Jesuits in China, 5, 7, 159
Jett, Stephen, 44
Jim Twins, 47, 120
Jordens, J.F.T., 104
Jordan, Pasqual, 107
Jenkins, Stephen, 124–27, 135
Jones, Jack, 131
Jeffries, Richard, 158–59
Janus, 165
Jung, C.G., ix–x, 1f, 30, 38, 48–49, 54, 64–65, 71, 73, 87–89, 93, 98–99, 104f, 114, 117–19, 122f, 133–35, 137, 142f, 155, 158, 161–62, 164, 172–73, 176
  archetypes, 17–18, 22, 145
  causality, 1, 5, 12, 14, 88, 150
  defines synchronicity, 4, 8, 14, 49
  epistemological openness, 133–34
  and Freud, 9
  and Kammerer, 4
  and Leibniz, 6–7, 14–15, 73, 142
  and Pauli, ix, 3, 9–11, 14, 16–17, 22, 25, 64–65, 87–88, 98–99, 143–45, 176
  parapsychology, 9, 15–16, 19, 24–25, 48–49, 88, 117–19, 145
  and Rhine, 8–9, 15–16, 25, 49
  and Schopenhauer, 5, 9–10
  tao, ix–x, 11–12, 26, 118, 134, 145f, 161–62, 164
  unus mundus, x, 14, 55, 104, 118–19, 123, 128, 137, 142f, 149–50, 155, 172, 176
  and Wilhelm, ix, 8, 11–12, 20, 22, 25–26, 145–47, 161–62
Jupiter, 60

Kafatos, Menas, 109
Kaku, Michio, 61
Kammerer, Paul, 3–5, 38, 117–19, 130
Kelly, Kevin, 43–44
King, Brian, 113–15, 117
Koestler, Arthur, 4, 48–49, 52, 86–88, 93, 117–18, 120–21
  coincidence categories, 52
  on Kammerer and Jung, 4, 118
  physics and parapsychology parallels, 86–87
Krauss, Lawrence, 75, 79
Kuhn, Robert Lawrence, 69–70, 80
Kuttner, Fred, 94–96, 98, 104

Lao Nai-hsüan, 160
Lao Tzu, 134–35, 154, 159–60, 164, 166
Lau, D.C., 146–47, 149, 153, 156
Laplace, Pierre-Simon, 36, 68
law of large numbers (Bernoulli), 33, 38
law of truly large numbers (Diaconis and Mosteller), 38–39
Legge, James, 160–61
Leibniz, Gottfried, 3, 6–8, 14–15, 73, 142, 159–60
  Monadology, 6–7, 73

Lennon, John, 78, 131
Leonard, Tom, 86
Leslie, John, 62
Lovelock, James, 79

M. de Fortgibu and the plum-pudding, 2–3, 11, 13, 171
Magruder, Kerry, 171, 174
Main, Roderick, 124–25
Malebranche, Nicholas, 159
Malthus, Thomas, 43
Mansfield, Victor, 12, 15–16, 24, 49, 54, 88, 100, 107
Manson, Charles, 131
McCartney, Paul, 132
meaning (in meaningful coincidences), ix, 4–5, 11–12, 16, 21, 30, 38, 49, 54, 88, 104, 114, 117, 119, 122, 125, 130
   as *tao*, ix, 11–12, 21
   -correspondence, 11, 49, 73
   -equivalence. *See* equivalence of meaning
measurement problem, 98, 107, 123
mega-synchronicity, 73
Meier, C.A., 87–88, 145
Mencius, 163–64
Mill, John Stuart, 36
Miller, Arthur I., 64–65
Minnesota Study of Twins Reared Apart, 46–47
Mlodinow, Leonard, 68, 72
monad (Leibniz), 6–7, 14
Moon (Earth's), 60–61, 70, 77–78, 81, 89, 98
Moss, Robert, 10
Mosteller, Frederick, 38–40, 55
Moyers, Bill, 23
multiverse, 68f, 80, 113, 122, 143, 179

Nash, Ogden, 120
Nature, 108
Needham, Joseph, 6–7, 151–52
New Scientist, 48, 101
Newton, Isaac, 7, 63, 90, 101
Nominalists, 149
numinosity, numinous, ix, 2, 12, 17, 73, 105, 124, 127, 129, 150, 158, 179

Otto, Rudolf, 12
Oxford English Dictionary, 72, 146

panpsychism, 107
parallel discoveries, inventions, 10, 43–45, 52
participatory universe, 98, 123
Pascal, Blaise, 36
Pauli, Wolfgang, ix–x, 3, 9–11, 14, 16–17, 21–22, 25, 64–65, 87–88, 98–99, 103, 110, 119, 133, 143–45, 176
   137, 64–65
   and Jung. *See* Jung and Pauli
   Pauli Effect, 10, 23, 53
Pauli-Jung Conjecture (Atmanspacher), 145
Paulos, John Allan, 37–38
Peat, F. David, 90–92, 143–44
Penrose, Roger 69–70, 122
photon(s), 63, 90f, 99–100, 103, 123
physicalist (interpretation), 2, 105, 107, 109, 119, 176
Physics World, 93
Planck, Max, 10, 102
   Planck length, time, 63
   Planck's constant, 63–64
Platonic (conception), 17, 80, 108, 148–49, 159
Playfair, Guy Lyon, 177
Plimmer, Martin, 113–15, 117
Poe, Edgar Allan, 36–37
Polanski, Roman, 131
prakriti, 103–04
prayer, 26, 158–59
pre/post fallacy (Wilber), 132
pre-established harmony, 5–7, 14, 142
premonition, 53, 59, 121
Primack, Joel, 74–77, 79, 82
probability, ix, 1, 4, 13, 18, 30–31, 33, 35f, 49, 51, 55, 69–71, 79, 86, 95, 105, 114–17, 121–22, 143
Progoff, Ira, 14, 25
psi, 55, 101
psychokinesis, 10, 23, 53, 119, 127
psychophysical (conception, unity), x, 14, 105f, 119, 123, 144, 150, 176–78
psychophysical parallelism, 73

quantum entanglement, 99–101, 106, 123, 177
   spin direction, 99
quantum leap, 88, 90

quantum physics, x, 1, 10, 15, 25, 51, 63, 66, 68, 72, 80, 87f, 113, 119, 121, 123, 142-45, 177-78
  anomalies and enigmas, x, 1, 80, 87f, 119, 121, 142, 178
  conceptual parallels, 87-88, 98-101
  misconstrued, 87-88, 98
  predictive power, 88

Radin, Dean, 101
Rainmaker, 26, 134, 137-38
Ramana Maharshi, 132
Realists, 149
Reichenbach, Hans, 42
Reps, Paul, 152
Rhine, J.B., 8-9, 15-17, 22, 25, 49, 55
Rhine-Feather, Sally, 15-16
Ricci, Mateo, 159
Richo, David, 51, 82
riffle shuffle (Hill), 33, 37
Rosen, David, 134
Rosenblum, Bruce, 94-96, 98, 100-01, 104
Rosenthal, Jeffrey, 43
Ross, Kelley, 152-53
Russell, Bertrand, 5-6

scepticism, sceptics, 1, 61-62, 88-89, 101, 125
Scherrer, Robert, 75, 79
Schopenhauer, Arthur, 3, 5-6, 10
Schrödinger, Erwin, 102, 107
scientism, 102-03
Segal, Nancy, 45, 47
serendipity, 51, 120
seriality (Kammerer), 4, 117-19, 130
Shaw, Albert, 131-32
Sheldrake, Rupert, 102
Smith, Huston, 102
Smullyan, Raymond, 148-49
Sober, Elliott, 39-42, 179
Spinoza, Baruch, 80-81, 144
Stenger, Victor, 68
Strogatz, Steven, 19
sufficient statistics (Fisher), 41
Surprise, Kirby, 126-27, 129-31
synchronicity, ix-x, 1f, 30, 38, 48f, 72-73, 80, 82, 87-88, 98-100, 104-06, 110, 114, 116f, 142f, 150, 155, 158, 161, 163, 165, 171-74, 176, 178
  as coincidence category, 30, 51-54, 72, 80, 116, 119, 176
  definitions and clarification, 1, 4-5, 8, 12, 14-17, 49, 73, 105, 127f, 158, 165
  and individuation, 23
  and intent, 24
  principle of, 1, 7-8, 14-15, 26, 48, 104, 118, 124, 128, 150
  stages, 135-38
  and synchronism, 4, 130-31
synchronistic events, experiences, x, 1-4, 7-8, 11f, 48-51, 54, 73, 104-06, 110, 114, 117-19, 123-24, 127f, 135-37, 142-43, 150, 155, 173, 179
  induced, 21, 134
synchronistic thinking, 20-21, 25-26, 133-35, 145, 150-51, 157-58, 163
Sze Mai-mai, 157, 166

Taleb, Nassim Nicholas, 47-48
Tanzi, Rudolf, 109
tao, ix-x, 11-12, 21, 26, 71, 81, 118, 134, 138, 145f
  definitions, 146-47, 164
  'man of *tao*', 134, 156
  misappropriation of, 152-53
  primordial intuition of, 155-56
Tao Te Ching, 12, 71, 145f, 153-55, 159-60, 162, 164
Taoism, 20, 145f, 161, 164
  alchemy, meditation, 147-48, 153-55
  classical, philosophical, 145, 148-49, 154-56, 161
  magical, ritualistic, 153-54, 156
  painting, poetry, 152, 154f
Tarnas, Richard, 16, 132-33, 135-37
Tart, Charles, 103
Tate, Sharon, 131
telepathy, 48, 50, 52, 72, 89, 93, 102, 106, 121, 172, 177
Temple, Archbishop William, 26
Tenenbaum, Joshua, 114
Tokuriki, Tomikichiro, 136
Trappist-1 (dwarf star), 62
trickster, 3, 13, 54
Tryon, E.P., 72
twins, 45-48, 55, 115-16, 120, 133, 177
  separated identical, 45-47, 115-16, 120

twin telepathy, 48, 177

unus mundus, x, 14, 18, 55, 104f, 118–19, 123–24, 128, 137–38, 142f, 155, 165, 172–74, 176
  cf. *tao*, 145–46, 149–50, 155, 165

Velmans, Max, 144
Venn, John, 37
Vogt, Steven, 62
Voltaire, 159
von Franz, Marie-Louise, 1–2, 5, 11–12, 14, 16, 18, 21, 26, 105, 110, 118, 124–25, 155, 172–74
  defines synchronicity, 5
  field thinking, 21
  Flammarion Woodcut symbolism, 172–74
  meaning, 11–12, 125
  unus mundus, 14, 118, 124, 155

Waley, Arthur, 146, 160
Wallace, Alfred, 43
Wallace, Alan, 165
Ward, Keith, 68
Ward, Peter, 60
wave function, collapse of, 94–95, 98, 123
Weaver, Warren, 30f, 55, 59, 86
Weinberg, Steven, 66
Wheeler, John, 92, 96–98, 123
which-box? experiment (Rosenblum and Kuttner), 95–96, 98, 104
Wilber, Ken, 132
Wilhelm, Richard, ix, 8, 11–12, 20, 22, 25–26, 145–47, 159–62
  I Ching translation, 8, 20, 22, 146, 160–61
  impact on Jung, ix, 8, 25–26, 145–46, 161–62
  Tao Te Ching translation, 11–12, 159–60
Wilson, E.O., 102
Wilson, Robert Anton, 106
Wolf, Fred Alan, 93, 97
Wolff, Christian, 159
wu wei, 134, 151

yin and *yang*, 20, 145, 153
Young, Thomas, 89–91

Zeilinger, Anton, 103, 107
Zen oxherding pictures, 135–38

www.ingramcontent.com/pod-product-compliance
Lightning Source LLC
Chambersburg PA
CBHW081215230426
43666CB00015B/2743